THE TEMPTATIONS OF JESUS
IN MARK'S GOSPEL

The Temptations of Jesus in Mark's Gospel

Susan R. Garrett

WILLIAM B. EERDMANS PUBLISHING COMPANY
GRAND RAPIDS, MICHIGAN / CAMBRIDGE, U.K.

© 1998 Wm. B. Eerdmans Publishing Co.
255 Jefferson Ave. S.E., Grand Rapids, Michigan 49503 /
P.O. Box 163, Cambridge CB3 9PU U.K.

Printed in the United States of America

03 02 01 00 99 98   7 6 5 4 3 2 1

Library of Congress Cataloging-in-Publication Data

Garrett, Susan R., 1958-
The temptations of Jesus in Mark's Gospel / Susan R. Garrett.
p.   cm.
Includes bibliographical references and index.
ISBN 0-8028-4259-3 (alk. paper)
1. Jesus Christ — Temptation.
2. Bible. N.T. Mark — Criticism, interpretation, etc.
I. Title.
BT355.G37 1998
226.3'06 — dc21   97-32349
                                            CIP

Contents

Preface

Writing this book was always a joy and never a trial, though I may well have tested the patience of others. In any case, I have many persons to thank for their assistance.

I begin by thanking the Association of Theological Schools for a Young Scholar Theological Scholarship and Reseach Grant, awarded to me for 1991–1992; the grant enabled me to hire two highly competent research assistants (Allen Hilton and William Alexander), each of whom contributed to the definition and development of the project. The grant also made it possible for me to travel to Duke University, where I had fruitful conversations with both Richard B. Hays and Dale B. Martin about the book. I also offer thanks to the faculty and administration of Union Theological Seminary in Richmond, Virginia, for the opportunity to offer lectures on my research during July 1992; and to the faculty and administration of Luther Seminary in Saint Paul, Minnesota, where I lectured in January 1995. On both occasions the opportunity to present my work in a public forum and to obtain feedback from my hearers helped me greatly to focus and refine the work-in-progess.

Several persons read the manuscript at key moments in its evolution and made comments that were extensive or trenchant or both; without their assistance I would have written a different book. Students in a course on literary criticism and New Testament exegesis (taught at Yale Divinity School in the spring of 1994) read the earliest complete draft of the book; these students were graciously indulgent but also incisively critical in their comments. One of these students, Regina Plunkett Dowling, offered additional, invaluable critiques as I began to revise the manuscript over the

ix

subsequent year. David R. Adams read a revised version of the work and convinced me that "leaner is better." Luke Timothy Johnson read a still later draft of the manuscript and made sparing but acute critiques and suggestions, to which I have tried to respond in the finished work. (Of course the usual caveat about errors and weaknesses of the work being my sole responsibility certainly does apply.)

During the final stages of the writing, members of the faculty, administration, staff, and student body here at Louisville Presbyterian Theological Seminary have been helpful and supportive. Amy Plantinga Pauw read parts of the manuscript and helped me to discern more clearly some of the theological implications of my reading of Mark's Gospel. Melissa Nebelsick proved herself to be the kind of secretary scholars dream of having; without her help in tracking down various pieces of bibliographic and other information and in preparing the final manuscript, the publication of the book would have been delayed considerably. Angela Morris procured needed items on interlibrary loan. Emily Rodgers prepared the indexes for the volume. More generally, President John Mulder, Dean Eugene March, and all of my colleagues and students at LPTS have helped to foster a very collegial and stimulating work environment. To them I extend my thanks.

Last, but far from least, I must thank my husband, Jim, and my daughters, Laura and Kate, for their constant support and love, demonstrated daily in ways too numerous to count. It is to Jim that I dedicate this book.

Introduction

The first Christians remembered Jesus as one who had faced and endured temptation. "We do not have a high priest who is unable to sympathize with our weaknesses, but we have one who in every respect has been tested as we are, yet without sin." So writes the author of Hebrews (Heb. 4:16; cf. 2:12). And Matthew, Mark, and Luke all depict Jesus as tested by Satan in the wilderness. From the early Christians' perspective, the tempting or testing of Jesus would not have seemed unusual or offensive,[1] for Christians and Jews of this era taught that *all* persons who strived to walk the straight and narrow path would be put to the test. "My child, when you come to serve the Lord, prepare yourself for testing," advises Jesus the son of Sirach (Sir. 2:1). Far from signifying sin or failure, life's inevitable trials are in many ancient writings viewed as opportunities for persons to prove the genuineness of their faith and obedience. Such authors took it for granted that enduring trials would make one acceptable to God. "Set your heart right and be steadfast, and do not be impetuous in time of calamity. . . . For gold is tested in the fire, and those found acceptable, in the furnace of humiliation" (Sir. 2:2, 5).[2]

---

1. Compare the offense caused in the modern era by the release of the movie *The Last Temptation of Christ*. In part the movie offended because the so-called "last temptation" included a scene in which Jesus imagines that he and Mary Magdalene lived together as husband and wife. But perhaps at a more basic level, the movie struck a nerve in some persons because it dared to presume that Christ could be tested (or "tempted") at all.

2. The New Testament authors did not consider the notion that Jesus was tested to be scandalous; on the other hand, they *were* apparently offended by the memory of his baptism:

1

In this book I shall argue that Mark depicts Jesus as tempted or tested, not only in the wilderness at the start of his earthly ministry, but also throughout the course of that ministry. In Mark's portrayal, Jesus was tempted by Satan, by his earthly adversaries, and even by his own disciples. All these characters served as "agents" of temptation or testing. That is, they served as ones who tried to lead Jesus astray from the straight and narrow path that extended from the river Jordan to the cross — a straight and narrow path that Mark calls "the way of the Lord." *The cross* was the climactic and most severe test that Jesus faced as he traveled on "the way of the Lord," for as he hung on the cross Jesus was alone, forsaken by God. But Jesus persevered till he reached his destination. And, *because Jesus was faithful when tested,* God regarded his death as a saving, sacrificial death. Mark's Jesus is "tried and true," the "proven" son of God whose perfect obedience in time of trial made him an acceptable sacrifice before God, which ransomed persons from sin. By ransoming persons from the grip of blinding sin — thereby enabling them to "see clearly" and to "think the things of God" — Jesus has empowered his followers to persevere during their own times of trial, without being led astray.

Thus my presentation is to be a study of Mark's *Christology* (his view of Christ) and also of Mark's *soteriology* (his view of the salvation wrought by Christ). But Mark's story of Jesus as one tested is of far more interest than these scholarly terms might seem to suggest. Indeed, Mark's story of Jesus as "tempted" or "tested" is profoundly relevant to persons in the church today. For, in telling this story, Mark speaks not only to the academic question "Who *was* Jesus," but also to the living question of all disciples — "Who *is* Jesus, for me, in my life, today?" Mark's answer, I shall suggest, is that Jesus is one who by his death and resurrection *made it possible* for disciples to follow him in the straight and narrow way, the "way of the Lord." By his endurance of testing Jesus opened up the path, and now Jesus gives guidance and fortitude to those who wish to travel on it.

---

see D. H. Juel, *A Master of Surprise: Mark Interpreted* (Philadelphia: Fortress Press, 1994), 38-39. On the collective memory of Jesus as one who was tempted, see J. H. Korn, ΠΕΙΡΑΣΜΟΣ, *Die Versuchung des Gläubigen in der gr. Bibel* (Stuttgart: W. Kohlhammer Verlag, 1937), 76-88.

Testing as an Interpretive Model

The notion of "testing" is an "interpretive model," or "interpretive convention." (The same may be said for "temptation" and "trial," which — along with "testing" — are possible translations of the single Greek noun *peirasmos.*) The model is *interpretive:* in other words, it is a pattern or construct that guides its user in interpreting diverse events or circumstances. The model is *conventional:* in other words, it has currency in a given culture.[3] The particular interpretive model associated with testing in formative Christianity and Judaism takes the form of a *narrative,* or *story,* with elements such as roles, plot, and point of view. These elements are variables, which can be filled in different ways. At an abstract level, the roles of the narrative pattern include a protagonist, who is striving to achieve a culturally approved goal, and an antagonist, or "agent of testing," who seeks to disrupt that striving. The protagonist may persevere despite the agent's interference, or he or she may succumb to the testing/temptation. In Judeo-Christian writings, the plot is most often expressed through

3. In my remarks about "interpretive models," I have especially been influenced by recent work in cognitive anthropology on the topic of "cultural models" in language and thought (see D. Holland and N. Quinn, eds., *Cultural Models in Language and Thought* [Cambridge: Cambridge University Press, 1987]; and S. R. Garrett, "Paul's Thorn and Cultural Models of Affliction," in *The Social World of the First Christians: Essays in Honor of Wayne A. Meeks,* ed. L. M. White and O. L. Yarbrough [Minneapolis: Fortress Press, 1995] for application to a New Testament passage). I have also been influenced by the article of literary critic Stanley Fish, "Interpreting the *Variorum*" (in Fish, *Is There a Text in This Class? The Authority of Interpretive Communities* [Cambridge: Harvard University Press, 1980], 147-73), in which he introduces the notion of "interpretive communities." Fish writes, "Interpretive communities are made up of those who share interpretive strategies not for reading (in the conventional sense) but for writing texts, for constituting their properties and assigning their intentions. In other words, these strategies exist prior to the act of reading and therefore determine the shape of what is read rather than, as is usually assumed, the other way around" (171). Fish is primarily concerned with strategies governing the *rhetorical* or *formal* features of a given text (compare M. A. Tolbert, *Sowing the Gospel: Mark's World in Literary-Historical Perspective* [Philadelphia: Fortress Press, 1989], 9-10, 49-50, with reference to literary critics other than Fish). In my own usage, the interpretive models shared by a given interpretive community comprise not only the cultural conventions determining rhetorical or formal features of a text, but also those determining the *content* or *story* told by it. These latter conventions determine how persons interpret much that goes on in day-to-day life as well as in written texts. Thus the conventions are part of what might be called a community's "worldview" (but see Garrett, "Paul's Thorn," 86-87).

the metaphor of travel along a "straight and narrow path": the agent of testing either tries to *seduce person(s) away* from the path by making a deceptive offer of benefit or pleasure, or else afflicts person(s), in an effort to *impede forward movement on the path*. But the plot can also be expressed through other figures of speech. For example, Mark's parable of the sower and the seed (4:3-9, 13-20) may be read as a plot about "trials": the seed (which stands for the word that is sown) ought to "grow" and "bear fruit." Various agents, however, disrupt the growth and prohibit some of those in whom the word is sown (represented by the types of soil)[4] from achieving their proper goal: Satan may snatch the word away; or affliction and persecution may prompt those without deep roots in themselves to fall away; or the cares of the world, the lure of wealth, and the desire of other things may choke out the word before it bears fruit.[5] But some of the seed is sown on good soil: "They hear the word and accept it and bear fruit, thirty and sixty and a hundred-fold" (Mark 4:2-20).

In ancient Jewish and Christian writings, elements of the narrative schema associated with "testing," or "temptation," vary in set ways. These variations reflect the influence of both biblical and extrabiblical traditions. For example, the "agent of testing" in the story may be God, acting to test the fidelity of the righteous or to discipline them for their own good. Or the agent may be Satan, viewed as adversary of God, who tries to lure persons away from God's dominion. Or again the agent may be Satan, but viewed now as a servant and proxy of God, who implements trials that God has already authorized. Writers (and presumably readers) did not fill out each variable in the testing-plot in the same way every time: rather, they alternated, or combined elements from different patterns (for example, now naming Satan as agent of their trials, now naming God). Thus

---

4. Mark's account of the referents for the symbols "seed" and "soil" seems slightly confused; on the confusion see, e.g., Juel, *Master of Surprise*, 55.

5. These are the sorts of factors regularly labeled as tests or temptations in Jewish and Christian literature. Significantly, Luke substitutes the single word *peirasmos* (test/temptation) for Mark's phrase "affliction or persecution" (Luke 8:13 [par. Mark 4:17]) and also refers to the "patient endurance" of the good seed (Greek *hypomonē*, widely assumed to be the ideal response to testing [Luke 8:15]). These alterations suggest that Luke read the parable of the sower as a parable about endurance in time of trial (as I myself am reading the parable here; cf. K. G. Kuhn, "New Light on Temptation, Sin, and Flesh in the New Testament," in *The Scrolls and the New Testament*, ed. K. Stendahl [New York: Harper and Bros., 1957], 108).

the narrative pattern was highly flexible: it could be adapted to explain widely varying events and to address varying rhetorical situations.

Modern English usage does not make a strong connection between trials of affliction and trials of seduction: English speakers often interpret suffering as a "test" of faith, but view seductive persons or things as "temptations," which they regard as fundamentally different. But use of the noun *peirasmos* and its cognates by early Christians and Jews suggests that they regarded "tests" and "temptations" as integrally related. This ancient perspective can be summarized in this way: *seduction afflicts, and affliction seduces.* To the one who is afflicted, the option of apostasy from faith (or even suicide) may present itself like tempting fruit, ripe for plucking; to ones who long for forbidden fruit, "desire" *(epithymia)* may burn within like a painful and consuming fire. Thus, affliction and desire pose equally serious — and closely related — threats to the life of faith and obedience. Dietrich Bonhoeffer recognized this paradoxical relationship between affliction and desire in his 1937 lectures on temptation. He wrote, "Temptation to desire always includes the renunciation of the desire, that is to say, suffering. Temptation to suffering always includes the longing for freedom from suffering, that is to say, for desire. Thus temptation of the flesh through desire and through suffering is at bottom one and the same."[6]

Readers have usually assumed that Mark's Gospel emphasizes trials of affliction.[7] Mark, it is said, wrote to encourage persons who were persecuted, even in danger of being martyred. Such a reading draws especially from Mark 13. In this book, I concur that Mark anticipates a time in the near future when "there will be affliction, such as has not been from the beginning of the creation that God created until now, no, and never will be" (13:19). This affliction will indeed threaten Jesus' followers' perseverance in the way of the Lord. But I shall try to nuance this reading, by arguing that Mark is as concerned about present or imminent *trials of seduction* as he is about trials of affliction. For example, Mark has Jesus refer to the enticing power of "the cares of the world, and the lure of wealth, and the desire for other things," which may choke out the seed *13:19*

4:19

6. D. Bonhoeffer, *Creation and Fall, and Temptation: Two Biblical Studies* (New York: Macmillan, 1959), 118.

7. For a list of scholars who hold to the view that Mark's community was persecuted, see W. T. Shiner, *"Follow Me!" Disciples in Markan Rhetoric* (Atlanta: Scholars Press, 1995), 272 n. 22. For further reflection on the type of testing faced by the Markan community, see below, Chap. 4 n. 35.

before it matures (4:19). Such imagery points to a life-context in which not only affliction but also worldly goods and routine cares of life pose a serious threat to perseverance in the way. Jesus' parable of the absent master, who has put his slaves in charge of his estate, also may point to a settled life-context. Jesus asks, will the master return to find that his doorkeeper and slaves have succumbed to the seductive allure of "sleep"? That is, will they have given in to the temptation of business-as-usual, rather than having stayed watchful and vigilant (13:33-37)?[8] Finally, Mark has Jesus prophesy that the time of eschatological affliction will itself be marked by the appearance of agents of seduction — false messiahs and false prophets who will "produce signs and omens, to lead astray, if possible, the elect" (13:22). Mark strives to prepare his readers to face and endure trials of affliction *and* trials of seduction. Mark views the two sorts of trial as closely related, and equally threatening to singleminded faith.

On the "Correct" Reading of Mark

In this book I focus on interpreting (literarily and theologically) the story "in front of" the text of Mark, rather than on constructing either the supposed sources used by Mark or a history of events "behind the text." Thus the book could best be classified as an essay in "narrative criticism" of Mark, though I have also been influenced by anthropological perspectives. Below I shall contend that key narrative motifs in Mark become evident and explicable only when certain interpretive models specific to ancient Jewish and Christian subcultures (or in some cases to ancient Greco-Roman culture more broadly) are brought into play.[9]

8. For a similar reading of the parable, see Juel, *Master of Surprise,* 77-88. Compare Luke 12:35-40 (par. Matt. 24:42-51).

9. For a description of the purposes and methods of narrative criticism, see M. A. Powell, *What Is Narrative Criticism?* (Minneapolis: Fortress Press, 1990); for a critique of such methods, see S. D. Moore, *Literary Criticism and the Gospels: The Theoretical Challenge* (New Haven: Yale University Press, 1989), 3-68; on anthropological perspectives pertinent to biblical study, see n. 3 above; also S. R. Garrett, *The Demise of the Devil: Magic and the Demonic in Luke's Writings* (Minneapolis, Fortress Press, 1989), 5-9; and S. R. Garrett, "Sociology of Early Christianity," in *Anchor Bible Dictionary* (hereafter *ABD*), vol. 6 (New York: Doubleday, 1992), 91-92. My interpretive stance in this book is fundamentally the same as the one I took in *The Demise of the Devil,* though in the present work I make a more deliberate attempt to utilize literary critical concepts and categories in my analysis. I am more

Robert Fowler compares Mark's Gospel to lace, which creates its effect "as much by its open spaces as by the tangible threads that outline them."[10] Even Mark's earliest readers recognized that the narrative of this Gospel is ambiguous at many points: Matthew and Luke both filled gaps and in other ways clarified Mark's story. Scholars in the early part of the twentieth century perceived an "incompleteness" about Mark's narrative, viewing its author as a clumsy compiler of oral tradition, with no literary or theological finesse.[11] Lately, however, the scholarly tide has shifted: now the author of this Gospel is given not criticism for his clumsiness, but kudos for his creativity. Fowler lauds Mark's so-called strategies of indirection — rhetorical features such as the use of irony, ambiguity, paradox, opacity.[12] Wherein does the truth lie? As rhetorician, was Mark a master of indirection or a rank amateur? The answer, I suspect, is "something in between." Some of the rhetorical "strategies" that Fowler and other recent interpreters identify — especially certain uses of irony — do indeed seem too artful to be accidental. On the other hand, some of this Gospel's ambiguities may not be "strategies of indirection" at all, but the result of hasty or careless writing or of the unreflective combining of sources (as was believed a generation or two ago).[13]

---

willing than are some other literary critics of Mark to theorize on how circumstances that came about after the events narrated in Mark 16:1-8 (for example, the rise of certain disciples to high-status positions within the church) might have influenced interpretations of Mark by early flesh-and-blood readers of the text.

10. R. M. Fowler, *Let the Reader Understand: Reader-Response Criticism and the Gospel of Mark* (Minneapolis: Fortress Press, 1991), 136; see also 46, 89; cf. Tolbert, 7-10.

11. For a brief and helpful overview of scholarship on Mark, see Juel, *Master of Surprise*, 11-30. I have put the word "incompleteness" in quotation marks because the "incompleteness" of a given narrative is a relative matter: narratives always leave some things out, and so no narrative is ever "complete." But some narratives give a greater sense of amplitude than others.

12. Fowler; cf. D. Rhoads and D. Michie, *Mark as Story: An Introduction to the Narrative of a Gospel* (Philadelphia: Fortress Press, 1982); Tolbert, esp. p. 43.

13. See especially the examples of ambiguity in Fowler's chapter entitled "Moves of Greater Uncertainty." Stanley Fish argues that each reader "writes" a given text anew, calling formal features into view in accordance with the interpretive strategies that he or she shares with the members of a given interpretive community (Fish, e.g., 164-65, 169-72). Fowler's work is sometimes unconvincing because he makes no effort to show that the interpretive strategies he *himself* uses would have been available in any first-century interpretive community: one has the sense that Fowler is "reading into the text" (put in quotation marks because *all* interpretations "read into the text"). Tolbert does try to interpret Mark in light of *first-century* interpretive strategies, but in my estimation Tolbert (like Fowler) attributes too much rhetorical subtlety to the implied author of the Gospel.

Each gap in Mark's narrative requires us to make an interpretive decision. Take, for example, Mark's account of the testing in the wilderness: Mark never explicitly tells us the outcome of the testing. We might therefore be prompted to ask, did Jesus on that occasion bind the strong man, Satan — or would that event take place only later in the story?[14] If later, then when? In the exorcisms that Jesus performed? When Jesus was in Gethsemane? When he was on the cross? At the resurrection? Or is the binding perhaps not to occur within the frame of the narrative at all, but only at the eschaton? Mark does not explicitly answer such questions for us, and so we ourselves must decide. But *how* we fill this particular gap in the narrative will in turn profoundly shape our reading of the rest of the story. Ernest Best argues that Mark does indeed portray Jesus as having defeated Satan at the temptation in the wilderness; hence, Best infers, there is no further struggle between Jesus and the devil (or between Jesus and any other cosmic power) in the remainder of the narrative.[15] By contrast, Joel Marcus reads the wilderness episode as merely one encounter in what amounts to a virtual apocalyptic "holy war" of Jesus against Satan and his forces, a war that extends from the beginning of Jesus' earthly ministry, beyond the readers' own horizon, to the coming of the Son of Man in power.[16] Such interpretive decisions are required at many points in the narrative. If one thinks of each of these places in Mark's account as a fork or crossroads, with alternative readings leading off in several directions, one can see how quickly the potential for very different interpretations of the Gospel expands. This situation may strike some readers as distressing. How, such readers may ask, are we to find the "right" path — the one that leads to the "correct" reading of Mark's Gospel?

My answer is to deny the validity of the question: there is not now (nor was there ever) a single, clear, unequivocally "correct" way of reading this

14. In assuming (as I do) that the strong man is Satan and that Jesus has bound (or will bind) him in some way, I have already made a prior interpretive decision. Tolbert suggests that one can read Jesus' words about the binding of the strong man in Mark 3:23-27 as having a different referent (and hence, an ironic cast): *Jesus* is the "strong man," who will be soon be "bound" (Tolbert, 100-101, 104).

15. E. Best, *The Temptation and the Passion: The Markan Soteriology,* 2nd ed. (Cambridge: Cambridge University Press, 1990), xviii-xxiii, 12, 15 (and throughout).

16. J. Marcus, *The Way of the Lord: Christological Exegesis of the Old Testament in the Gospel of Mark* (Louisville: Westminster/John Knox Press, 1992), 26-27 (see esp. n. 57), 66-69, 76.

or any other Gospel. Even Mark's very first readers had to make interpretive decisions as they read through the narrative; even they disagreed about where interpretive crossroads were to be found and about how best to traverse them. The differing usages of Mark's material by Matthew and Luke illustrate the point. "But," we may ask hypothetically, "what if Mark himself had been present among such readers or hearers of his work? Would not he have been able to resolve such interpretive disputes?" In other words, should not the author's intention be regarded as the decisive answer to questions about "the correct reading" of the text? The answer, I think, is both "yes" and "no." The time is now past when all literary critics categorically reject the quest for authorial intent. Some critics again acknowledge what seems "common sense" to many persons: that knowledge of an author's intent may indeed help readers/hearers to interpret a text.[17] But in the case of Mark's Gospel, such intent cannot be learned directly: we cannot interrogate the flesh-and-blood author of this Gospel about his purpose(s) in telling the story in just such a way.[18] Even if we could do so, knowledge of "authorial intent" would not exhaust the meaning of Mark's text, because Mark (like all other speakers and writers) could scarcely have recognized *all* the implications of his words. In this book I am willing to talk about "authorial intent" where I think that rhetorical or narrative features make the positing of such intent plausible — but I always recognize (even where my own rhetoric is not explicit) that the meaning of the text overflows the bounds of "authorial intent."

Occasionally, I speak not of the author but of "implied" or "ideal"

17. The denial of authorial intent as relevant to the task of literary interpretation is associated especially with the literary critical movement known as "New Criticism." Powell remarks that "most literary critics today have moved beyond the initial concerns of New Criticism" and that many today would regard the exclusion of authorial intent as "extreme." Powell continues, "Even so, it is now accepted as axiomatic in literary circles that the meaning of literature transcends the historical intentions of the author" (Powell, 4-5; cf. Tolbert 1989, 12; and Fowler 1991, 43 n. 9 [both include citations of works by literary critics]).

18. Hence we cannot know the intentions of the flesh-and-blood author of Mark's Gospel, but only those of the "implied author." In Donald Juel's succinct formulation, the "implied author" is "the sum total of the judgments and outlook that result from literary analysis rather than historical reconstruction" (Juel, *Master of Surprise*, 25). Further discussion of the notion of "implied author" may be found in Powell, 5-6; Tolbert, 51-52 (includes citations of works by literary critics); Fowler, 31-32 (likewise includes citations of works by literary critics).

readers — those outside the story, whom Mark signals by means of rhetorical moves at the discourse level.[19] The most explicit instance of such a rhetorical signal is the instruction at 13:14, "Let the reader understand." In Chapter 4, I argue that Mark includes other such signals, especially in Mark 13, which serve to identify certain exhortations or other teachings of Jesus as pertinent for the readers of the Gospel. The sum of such rhetorical signals can be fashioned into a profile of persons for whom Mark tailored his message. These readers are labeled "ideal" because they are a mirror image of the author's own "ideal" or "intent": they are persons who need (and are able) to hear precisely what the author has to say.[20] The situation of ideal readers as represented by Mark may or may not have corresponded to the life-situation of early flesh-and-blood readers of the Gospel. But even if we can no longer measure the degree of correspondence or fit between Mark's ideal readers and the flesh-and-blood readers who (by chance or providence) first read Mark's work, attention to the way Mark constructed his readers may help us to make sense of his rhetorical and theological strategies throughout the Gospel.

At other times in this book, instead of remarking about authorial intent or ideal readers, I find it more helpful to talk about ways that early "real readers" (or "flesh-and-blood readers") of Mark's Gospel would likely have construed the text. I generally base such assertions on my identification of cultural parallels for a particular Markan narrative pattern. In other words, I make such assertions in cases where I find ancient interpretive conventions that seem to make sense of the Markan story and that could

19. Powell writes, "*Story* refers to the content of the narrative, what it is about. A story consists of such elements as events, characters, and settings, and the interaction of these elements comprises what we call the plot. *Discourse* refers to the rhetoric of the narrative, how the story is told" (Powell, 23). The story/discourse distinction draws especially on S. Chatman, *Story and Discourse: Narrative Structure in Fiction and Film* (Ithaca: Cornell University Press, 1978). Two studies of Mark's Gospel making use of the story/discourse distinction are Rhoads and Michie ("story/rhetoric") and Fowler. Fowler overdraws the distinction, however, writing as if "story" and "discourse" were separable parts of the narrative (see, e.g., 57, 76, 88, 102). Fowler dismisses attempts to make sense of certain passages and problems in Mark's *story* (e.g., the "messianic secret"; the disciples' incomprehension), claiming that the passages/problems function solely or primarily at the *discourse* level (see, e.g., 125, 130, 155-56).

20. One could say that they are also a reflection of the *reader's own* "ideal" or "intent," insofar as the interpretive conventions employed by the reader control his or her very perception of "rhetorical signals to the reader." See Fish, 161, 165; for a useful, general overview of "real readers," "implied readers," and "narratees," see Fowler, 31-40.

have been known to early real readers of Mark's Gospel.[21] Thus, for example, I cite several Jewish and Christian claims that Satan "blinds" persons; this cultural evidence underlies my hypothesis that some early readers of Mark would have inferred that it was Satan who prevented the twelve disciples from comprehending Jesus' instruction. Shifting from remarks about the author or about ideal readers to remarks about how real, flesh-and-blood readers might have interpreted the text is an especially useful strategy in cases where a passage (or set of passages) is too ambiguous to argue that an author must have meant for it to be read one way rather than another: in such instances it makes sense to talk about the *range* of meanings a text may have had for various early readers. Talking about real readers serves other purposes as well. Such talk helps us to remember that meaning is always negotiated between authors or speakers on the one hand, and readers or hearers on the other. Writing about "readers" (in the plural) reminds us that even the simplest utterance would have had different meanings for different readers. Any reading necessarily simplifies, and silences alternative readings.[22]

By noting Mark's signals to ideal readers and identifying interpretive models or conventions that might have guided real ancient readers, one can delimit the range of meanings of the text and arbitrate some interpretive disputes.[23] For example, Joel Marcus identifies first-century interpre-

---

21. I use such expressions as "would likely have construed the text" and "could have been known to early readers" because we cannot know how any *particular* flesh-and-blood reader of the first century interpreted Mark's text. Whether a given interpretive convention "could have been known" to first-century readers is always a historian's judgment call: the more striking the parallel, and/or the wider the attestation, the greater the likelihood that flesh-and-blood readers shared the interpretive model in question.

22. Additionally, in some instances deliberate attention to disparities between what the implied reader knows (say, that Jesus is the "son of God" [Mark 1:1]) and what characters in the story know — or don't know — can help to disclose ironies or other narrative strategies. See Powell, 30-32; Fowler, 163-75.

23. Compare Fish's argument that it is the existence of "interpretive communities" that gives relative stability to the interpretation of texts (Fish, 171). I am suggesting here that the more one adopts ancient interpretive conventions that likely directed the "writing" (i.e., writing/reading) of Mark's Gospel in the first century, the more stable the meaning (Fish would say "the text") of that Gospel will become. Readers/critics of the late twentieth century can only approximate the "historical meaning(s)" of the Gospel ("what it meant"); they can never actually replicate such meaning(s), because they cannot fully escape the control over perception exercised by their own (modern) interpretive conventions. (See my related comments on "the problem of subjectivity" in ethnographic

tive conventions for scriptural texts quoted or alluded to by Mark, and shows how these conventions might have shaped early readings of the Gospel. It is this *attention to ancient interpretive models* that makes Marcus's reading of Mark as a narrative about "holy war" more plausible than Best's de-eschatologized interpretation of the Gospel. Even so, any resemblance between Marcus's reading of Mark and the actual interpretations of Mark by early real readers of the Gospel could at best be a family resemblance, since no two readings of the text are in practice ever identical.

My reading of Mark's story of Jesus as "tested as we are" is dependent on the work of others at many points; still, in its totality the reading is uniquely my own. In constructing this reading, I have tried to be informed by such rhetorical and cultural conventions as I think may have been available to Mark and early readers of the text. This attention to ancient interpretive models reflects my own historical interest/bias as a reader of biblical texts. But I am always acutely aware that, considered in its entirety, my reading would not correspond perfectly to anyone else's, be that person Mark, his contemporaries, or my own contemporaries. What I offer here is not "the correct" reading of Mark; nonetheless, I hope that my own flesh-and-blood readers will find it to be a cogent and compelling reading. One of my goals for the work is that it show how Mark used the resources of Scripture and of culturally-given interpretive conventions about testing/temptation to fashion a story that could account for Jesus' trials and the trials of his followers. Another goal is that the work stimulate theological and pastoral thinking about how Christians today may interpret their own diverse trials of faith and obedience.[24]

---

analysis, in Garrett, "Sociology," 92-93; my own position is closest to that of the "interpretive anthropologists" mentioned therein.) For readers/critics who choose not to attend to ancient interpretive models, the range of possible meanings explodes wildly; see, e.g., Stephen Moore's short deconstructionist reading of Mark, in J. C. Anderson and S. D. Moore, eds., *Mark and Method: New Approaches in Biblical Studies* (Minneapolis: Fortress Press, 1992), 84-102.

24. Author and pastoral counselor Wayne Oates remarks on "the scarcity of contemporary books and serious articles on temptation" (W. E. Oates, *Temptation: A Biblical and Psychological Approach* [Louisville: Westminster/John Knox Press, 1991], 11). His own work, directed toward a pastoral audience, has some very good insights. An older work that is still of immense value for theological thinking about temptation/testing is Bonhoeffer.

Theological and Pastoral Relevance of the Study

As just implied, I hope that this effort will be useful not only to biblical scholars, but also to theologians and to pastors ministering to those who are tested.[25] Reflection by academic theologians and by pastors on the subject of testing/temptation might offer at least two important benefits to the church. First, by speaking or writing about trials of faith and obedience, teachers and preachers might help to counteract moral ambivalence (what ancient authors would have called "doublemindedness"): a condition in which persons confronted with choices about right and wrong behavior are caught in indecision, unable to articulate what is at stake and unable to make the right choice if it entails any sort of personal deprivation or sacrifice. Second, by teaching about trials, theologians and pastors might offer believers valuable resources for coping with affliction when it inevitably strikes. This is not to say that a few prior sermons on testing will lessen the shock and devastation caused by a traumatic event; on the other hand, instruction on the subject may help sufferers to put the pieces back together in the days, months, and years after such an event. Theologians and pastors can equip persons with the cognitive resources — the vocabulary and narrative patterns — to think and to talk about crises of perseverance (be they trials of seduction or of affliction) both before and after they arise.

Kenneth Surin draws on the book of Job to argue that unwarranted suffering can engender a personal or communal crisis, in which persons question the schemata that have previously informed their interpretations of social and religious life. Such a crisis may be viewed as an *epistemological crisis* — that is, a crisis in which the interpretive models used to make sense of life have collapsed or are threatening to collapse. When Job finds that his previous understanding of his relationship to God is not adequate to explain his worsened situation, he must "seek a new vision of divinity." Surin writes,

> To begin with, he is content to curse the day he was born (Job 3:1), and to wish that God would end his agony by annihilating him (6:8-9). His wife advises him to curse God for afflicting him (2:9), but Job

25. Because I am trying to appeal to a wider audience, I have often relegated the discussion of technical or methodological points to the notes; even in the notes, I have tried to make my remarks comprehensible to those who are not professional New Testament scholars.

steadfastly refuses to "sin with his lips" (2:10). However, when his friends Eliphaz, Bildad, and Zophar arrive to comfort him, Job finds himself confronted by more than one schema for interpreting his new situation. His impeccably orthodox friends are anxious to justify the ways of God. In a series of homilies they present him with a variety of schemata, each amounting to a kind of theodicy. . . . Job is in a position where he not only has to decide which of these schemata to apply, he has also to address the question: whom now do I believe? My wife? My friends (and if so, which of the several schemata enunciated by them?) Or do I trust my own instincts? Until he has adopted some schema Job will not be able to determine what he should regard as evidence; until he decides what to treat as evidence he cannot be sure which schema is the right one to adopt.[26]

In order to resolve this crisis, Surin observes, Job must fashion a new narrative schema, one that integrates both the former, personal narrative centered on himself as a devout and morally upright individual and an external "historical" narrative that recounts the succession of disasters that have befallen him. Surin argues that, in order to resolve an epistemological crisis triggered by suffering, a new narrative must enable the protagonist to understand "*both* how he or she could intelligibly have held his or her original beliefs *and* how he or she could have been so drastically misled by them."[27] In the present study I assume that the *skandalon* or "stumbling block" of Jesus' death triggered a series of epistemological crises for his circle of followers. Immediately after the crucifixion, Jesus' followers had to explain why God had permitted Jesus' opponents to kill him. After their experience of the resurrection, these followers had to explain how they themselves could have been so blind to God's design that they had failed Jesus in his hour of greatest need. In Mark's own day, the epistemological problem persisted, though in altered form: new generations of converts to "the way" had to be able to account for their *own* preconversion ignorance or obstinacy, as well as for the persistent blindness and hostility of nonbelievers. Moreover they had to make sense of ongoing experiences of suffering and seduction — experiences that called into question their deepest convictions

26. K. Surin, *Theology and the Problem of Evil* (Oxford: Basil Blackwell, 1986), 24-25.
27. Surin, 26; quoting from an article by Alasdair MacIntyre ("Epistemological Crises, Dramatic Narrative and the Philosophy of Science," *The Monist* 60 [1977]: 453-72).

about right belief and action. Mark comments on these interrelated crises of knowing through his varied and sophisticated use of the metaphors of blindness and sight. The resulting Gospel is a story in which Christian readers could locate Jesus, his first disciples, unbelieving antagonists, and themselves. Mark's Gospel is not a set of timeless truths about "the problem of evil," but a historically and culturally contingent product of real persons' grappling with the communal and personal catastrophes of Jesus' death; their own "blindness," or failure to comprehend; and present and future threats to their continuing perseverance in faith.

Though I see Mark's work as "historically and culturally contingent," I affirm that his depiction of Jesus' trials is relevant to Christians today. Mark's Gospel can furnish us with materials to fashion our own narrative patterns for coping with trials of faith. Thus, for example, Christians today may adopt for themselves the conviction of Mark and other early believers that Christ's death and resurrection have empowered them to endure trials of all sorts. But the challenge of transferring Mark's narrative schemata across centuries and cultures should not be minimized (as is done in fundamentalist appropriations of the New Testament).[28] With respect to Mark's teachings about trials, the most obvious hermeneutical challenge is the problem of Satan. To be sure, for some persons, Satan presents no hermeneutical "problem" at all: he is as much a player in the cosmic game today as he was in Jesus' day. But those who were never socialized into "believing in Satan" may find it impossible or undesirable to try to reconfigure that aspect of their worldview. My principle in confronting this and other hermeneutical challenges[29] is to

28. See, for example, Frank Peretti's enormously popular apocalyptic novel, *This Present Darkness* (Westchester, Ill.: Crossway Books, 1986).

29. Another challenge in appropriating biblical teachings about trials of faith is that such teachings presuppose fundamentally different construction(s) of the human self than the models that modern readers presuppose. Yet another hermeneutical challenge arises from the gender bias of ancient remarks about testing: in the ancient Mediterranean world, it was often assumed that women were less able to control their passions than men; hence women were viewed as more likely to fail to endure in time of trial and also more likely to act as "agents of seduction" for others. See A. Carson, "Putting Her in Her Place: Woman, Dirt, and Desire," in *Before Sexuality: The Construction of Erotic Experience in the Ancient Greek World,* ed. David M. Halperin et al. (Princeton: Princeton University Press, 1990), 135-69; S. R. Garrett, "The 'Weaker Sex' in the *Testament of Job," Journal of Biblical Literature* 112 (1993): 55-70.

take the biblical language seriously, even where I cannot adopt it as my own. As far as possible, I strive to understand the authors on their own terms and to find points of connection between their terms and mine.[30] But I must emphasize that in this book I do not aim to offer distilled, abstract teachings about trials, which can then be conveniently applied by all Christians in every situation. Rather, I aim only to point the way for modern (or "postmodern") Christians to appropriate and reconfigure the Markan narrative schema, so as to find a place in the story for themselves.

In a narrative, there are multiple roles that must be filled — multiple places where the reader can stand. In reading and construing a narrative such as Mark, it may seem natural for us to identify ourselves always with the ones tested (Jesus, or the followers of Jesus who are addressed in Mark 13 and elsewhere). One of my purposes in writing this book is to encourage such identification by Christian readers. "Trying on" such roles — for example, exploring what it would mean to "endure to the end" (13:13) *despite* affliction or forbidden attractions — may help Christians today to name and to persevere through the trials that they themselves face. At the same time, I recognize that there is inherent danger in such identification. The danger is that, by identifying always with the "victim" of seduction or affliction, we will be blinded to the myriad of ways that we play the role of "agent" in the trials of others (cf. Wis. 2:21). For example, we may (like disciples before us) continue to put God and Christ to the test: challenging God's grace through our own willful wrongdoing or demanding signs and wonders to assure us of Christ's faithfulness to us. We may put others to the test, encouraging them to take the easy way out when they find themselves in a moral or ethical dilemma. We may discriminate against (or even persecute) others, thereby moving them to despair. Or we may give direct or indirect support to oppressive regimes — perhaps even as we encourage the biblical virtue of "patient endurance" by the oppressed. But to take on the role of "tester" in these and other ways is to fall away from the path of righteousness, the "way of truth."[31] The Wisdom of Solomon teaches

---

30. Analysis that is *exclusively* emic (done entirely "from the native's point of view") is in my opinion impossible. See Garrett, "Sociology," 92-93; also the comments in n. 23 above.

31. Cf. Oates, 67-78 and *passim*.

that, at the judgment, such oppressors will finally confront their own misdeeds:

> So it was we who strayed from the way of truth, and the light of righteousness did not shine on us, and the sun did not rise upon us. We took our fill of the paths of lawlessness and destruction, and we journeyed through trackless deserts, but the way of the Lord we have not known. (Wis. 5:6-7)

Those teaching and preaching about trials of faith and obedience have the opportunity to encourage a bifocal vision among those to whom they minister: a vision that discerns not only how such persons may themselves be empowered to persevere in their journey along the way of truth, but also how they might empower others to do likewise. Whether pastor or layperson, we must ask ourselves, how can we cast off the role of "tester" and take on the role of one who "makes paths straight" for those who seek to walk upon the way of the Lord?

In portraying Jesus as tested or tempted, Mark entered into a rich and varied conversation about the suffering and seduction of the righteous, a conversation involving countless participants from several cultures and extending over centuries. In Chapter 1, I discuss some of these "traditions about testing," as a way of bringing my own readers into this conversation, of helping them to discern the sorts of issues that would have been pressing for ancient readers who read (or wrote) the story of Jesus as one tested. In Chapter 2, I study three of the characters (or groups of characters) who serve as "agents of testing" in Mark's narrative: Satan, the (Jewish) authorities, and the twelve disciples of Jesus. I contrast the actions of these characters with those of John the Baptist and the woman who anointed Jesus — the lone figures in Mark who do attempt to help Jesus rather than to hinder him on the way to the cross. In Chapter 3, I examine Mark's depiction of Jesus' betrayal "into the hands of sinners" — that is, his entry into the most severe testing of his earthly existence, initiated at the end of his time in Gethsemane and culminating in his death. (Here I also examine the role played by Roman authorities in the tempting or testing of Jesus.) And in Chapter 4, I consider Mark's message to "disciples on trial" — his own readers, who are persons who strive to follow in the way of Jesus, but who face their own tests of affliction and of seduction. To these readers — among whom we ourselves are numbered — Mark delivers a message that is both realistic (refusing to minimize or whitewash the looming dangers to faith) and abounding with Good News. The Good News is that by his own endurance Christ has empowered followers to persevere in the straight and narrow way of the Lord. In Bonhoeffer's words, "the power of temptation is broken in the temptation of Jesus."[32]

32. Bonhoeffer, 107.

CHAPTER 1

Traditions about Testing

Early Christians taught that followers of Jesus should not only expect trials, but embrace them. "My brothers and sisters, whenever you face trials of any kind, consider it nothing but joy, because you know that the testing of your faith produces endurance; and let endurance have its full effect, so that you may be mature and complete, lacking in nothing" (James 1:2-4; cf. 1 Pet. 1:6-7; Rom. 5:3-4). Trials *(peirasmoi)* are inevitable in the Christian life. By using them as opportunities to practice endurance *(hypomonē)*, believers progress toward maturity and perfection.

But who causes trials? Is it God or some other force? Apparently this question concerned the author of the epistle of James, who also wrote the following:

> Blessed is anyone who endures testing [or "temptation"]. Such a one has stood the test and will receive the crown of life that the Lord has promised to those who love him. No one, when tested [or "tempted," here and throughout], should say, "I am being tested by God"; for God cannot be tested by evil and he himself tests no one. But one is tested by one's own desire *[epithymia]*, being lured and enticed by it; then, when that desire has conceived, it gives birth to sin, and that sin, when it is fully grown, gives birth to death. Do not be deceived, my beloved. (James 1:12-16)

The author denies that God is the source of *peirasmoi*, "tests" or "temptations." By pointing the finger at desire, this author tries to shift the blame for testing/temptation away from God onto an evil passion or

19

impulse within the human self.[1] Others writers followed different strategies in the attempt to relieve God of blame for testing, naming not desire but Satan as the agent of testing or temptation. In this chapter I shall present and discuss scriptural and other ancient Jewish and Christian texts that illustrate beliefs about the origin of testing, focusing especially on texts that assume God or Satan to be the provoking agent in trials. This discussion will provide the necessary background to my reading (in Chapters 2–4 below) of Mark's portrayal of Jesus as one who was "tested as we are."

God as the Agent of Testing

Throughout the Hebrew Scriptures (and also in noncanonical texts) God is described as "testing" individuals or the whole people of God. Sometimes the emphasis in accounts of divine testing falls on their character as *acts of investigation:* God "tests" so as to determine whether persons are indeed faithful and obedient. Other accounts stress the character of tests as beneficial (though painful) *acts of divine chastisement or discipline.* In still other texts, the investigative and disciplinary aspects of testing cannot be distinguished.[2]

---

1. On the "evil impulse" in James, see J. Marcus, "The Evil Inclination in the Epistle of James," *Catholic Biblical Quarterly* 44 (1982): 606-21; cf. H. Seesemann, "πεῖρα κτλ.," in *The Theological Dictionary of the New Testament* [hereafter, *TDNT*], vol. 6 (Grand Rapids: William B. Eerdmans, 1968), 29, who (like Marcus) identifies *epithymia* in this passage with the evil impulse. Space does not permit me to explore the background and meaning of James's reference to "desire" as an agent of testing; the notion has affinities not only to Jewish ideas about the evil impulse, but also to Greek philosophical notions about the passions (on which see especially M. C. Nussbaum, *The Therapy of Desire: Theory and Practice in Hellenistic Ethics* [Princeton: Princeton University Press, 1994]). See D. Bonhoeffer, *Creation and Fall, and Temptation: Two Biblical Studies* (New York: Macmillan, 1959), and L. T. Johnson, *The Letter of James* (New York: Doubleday, 1995), for insightful discussions of what it means *theologically* to name "desire" as an agent of testing. See J. D. Levenson, *Creation and the Persistence of Evil* (San Francisco: Harper and Row, 1988), 44-45, on the tendency in later Jewish writings to exculpate God from any role in the bringing about of "evil" events or circumstances, including those which "tempt" or "test" persons.

2. On divine testing as investigation, see also B. Gerhardsson, *The Testing of God's Son* (Lund: C. W. K. Gleerup, 1966), 27-28; on divine testing as chastisement, see Gerhardsson, 31-35. In general on the notion of "testing" *(peirasmos)* in the LXX and the NT (with careful attention to lexical issues), see J. H. Korn, ΠΕΙΡΑΣΜΟΣ, *Die Versuchung des Gläubigen in der gr. Bibel* (Stuttgart: W. Kohlhammer Verlag, 1937).

Divine Testing as Investigation

The story about Abraham's near-sacrifice of Isaac — surely one of the most memorable stories in the Bible — centers on the theme of the patriarch's obedience when tested by God. The account begins, "After these things God tested Abraham" (Gen. 22:1). In response, Abraham prepared to sacrifice his only (LXX: "beloved" *[agapētos]*) son, and by his readiness proved that he feared God (22:12). At the time of the Jesus-movement or shortly thereafter, Jews began to elaborate this story of the "Akedah," or "binding of Isaac," and to invest it with new meanings. Increasingly, persons supposed that Isaac was an adult at the time of the testing. Thus, God's command to Abraham was a test not only of the father but also of the son, who showed his faithfulness by facing death willingly — even joyfully. Isaac's willingness (as was supposed) to *offer himself* upon the altar made even his near-death count as a genuine sacrifice, pleasing to God. (Some rabbinic accounts refer to "the blood of Isaac," thereby defying the biblical testimony that Isaac was spared.) Full development of the Akedah-doctrine took place in the period after the emergence of Christianity, though there is evidence that already in Jesus' day important pieces of the story/doctrine were in place.[3] Here it is important simply to note that in this very prominent biblical story, God is described as *putting Abraham to the test,* investigating to see what was in his heart and whether he would obey God.

With "trials, signs, and wonders" God brought the Israelites out of the land of Egypt and led them through the wilderness (Deut. 4:34; 7:19; 29:3). The stated or implied purpose in this extended period of testing was to assay or prove the purity of the Israelites' hearts and their fidelity to God's law. For example, Exodus reports that when the Israelites complained against Moses and Aaron, God sent the manna from heaven, saying, "In that way I will test them, whether they will follow my instruction or not" (Exod. 16:4; cf. 15:25; cf. Ps. 66:10). Likewise in Deuteronomy 8:2-5, Moses explains that God tested the Israelites in the wilderness to see whether they would obey the divine commands:

---

3. See esp. Rom. 8:32, together with N. A. Dahl, "The Atonement — An Adequate Reward for the Akedah? (Ro 8:32)," in *Neotestamentica et Semitica: Studies in Honor of Matthew Black,* ed. E. E. Ellis and M. Wilcox (Edinburgh: T. and T. Clark, 1969); for further discussion, see Chap. 3, n. 61.

> Remember the long way that the Lord your God has led you these forty
> years in the wilderness, in order to humble you, testing you *to know
> what was in your heart, whether or not you would keep his commandments.*
> He humbled you by letting you hunger, then by feeding you with
> manna. . . . Know then in your heart that as a parent disciplines a child
> so the Lord your God disciplines you. (Deut. 8:2-5 [emphasis added];
> cf. Deut. 8:16)

God's testing of the Israelites in the wilderness was designed to evaluate,
or "prove," the Israelites, whether they would be obedient; moreover,
Moses explains, the testing was intended to "improve" them, by chastising
or disciplining them as a parent disciplines a child. (I shall say more about
this second purpose of divine testing below.)

Through such interventions, God learned that the Israelites would not
be fully obedient to the divine commands. Time and again, the Scriptures
recount, the members of the wilderness generation failed God's tests.
Repeatedly they murmured against God's servant Moses and turned back
to Egypt in their hearts — thereby demonstrating that they were not
singleminded in their devotion to God. For example, at Rephidim the
people quarreled with Moses when there was no water to drink, to which
Moses responded:

> "Why do you quarrel with me? Why do you test the Lord?" But the people
> thirsted there for water; and the people complained against Moses and
> said, "Why did you bring us out of Egypt, to kill us and our children and
> livestock with thirst?" So Moses cried out to the Lord, "What shall I do
> with this people? They are almost ready to stone me." (Exod. 17:2-4)[4]

By challenging Moses' leadership, the members of the wilderness generation were themselves *putting God to the test.* Similarly, when it was time
to enter into Canaan, the Hebrews failed to trust God, and so put God
to the test: all except Caleb doubted that they could overtake the inhab-

---

4. See also Num. 14:22; Deut. 6:16; Pss. 78:18, 41, 56; 95:8-10; 106:14. Wisdom
11:9-10 seems to allude to Deuteronomy 8:2-5, referring to the "tests" and "chastisements"
of the Israelites (in contrast to the torments suffered by the ungodly), but remarkably omits
all references to the Israelites' failings. The theme of the Israelites' failure to endure God's
tests is picked up by New Testament authors: see Acts 7:39-43 (regarding which see S. R.
Garrett, "Exodus from Bondage: Luke 9:31 and Acts 12:1-24," *Catholic Biblical Quarterly*
52 [1990]: 656-80); 1 Cor. 10:1-11; Heb. 3:7-19.

itants of the land (Num. 13:27-29; 14:24; cf. Deut. 1:26-33). In both these instances the Israelites were demonstrating that their hearts were divided and that they did not fully trust in God's promise to sustain. As H. Seesemann remarks, "To test or tempt God is not to acknowledge His power, not to take seriously His will to save. This finds expression in complaint against His guidance, in the failure to see His glory or to note His signs and wonders. To test God is thus to challenge Him. It is an expression of unbelief, doubt, and disobedience."[5] In Mark's Gospel, Jesus' adversaries put him to the test and seek from him signs from heaven; when they do so, Jesus tells them that no sign is to be given to "this generation." Thus Mark associates Jesus' adversaries with the "generation" that tested Moses in the wilderness, exhibiting faithlessness and idolatry (Deut. 32:4-5, 20; Mark 8:12; cf. 8:38; 9:19).[6]

Later authors highlighted the connection between *putting God to the test* and *failing to trust God in one's own time of trial*.[7] The author of Wisdom of Solomon, for example, instructed readers to seek God with singleness of heart, "because he is found by those who do not put him to the test, and manifests himself to those who do not distrust him" (Wis. 1:2). In Chapters 2–3 below, I shall demonstrate that this complex of ideas is important also for the Gospel of Mark: as portrayed in this Gospel, Jesus' adversaries and his disciples are not singleminded in their commitment to God, and consequently they put Jesus (and, through Jesus, God) to the test.

Also outside the Exodus traditions, the Hebrew Scriptures sometimes portray God as one who tests persons' minds and hearts to investigate whether they are obedient. Judges, for example, reports that God refused to drive out all the nations from the land, so as to test Israel and see if they would walk in the way of the Lord or not (Judg. 2:22; 3:1, 4). Second

5. Seesemann, 27. On human testing of God, see also Korn, 31-43; Gerhardsson, 28-31, 46-48, 59-60; Bonhoeffer, 104-5.

6. Note how the Lukan and Matthean parallels to Mark 9:19 strengthen the allusion to Deuteronomy by adding the qualifier *diestrammenē*. I am grateful to my former student James L. Weaver for pointing out these allusions to me.

7. Thus I disagree with Seesemann, 27 n. 27, who sees no inherent connection between God's testing of humans and humans' testing of God: on the contrary, it is precisely in times of crisis or trial that humans are most likely to put God to the test (see Jth. 8:12-13, 16, 24-27). For more on the connections between "testing God" and being "double-minded," and also on the connection between "testing God" and "seeking signs," see S. R. Garrett, " 'Lest the Light in You Be Darkness': Luke 11:33-36 and the Question of Commitment," *Journal of Biblical Literature* 110 (1991): 101-3.

Chronicles indicates that God departed from Hezekiah for a time, so as to test him (2 Chron. 32:31). (This notion that God might "depart from" righteous persons for a time, to test them, is picked up by later authors and may be relevant to Mark's portrayal of Jesus as forsaken by God, as we shall see in Chapter 3 below.) The Psalms describe God as one who "searches" minds and hearts, who "tries" or "proves" mortals.[8] In an especially striking passage, the psalmist pleads with God to try his heart, and thereby to show forth the writer's integrity:

> Vindicate me, O Lord, for I have walked in my integrity, and I have trusted in the Lord without wavering. *Prove me, O Lord, and try me; test my heart and mind.* For your steadfast love is before my eyes, and I walk in faithfulness to you. (Ps. 26:1-3 [emphasis added]; cf. 17:3)

In this passage, to "test" means to assess or judge, rather than to seduce or afflict (though in some other writings seduction and/or affliction are the very means of assessment). The psalmist is so certain of his own faithful obedience (vv. 1, 3) that he is confident he can only be helped, and not harmed, by divine scrutiny. Finally, the book of Job portrays God as testing the righteous man (at the instigation of the *satan*) to see whether Job will persevere in his faithfulness toward God. God's test of Job was designed "to reveal whether Job would stand fast by his innocence, honesty and faith, or whether in such a situation he would reveal himself unrighteous by breaking out into curses against God."[9]

Divine Testing as Discipline (paideia)

Deuteronomy 8:12 (quoted above) gives another reason for God's testing of the Israelites in the wilderness. Besides desiring to know their hearts and minds, the author says, God wished to *humble* the Hebrew children and to *discipline* them. "Know then in your heart that as a parent disciplines a child so the Lord your God disciplines you" (8:5). The notion that God uses affliction to serve the positive purpose of disciplining and so improving God's children is found throughout the Hebrew Scriptures,

---

8. Pss. 11:5; 17:3; 26:1-3; 66:10; 94:9-11; 139:1-4, 23-24.
9. Gerhardsson, 28.

though it is not always explicitly connected with divine *testing* (as it is here).[10] Human parents use corporal discipline to express their love for their child, as noted in Proverbs 13:24: "Those who spare the rod hate their children, but those who love them are diligent to discipline them" (cf. 19:18; 22:15; 23:13; 29:17, 19). So, by analogy, the Lord disciplines the one whom he loves: "My child, do not despise the Lord's discipline *[mûsār]* or be weary of his reproof, for the Lord reproves *[yākach]* the one he loves, as a father the son in whom he delights" (Prov. 3:11-12). Other texts employ not the parental metaphor, but the image of the refiner's fire, which "proves" (or "improves") silver or gold by burning away the dross.[11] Both the metaphor of parental discipline and that of the refiner's fire assume an element of violence, the inflicting of pain, and so are suited to account for trials of affliction.[12]

Certain Jewish intertestamental writings also interpret affliction as divine discipline or correction of God's children. The narrator of one of the Qumran hymns regards his enemies' affliction of him as discipline or rebuke by God; this discipline tests and purifies him, and will lead to his salvation (1QH 9.23-25; cf. 1QH 17.21-22). The author of the *Psalms of Solomon* declares God to be "the God of righteousness, judging Israel in

10. Some of the other passages in the Hebrew scriptures that refer to divine discipline or punishment include: Deut. 4:36; 8:5; 11:2; Lev. 26:18, 23, 28; Job 5:17; 33:19; Hos. 7:12; 10:10; Isa. 26:16; 53:5; Jer 2:30; 5:3; 7:28; 10:24; 30:11, 14; 31:18; 46:28; Zeph. 3:2, 7; Prov. 3:11; 15:10; Pss. 6:1; 38:1; 39:11; 50:17; 94:10, 12; 118:18. Important references to divine discipline in the apocrypha include Sir. 18:13-14; 22:27–23:3; Wis. 3:5 (equates "discipline" and "testing"); 11:9-10 (also equates "discipline" and "testing"); 12:18-22 (cf. 12:9-10); Jth. 8:25-27 (discussed below). Secondary treatments of the theme of divine discipline in the Hebrew scriptures and later Jewish and Christian literature include especially J. A. Sanders, *Suffering as Divine Discipline in the Old Testament and Post-Biblical Judaism,* Colgate Rochester Divinity School Bulletin, special issue, vol. 28 (Rochester: Colgate Rochester Divinity School, n.d.); also G. Bertram, "παιδεύω κτλ.," in *TDNT,* vol. 5 (1967), 596-625; C. H. Talbert, *Learning through Suffering: The Educational Value of Suffering in the New Testament and Its Milieu* (Collegeville, Minn.: Liturgical Press, 1991); J. M. Gundry-Volf, *Paul and Perseverance: Staying In and Falling Away* (Louisville: Westminster/John Knox Press, 1990), 107-11.

11. The fire- or refining-metaphor is found in Ps. 66:10; Prov. 17:3; 27:21; Ezek. 22:17-22; Zech. 13:9; Mal. 3:2-3; Sir. 2:5; 1 Pet. 1:7; Rev. 3:18 (cf. Dan. 11:35; 12:10; 1 Cor. 3:13-15); 1QH 5:16; Philo, *Sacr.,* 80; Seneca, *De Prov.,* 5.10.

12. Such a view of affliction as painful but beneficial discipline is taken up by the character C. S. Lewis in the play and movie "Shadowlands." Explaining why God lets us suffer, Lewis says, "The blows of God's chisel, which hurt us so much, are what make us perfect."

discipline" (*Pss. Sol.* 8:26; cf. v. 29). Israel for its part affirms its submission to God's correction by declaring, "We are under your yoke forever, and under the whip of your discipline" (7:9; cf. 10:2, 3; 13:7-10; 14:1). Elsewhere the pious "Solomon" prays to God, "If I sin, discipline (me) that (I may) return" (16:11).

When the Scriptures were translated into the Greek of the Septuagint (LXX) edition, in the third century B.C.E., the Hebrew terms for "discipline" or "to discipline" (noun: *mûsar;* verb: *yasar*) were often rendered into the Greek terms *paideia* and *paideuein*. As used by Greeks, *paideia* and related words referred primarily to *education* — that is, to the transmission of knowledge and cultural values — rather than to physical chastisement or discipline per se.[13] Thus, by employing these Greek terms to designate "chastise(ment)," "discipline," or even "punish(ment)," the translators of the LXX were expanding the range of meanings of *paideuein* and cognates beyond their typical usage in pagan Hellenistic writings of that era.[14] On the other hand, the brutal physical discipline and also the regular athletic training that were customary features of Hellenistic educational practice made the LXX translators' likening of divine "discipline" to "education" an easy and obvious comparison.[15] Plato had already used

13. On the various Hebrew terms pertaining to education, see A. Lemaire, "Education (Israel)," in *ABD,* vol. 2 (1992), 305. Conventional Hellenistic theory about *paideia* (as expounded around the turn of the millenium) can be found in Quintilian, *Institutio Oratoria;* and Pseudo-Plutarch, *On the Education of Children.* The classic secondary discussion of *paideia* in the Greek context is W. Jaeger, *Paideia: The Ideals of Greek Culture,* trans. Gilbert Highet (Oxford: Basil Blackwell, 1939); see also H. I. Marrou, *A History of Education in Antiquity* (New York: Mentor Books, 1964), esp. 137-308 on classical education in the Hellenistic age; and J. T. Townsend, "Education (Greco-Roman)," in *ABD,* vol. 2 (1992), 312-17, for a concise recent treatment with bibliography. With respect to the Hellenistic epoch, M. Hengel, *Judaism and Hellenism: Studies in Their Encounter in Palestine during the Early Hellenistic Period* (Philadelphia: Fortress Press, 1974), 65, identifies *paideia* as "the key concept" in a new picture of humanity: "Alexander's victorious expedition gave new possibilities to the idea of 'Greeks by *paideia*'" (cf. Marrou, 143). Townsend, 312-13, notes the essential unity of education in the Greco-Roman world "until the barbarian overthrow of the West and the Muslim conquest of the East."

14. The point is made by Bertram, 608.

15. Marrou, 221, stresses the inseparability of education and corporal punishment in the view of Hellenistic Greeks, and suggests that this link facilitated the LXX translators' rendering of the Hebrew *mûsar* ("education" or "discipline") with the Greek *paideia.* On the central role of athletic training in Hellenistic education, see Marrou, 154-57, 165-86. Marrou argues (183-86) that the role of athletics in education declined as the Hellenistic

references to gymnastic exercises as a metaphor for the rigor of serious study; many other philosophers, too, compared training or education in the philosophical life (especially the quest for mastery over the passions) to the physical challenges and abuses of athletic and military contests.[16]

By their seeming equation of divine "discipline" or "chastisement" on the one hand and "education" on the other, the LXX translators/authors permitted readers to infer that chastising affliction by God was not an exceptional event, but — like secular education — a *routine mechanism by which persons learned obedience.* The book of Sirach offers a striking illustration of this merging of Hebrew notions of divine discipline and Greek views of education.[17] The author portrays Wisdom, personified as a woman, as an *agent of affliction:*

> At first she [Wisdom] will walk with [the righteous] on tortuous paths;
> she will bring fear and dread upon them, and will torment them by her

---

age progressed, but Townsend, 313-14, contends that one should not exaggerate this decline: "In New Testament times, [athletics] still played a significant role in all levels of education, particularly in the East."

16. Plato had written that "souls are much more likely to flinch and faint in severe studies than in gymnastics, because the toil touches them more nearly, being peculiar to them and not shared with the body" (*Rep.* 7.535b, trans. Paul Shorey, in Plato, *The Collected Dialogues of Plato,* ed. E. Hamilton and H. Cairns [Princeton: Princeton University Press, 1961], 767). An especially pointed example of such imagery in a New Testament–era document is Epictetus, *Dis* 1.29.33-35. For examples of pre-Socratic emphasis on the "exercise of the soul," see V. C. Pfitzner, *Paul and the Agon Motif* (Leiden: E. J. Brill, 1967), 25. At points Pfitzner's important book effectively brings out the connotation of the *agōn* as a test or trial (see, e.g., 27, 32, 70, 96).

17. The author of the work, Yeshua ben Sira (Jesus the son of Sirach), wrote the book in Hebrew around 180 B.C.E.; his nephew translated the work into Greek, publishing his rendition sometime after 117 B.C.E. Greek-influenced ideas about education are evident even apart from use of the term *paideia* in the LXX version, and must have been present already in the original: like the Greeks, Ben Sira viewed education as a long-term process of instruction and striving, which molded the student into an ideal form. Ben Sira had himself been a scribe and schoolmaster who educated young men in Jerusalem (see Sir. 51:23, 28). His life's work as a scribe and a teacher of wisdom must be seen as part of a larger, democratizing educational movement in formative Judaism, which stressed education of the masses as a defense against the lure of Hellenistic culture. Martin Hengel calls the formation of Jewish schools "the richest fruit of what was at first such a threatening encounter with 'Greek education' " (Hengel, *Judaism and Hellenism,* 78; see his excursus, "The development of the Jewish school," 78-83). Thus, Ben Sira's very emphasis on "education" or "instruction" had itself already been shaped by the culture whose influence he sought to stem.

discipline *[paideia]* until she trusts them, and she will test *[peirasai]* them with her ordinances." (Sir. 4:17)

Here it is taken for granted that affliction naturally accompanies education into God's ways or God's wisdom: *education requires discipline; conversely, discipline or chastisement educates.* Later authors would likewise presuppose an inseparable tie between discipline and education into God's ways.[18]

The book of Judith (ca. 150 B.C.E.) includes a passage that combines several of the themes discussed above, and that therefore serves as an apt summary of this discussion of God as one who tests humans. The heroine of the story reprimands the leaders of the town of Bethulia (under seige from the Assyrians), for vowing to surrender to the enemy if God did not rescue them within five days. She asks, "Who are you to *put God to the test today,* and to set yourselves up in human affairs?" (Jth. 8:12 [emphasis added]). No, she continues, the Bethulians ought not to try to bind the purposes of God, "for God is not like a human being, to be threatened, or like a mere mortal, to be won over by pleading" (8:16). Rather, the Bethulians must wait patiently for God's deliverance of them:

> In spite of everything let us give thanks to the Lord our God, who is *putting us to the test [peirazein]* as he did our ancestors. Remember what he did with Abraham, and how he tested *[peirasai]* Isaac, and what happened to Jacob in Syrian Mesopotamia, while he was tending the sheep of Laban, his mother's brother. *For he has not tried us with fire,* as he did them, to search their hearts *[hoti ou kathōs ekeinous epyrōsen eis etasmon tēs kardias autōn],* nor has he taken vengeance on us; but the Lord scourges those who are close to him in order to admonish them *[eis nouthetēsin mastigoi Kyrios].* (Jth. 8:25-27 [emphasis added])

Noteworthy motifs in this passage include the assumption that God tests persons both to investigate ("search hearts") and also to admonish; the assumption that it is unacceptable to put God to the test; and the assumption that not only Abraham but also Isaac was tested.

---

18. See, for example, Heb. 12:3-11.

The Endurance of Testing

Various ancient Jewish and Christian texts reflect the belief that endurance of discipline or testing makes one acceptable to God, either here and now or at the judgment. In the words of the *Psalms of Solomon,* "the one who prepares (his) back for the whip shall be purified, for the Lord is good to those who endure discipline" (*Pss. Sol.* 10:2; cf. 14:1). But authors give various explanations of *how* or *why* God regards those who endure discipline or testing as worthy. Some passages seem to imply that divine testing merely *shows forth a righteousness already present.* Thus, by obeying God's command to take Isaac up on the mountain to sacrifice him, Abraham proves the unwavering commitment of his heart and mind. So also the psalmist who beseeches God to "test" and "prove" him is confident that the tests will demonstrate his own (prior) integrity. Other passages suggest that God's discipline makes one acceptable to God *by provoking needed repentance and reform.* Concerning human parents, Sirach wrote, "He who loves his son will whip him often, so that he may rejoice at the way he turns out. He who disciplines his son will profit by him, and will boast of him among acquaintances" (Sir. 30:1-2). So also God will "boast" of those who respond to divine discipline by mending sinful ways.[19] Finally, other texts suggest that through the endurance of divine discipline, persons *pay a debt of punishment owed to God on account of wicked behavior,* and thereby escape having to pay it at the judgment. On this point, the author of *Psalms of Solomon,* for example, contrasts the *disciplines* brought upon the righteous with the *punishments* brought upon the wicked:

> For the discipline of the righteous (for things done) in ignorance is not the same as the destruction of the sinners. In secret the righteous are disciplined lest the sinner gloat over the righteous. For he will admonish

19. Behind many or most passages in the Hebrew Bible referring to God's discipline lies the presumption that such discipline or instruction has repentance and reformation as its goal (Sanders, 101-2, 105, 108, 117). Wisdom of Solomon attests to this view that divine discipline and punishment lead to repentance: God corrects "little by little those who trespass," and reminds and warns them "of the things through which they sin, so that they may be freed from wickedness and put their trust" in the Lord (12:2). God judges even the ungodly little by little, so as to give them an opportunity to repent (12:10); how much more, then, does God govern the elect with "great forbearance," "judging" them now so as to give opportunity for repentance (Wis. 12:18-22). *Psalms of Solomon* 16:11 also assumes that divine discipline will issue in repentance or turning from sin.

the righteous as a beloved son and his discipline is as for a firstborn. For the Lord will spare his devout, *and he will wipe away their mistakes with discipline.* For the life of the righteous (goes on) forever, but sinners shall be taken away to destruction, and no memory of them will ever be found. (*Pss. Sol.* 13:7-11 [emphasis added])[20]

God is merciful and just, and so disciplines or chastises even the righteous for their (few) sins; by enduring God's discipline, the righteous pay their debt and then move on to eternal life. By contrast, the sinners' transgressions are of such magnitude that these persons can only meet with destruction.[21]

The books 2 Maccabees and especially 4 Maccabees (which used 2 Maccabees as a source) both presuppose that the faithful endurance of affliction by righteous persons can benefit others. In a description of the martyrdoms of a pious old man named Eleazar and of seven righteous Jewish brothers and their mother, the author of 2 Maccabees has one brother say to Antiochus Epiphanes:

"I, like my brothers, give up body and life for the laws of our ancestors, appealing to God to show mercy soon to our nation and by trials and plagues to make you confess that he alone is God, and *through me and my brothers to bring to an end the wrath of the Almighty that has justly fallen on our whole nation.*" (7:37-38 [emphasis added]; cf. vv. 32-33)

This remark assumes that God will show mercy to the whole nation because of the entreaties offered and chastisements endured by a few; nothing is said

---

20. Trans. R. B. Wright, in *OTP* 2.663.

21. Compare Wis. 11:9-10; 12:18-22; 2 Macc. 6:12-16. Gundry-Volf, 99-112, argues that the "chastisement" or "discipline" mentioned in Wisdom 12:22 and 1 Corinthians 11:27-34 is to be understood not as payment of a debt, but as evidence of *prior election by God* and hence as a sign or guarantee that God will be merciful at the final judgment. To defend this position, she must interpret the *hina mē* of 1 Corinthians 11:32 as introducing a logical result (". . . thus [or, it follows that] we will not be condemned along with the world"); she cites 2 Maccabees 6:12-16 and *1 Clement* 56.16 as parallel constructions (112). But in all three passages, the cited constructions could more readily be taken as expressing purpose: God chastens the righteous now, *in order that* they need not be punished at the judgment. Gundry-Volf's reading seems to be governed by her apologetic interest in denying that Paul could have viewed the present suffering of believers as atoning or redemptive (105). For a discussion of rabbinic (and some earlier) views of redemptive suffering, see E. P. Sanders, *Paul and Palestinian Judaism* (Philadelphia: Fortress Press, 1977), 168-72.

about the repentance and reform of the many.[22] The author of 4 Maccabees elaborated on the notion that the martyrs' deaths had vicarious effect. Before his death, Eleazar prays, "Be merciful to your people, and let our punishment suffice for them. Make my blood their purification, and take my life in exchange for theirs" (4 Macc. 6:28). Subsequently, the author describes the martyrdoms of Eleazar and the seven sons as pure sacrificial offerings that reconciled the nation to God by means of cleansing blood:

> These, then, who have been consecrated for the sake of God, are honored, not only with this honor [a life of eternal blessedness], but also by the fact that because of them our enemies did not rule over the nation, the tyrant was punished and the homeland purified — they having become, as it were, a ransom *(antipsychos)* for the sin of our nation. And through the blood of those devout ones and their death as an atoning sacrifice *[hilastērion]*, divine Providence preserved Israel that had previously been mistreated. (17:20-22)

Explicit cultic terminology is here used to describe the martyrs' sacrifice; further, the author of 4 Maccabees portrays Eleazar as a priest and the seven sons as sinless, implying their fitness to offer and be offered as sacrifice.[23] *By their courage and endurance unto death*, Eleazar, the seven

22. S. K. Williams (*Jesus' Death as Saving Event: The Background and Origin of a Concept* [Missoula, Mont.: Scholars Press, 1975], 196) argues that 2 Maccabees presents the expiation of the nation's sin not as a result of the martyrs' vicarious sacrifice, but "in terms of the victories of the Maccabees and their purifying of temple, city, and land"; 4 Maccabees then "telescopes this *extended* event and identifies it as the effect of the martyrs' faithful suffering unto death; it was *through their faith* that God delivered Israel; *because of them* the land was purified" (italics original). My point here is that even in 2 Maccabees (in the passage quoted above), the sacrifice of the martyrs is assumed to contribute to the restoration of God's favor to the sinful people. The sins that the martyrs concede are not their sins alone, but the collective sins of the people; the punishments they endure at the hand of God (cf. 6:12-17) are likewise endured on behalf of the people.

23. Besides 6:28-29 and 17:21-22, see also 1:11. On the portrayal of the martyrs' deaths as vicarious sacrifices, see H.-J. Klauck, *Unterweisung in lehrhafter Form: 4. Makkabäerbuch,* (Gütersloh: Gütersloher Verlagshaus Gerd Mohn, 1989), 670-72, who shows how 4 Maccabees heightens the emphasis (already present in 2 Maccabees) on the vicarious and sacrificial character of the martyrs' deaths. The reference to the *hilastērion* in 4 Maccabees 17:22 alludes to the ritual of the annual Day of Atonement, when the high priest enters the Holy of Holies and applies sacrifical blood to the so-called mercy seat (Lev. 16:13-15; cf. 4:1-35). Williams, 183, suggests that "the components of *antipsychon* (i.e., *anti* and *psyche*) make it an obvious synonym for lytron." Moreover, the words *haima* and *kathorizein* "are commonplace cultic-religious terms in the LXX."

brothers, and their mother conquer the tyrant Antiochus and become the means or cause of the purification of the land (1:11). In an important study, Sam K. Williams shows that the author of 4 Maccabees doesn't present the martyrdoms as sacrifices that God demands; rather, the deaths "are understood as acts of complete devotion, and so, *like* perfect sacrifices, God can regard them as effective for purification, expiation, ransom."[24] It is precisely by means of his emphasis on the martyrs' *endurance* that the author of 4 Maccabees shows that their deaths were acts of complete devotion. In Chapter 3 below, I shall argue that so also in Mark's Gospel, it is the *endurance of testing* by Jesus that caused God to regard him as "perfect," and his death as the ultimate, effective sacrifice.

Satan as the Agent of Testing

A few of the Hebrew Scriptures refer to a character "Satan," or more likely "the *satan*," or "a *satan*" (a Hebrew term meaning "adversary," or "accuser," depending on context).[25] In these texts the character is a mere functionary in the divine assembly.[26] But during the intertestamental period this figure

---

24. Williams, 196-97 (emphasis original); cf. 41, 46-47, 56, 167-69, 176-79. The assumption in 4 Maccabees that an individual could make a vicarious sacrifice to the deity by dying an unmerited death is paralleled in (pagan) Hellenistic writings of the era, as Hengel and Williams have shown (M. Hengel, *The Atonement: The Origins of the Doctrine in the New Testament* [Philadelphia: Fortress Press, 1981], 1-32; Williams, 137-63).

25. V. P. Hamilton, "Satan," in *ABD*, vol. 5 (1992), 985-89, offers a brief, helpful discussion of the usages in the Hebrew Bible of the noun *satan* (and also of the cognate verb); for a fuller discussion of the background and early usage of these terms, see especially P. L. Day, *An Adversary in Heaven: śāṭān in the Hebrew Bible* (Atlanta: Scholars Press, 1988). The noun refers sometimes to a human adversary or accuser (1 Sam. 29:4; 2 Sam. 19:22 [MT 19:23]; 1 Kings 5:4 [MT 5:18]; 11:14, 23, 25; Ps. 109:6), and sometimes to a celestial one (Num. 22:22, 32; 1 Chron. 21:1 [occurs without the article]; Job 1-2 [14x]; and Zech. 3:1, 2.

26. Biblical passages in which Yahweh appears in the context of the divine assembly include (besides Job 1-2): 1 Kings 22:19; Isa. 6:2-3; Zech. 3:4, 7. On ideas about the divine assembly in the ancient Near East (and in the Hebrew scriptures specifically), see P. D. Miller Jr., *The Divine Warrior in Early Israel* (Cambridge: Harvard University Press, 1973), 12-23, 66-74; E. T. Mullen Jr., "Divine Assembly," in *ABD*, vol. 2 (1992), 214-17. Day makes a strong case for her view that the Hebrew term *satan* does not refer to a distinct celestial personality in any of its occurrences in the Hebrew Bible; the few depictions of celestial satans refer to anonymous members of the divine assembly.

grew in prestige and ascribed authority, so that in some circles the influence of the *satan* on daily life came to rival that of the God of Israel. In such circles, the most characteristic activity of "Satan" (which came to be understood as a proper name) was believed to be that of testing the righteous. It was supposed that Satan used various techniques — including affliction, deception, and seductive offers of benefit or pleasure — in his effort to lead the righteous astray from God's kingdom and into Satan's own realm. This role as "tester" was derived especially from the prologue to the book of Job.[27] Although Satan is never directly called "the tempter/tester" in Job, he functions in that way, using affliction to test whether Job's piety deserves the high marks God gives it.[28]

But "Satan" and "the tempter" (or "the tester," *ho peirazōn*) are just two of many aliases assigned to the archfiend and enemy of God in the late second-temple period. Besides these two designations, "the devil" (*ho diabolos,* the Greek term used to translate *satan* in the LXX) is the label most frequently used in the New Testament itself; others include "Belial" (or "Beliar"), "Mastema," "Sammael," "the enemy," "the angel of darkness," and "the ruler of this world." Why was there such a bewildering variety of names and titles for this figure? The character of Satan as known in the first century was the end product of long reflection by Jews on a number of ancient mythic traditions pertaining to the adversaries of Yahweh and of humankind. The traditions were diverse with respect to both ethnic origin and content: they ranged from stories about the victory of pagan gods over the sea or over death, to related myths about Yahweh's primeval combat with Leviathan (a "chaos monster"), to accounts of rebel angels who descended to earth and mated with human women, to tales of gods or humans who sought to make themselves like the Most High and so were cast down, to the biblical stories of Job and of Adam and Eve.[29] As Jews from the exilic period onward confronted the oppression

---

27. Cf. Gerhardsson, 39: the opening chapters of Job played an important part in establishing the idea that Satan is the instrument of God for the temptation of the righteous.

28. While neither *peirasmos* nor *peirazein* appears in the LXX edition of Job, *peiratēs* ([16:9] and 25:3) and *peiratērion* are used (7:1; 10:17; and 19:12). Korn, 10-18, offers helpful philological analysis of these passages, arguing that the LXX introduces a consistent, coherent notion of "testing" where it was not present in the Hebrew text.

29. The Genesis account does not mention "Satan," for when Genesis was written, Satan-as-archfiend was not yet in view. On the other hand, the story of the clever serpent does incorporate ancient Near Eastern mythological motifs that contributed to the evolu-

of their land and people by foreign rulers, as well as the seductive appeal of other cultures, the mythic enemies of primeval times took on new life and form. By the turn of the millenium, many Jews had begun to identify the adversaries in the ancient traditions with the "Satan" known from Job, but the variety of names and functions derived from the different adversary-traditions persisted.

The daunting task of tracing particular strands of these mythic traditions back through the tangled web of multiple cultural intersections (which spanned hundreds of years) has been undertaken by others, and cannot be repeated in any detail here.[30] Still, it may be helpful very

---

tion of Satan's character, and by the first century some readers assumed that the serpent and Satan were one, as Wisdom of Solomon 2:23-24 probably indicates (regarding this passage, see S. R. Garrett, "The God of This World and the Affliction of Paul: 2 Cor 4:1-12," in *Greeks, Romans, and Christians: Essays in Honor of Abraham J. Malherbe,* ed. David L. Balch et al. [Minneapolis: Fortress Press, 1990], 109; regarding the mythological background of the serpent in Genesis, see K. R. Joines, "The Serpent in Gen 3," *Zeitschrift für die alttestamentliche Wissenschaft* 87 (1975): 1-11; and L. K. Handy, "Serpent [Religious Symbol]," in *ABD,* vol. 5 [1992], 1112-16). The author of Wisdom implies that the devil's allies test righteous persons in the present, just as the devil/serpent had tested Adam and Eve in the Garden. Paul makes similar assumptions in 2 Corinthians 11:3; here he probably identifies the serpent with Satan (see Garrett, "God of This World," 106-7 n. 37). I do not here have the space to explore in detail the influence of the Genesis account on evolving ideas about Satan. This influence was probably as great as that exercised by the Job-account: for example, the story of the serpent in Genesis probably contributed to the fundamental assumption that Satan used not only affliction but also deceptive offers of benefit or pleasure ("seduction") to try to lead the righteous astray. The Genesis account may also have contributed to the assumption that Satan can metamorphose into other forms (including, by common interpretive convention, the form of the serpent in the Garden). Despite such influence from the Garden-story, it was the book of Job that most substantively affected beliefs about Satan's *afflicting of the righteous,* and also beliefs about Satan's *relationship to God* — the matters most pertinent for my interpretation of "the trials of Jesus" in Mark.

30. The fullest treatment of the mythic evolution of the character of Satan out of these various streams of tradition is N. Forsyth, *The Old Enemy: Satan and the Combat Myth* (Princeton: Princeton University Press, 1987), which, however, gives insufficient attention to the influence of Zoroastrian traditions on the emergence and character of Satan. In general on the contact between Zoroastrians and Jews, see G. Widengren, *Quelques rapports entre Juifs et Iraniens a l'epoque des parthes* (Leiden: E. J. Brill, 1957), 197-241; G. Widengren, "Iran and Israel in Parthian Times with Special Regard to the Ethiopic Book of Enoch," in *Religious Syncretism in Antiquity: Essays in Conversation with Geo. Widengren,* ed. B. A. Pearson (Missoula, Mont.: Scholars Press, 1975), 85-129; D. Winston, "The Iranian Component in the Bible, Apocrypha, and Qumran: A Review of the Evidence," *History of Religions* 5 (1966): 183-216; J. Barr, "The Question of Religious Influence: The Case of Zoroastrianism, Judaism, and Christianity," *Journal of the American Academy of*

briefly to sketch several of the most prominent lines of tradition running from the more ancient mythic accounts to the "Satan" of the New Testament and other Jewish and Christian apocalyptic literature. *Only when one understands Satan's composite nature (that is, blending elements from diverse mythic accounts) do certain tensions in the New Testament portrayals of this character become explicable.* The most significant such tension is the seeming contradiction between Satan's role as eschatological adversary, who fights against God and God's servants (see, for example, Rev. 12:7–13:18; 2 Cor. 2:11; 2 Thess. 2:4), and his role as servant of God, who carries out certain unpleasant duties for God (1 Cor. 5:5; 2 Cor. 12:7). Satan's adversary- or archfiend-role traces back to ancient Near Eastern myths about combat among the gods and also Zoroastrian mythology; his servant-role derives in part from passages in Job that portray the *satan* as requiring divine authorization in order to oppose God's righteous servant(s).[31]

Religion 53 (1985): 201-35; on Zoroastrianism's influence on ancient Jewish ideas about Satan and (more specifically) on the ideology of the Qumran sectarians, see K. G. Kuhn, "Die Sektenschrift und die iranische Religion," *Zeitschrift für Theologie und Kirche* 49 (1952): 296-316; K. G. Kuhn, "New Light on Temptation, Sin, and Flesh in the New Testament," in *The Scrolls and the New Testament,* ed. K. Stendahl (New York: Harper and Bros., 1957), 94-113 (Kuhn, however, may overstate the case). Discussions by other scholars of mythic antecedents to the character of Satan include Day; Hamilton; A. Y. Collins, *The Combat Myth in the Book of Revelation* (Missoula, Mont.: Scholars Press, 1976); and Garrett, "Exodus from Bondage" (regarding specifically the influence of Isaiah 14 and Ezekiel 28–32 on Luke's view of Satan). The best treatment of the *satan*-passages in the Hebrew scriptures is Day. Despite the title of the book, E. Pagels's *The Origin of Satan* (New York: Random House, 1995) contributes little to the question of the mythic development of the character of Satan.

31. The portrait in Job and also in Zechariah 3 of the *satan* as subordinate to God is itself dependent on ancient Near Eastern traditions about the hierarchical ordering of the divine assembly (concerning which, see Miller, 12-23, 66-74; and Mullen); thus the stream of tradition represented in these two biblical books is not independent of the combat myths, which also presuppose a divine assembly of the gods. Miller, 72-74, contrasts Israel's view of Yahweh's absolute rule over the divine council with the more "democratic" divine council arrangements presupposed in Mesopotamian and Canaanite cultures. The theological tension between the ideal of YHWH as sovereign and the realization that YHWH continues to face opposition from the forces of chaos pervades the Hebrew scriptures, as Levenson demonstrates. The tension that I highlight in the following discussion is related but not identical: it pertains not to the sovereignty of Yahweh per se, but to the identity of Satan as both opponent of Yahweh (that is, one who tries to *thwart* God's purposes) and minion of Yahweh (one who serves to *advance* God's purposes).

The Combat Myths of the Ancient Near East

Scattered throughout the Hebrew Scriptures are references and allusions to opposition — even outright combat — between Yahweh and other deities or cosmic forces. Such notices reflect Israel's long period of contact with the mythologies of neighboring cultures. Especially influential on Israelite thinking were the Babylonian creation myth, the *Enuma Elish*, in which Marduk slays the goddess Tiamat and forms the earth and sky out of the halves of her body; and an Ugaritic combat myth, in which the god Baal defeats the powers of chaos embodied in the ocean, called Prince Yamm ("sea"), then returns to the heavens as victorious king. There are allusions in the Hebrew Scriptures to other myths as well: Isaiah 25:7 alludes to an Ugaritic tale in which Baal conquers the god Mot ["death"]; and Isaiah 14:12-20 incorporates motifs paralleled in the Ugaritic story of the god Athtar, who ascended to the "reaches of Zaphon" (= "in the far north") to usurp the throne of Baal, but failed in his attempted rebellion (compare Ezek. 28:1-19).[32] Though it was the various Babylonian and Ugaritic myths that influenced the Hebrew Scriptures most pervasively, other ancient cultures (including Greece and Rome) also knew of combat among the gods; some of these myths may have influenced Jewish (and then Christian) writers in the intertestamental period and into the common era.[33]

The allusions to ancient myths of divine combat occur in many parts of the Hebrew Bible, including narratives, psalms, and prophetic oracles.

---

32. English translations of the Babylonian epic (the *Enuma Elish*) and of the Ugaritic cycle of myths involving Baal may be found in J. B. Pritchard, *The Ancient Near East, Volume I: An Anthology of Texts and Pictures* (Princeton: Princeton University Press, 1958), 31-39, 92-118; or J. B. Pritchard, *Ancient Near Eastern Texts Relating to the Old Testament* (Princeton: Princeton University Press, 1969), 129-42, 60-72. The contribution of these myths to evolving ideas about Satan is discussed in Forsyth, 44-66, 126-30. Miller, 24, remarks that Baal's conflicts with Yamm and with Mot are clearly different battles, "though they are aspects of a single mythological motif — the conflict between cosmos or order and chaos." For discussion of specific similarities and differences between the Babylonian *Enuma Elish* and the Ugaritic Baal-myths, see Miller, 25-28; Levenson, 9-10, 12. For an English translation of the Ugaritic tale about Athtar the rebel, see Pritchard, *Ancient Near East*, 111-12; regarding the influence of the lament in Isaiah 14 concerning the fall of the king of Babylon on developing views of Satan, see Forsyth, 134-39; also the works cited in n. 39 below.

33. For discussion of these other streams of mythic tradition and their influence on the character of Satan, see Forsyth, esp. 76-85, 132-34; also Collins, *Combat Myth*.

These allusions function in various ways, four of which I shall mention
here. First, in the biblical "holy war" traditions, authors incorporate
elements from the combat myths into descriptions of earthly battles
waged by the Israelites. The mythic elements pertaining to combat
among the gods are reappropriated and adapted to the Israelite context:
Yahweh battles not monsters or other gods, but the nations who were
the historical enemies of Israel.[34] Second, biblical authors use traditions
about cosmic combat in recalling God's former victory over the forces
of chaos, as a basis or warrant for summoning God to intervene again
on behalf of the afflicted (as in Psalm 74).[35] Third, late prophetic and
early apocalyptic writers use cosmic combat traditions in portraying
God's future (eschatological) intervention for the afflicted people of
God. Such writers ponder the tension between the ideal of God's
sovereignty, demonstrated by Yahweh's primordial conquest of enemies,
and the reality of triumphant evil, evidenced by crises current in their
own day.[36] These writers expect God's intervention against the forces

34. Descriptions of Yahweh's intervention in battle on Israel's behalf weave together
what would be designated by modern readers as "historical" and "mythological" elements.
Miller offers a helpful discussion of the "holy war" passages, including the following: early
poetry: Deut. 33:2-5, 26-29; Judg. 5; Ps. 68; Exod. 15; Hab. 3:3-15; 2 Sam. 22:7-18 (= Ps.
18:7-18); Josh. 10:12-13. Early prose: Josh. 5:13-15; Gen. 32:2-3; 2 Sam. 5:22-25. Ninth
century prophets: 2 Kings 6:15-19; 7:6. Later prophetic writings: Isa. 13:1ff.; Joel 4:9ff;
Isa. 40:26; 45:12; Zech. 14. Miller also discusses some intertestamental developments of
the holy war motif.

35. For an interesting discussion of such texts (including Pss. 74:10-11, 18-20; 89:39-
40, 50; Isa. 51:7-8, 12-13), see Levenson, 14-25. Levenson argues that appeals to God for
action, such as occur in these passages and in apocalyptic texts, reflect a widespread and
persistent notion that the forces of chaos, though held at bay since God's primordial
triumph, continue to pose a genuine threat to God's sovereignty: "The confinement of
chaos rather than its elimination is the essence of creation, and the survival of ordered
reality hangs only upon God's vigilance in ensuring that those cosmic dikes do not fail,
that the bars and doors of the Sea's jail cell do not give way, that the great fish does not
slip his hook" (17). Later, Levenson suggests ways in which the motif of the survival of
the cosmic adversaries after their initial defeat serves to underscore Yahweh's sovereignty
(26-27).

36. Levenson writes, "It is the disjunction between the ideal world of liturgy and the
real world of innocent suffering that this apocalyptic eschatology shares with laments
such as Ps 74 and 89" (32). For discussion of differences between the lament-traditions
and apocalyptic eschatology, see Levenson, 32-33, 50. Levenson is certainly familiar with
the scholarly argument that the phenomenon of apocalyptic cannot be explained solely
as a response to suffering; see his comments in 161 n. 19. Miller argues that the

of chaos to take place during a great holy war in which the earthly and heavenly hosts will participate.[37] Fourth, the authors of Isaiah 14:12-20 and Ezekiel 28–32 use combat traditions to condemn the unjust actions of certain historical rulers and nations and to predict divine judgment against them. The author of Isaiah 14 portrays the king of Babylon as a rebellious god, who seeks to make himself equal to Yahweh but is cast down for his arrogance ("You said in your heart, 'I will ascend to heaven; I will raise my throne above the stars of God . . .' but you are brought down to Sheol, to the depths of the Pit" [vv. 13-15]). Ezekiel employs a similar myth of rebellion (and also other combat motifs) in a series of oracles against the Princes of Tyre, Egypt, and others. By describing the opposition of human foes in mythic terms, writers such as Ezekiel and the author of Isaiah 14 suggest that those foes represent forces greater than mere mortals — forces that oppose Yahweh's sovereignty over the created order.[38]

Portrayals of Yahweh as a warrior in combat with Israel's enemies — enemies who embodied the very powers of death and chaos — prepared the way for Satan's advent. Once certain Jews had accepted the notion that God was opposed by a *single* spiritual adversary or archfiend, then the various depictions of mythic opponents (such as those discussed immediately above) were reappropriated to give form and character to the cosmic enemy. The best example of such "reappropriation" involves Isaiah 14: sometime around the first century of the common era, Jews (and, in turn, Christians) would "remythologize" the Isaianic oracle against the king of Babylon, interpreting it as a poem about the fall from heaven of the rebel angel, Satan, on account of his effort to usurp the

---

ninth-century prophets (themselves closely associated with the traditions about holy war) formed a link between "the early association of holy war theology with the heavenly army imagery and the later association of prophetic eschatology and the Day of Yahweh with that same imagery" (132-33). Miller also argues that the notion of the "Day of Yahweh" has its origins in the traditions about holy war (135-41); for a brief history of scholarly debate on this issue, see K. J. Cathcart, "Day of Yahweh," *ABD*, vol. 2 (1992), 84-85.

37. See, for example, Isa. 13:1-22; 24:1–27:13; Joel 3:9-21; Zech. 14:1-21; 1 Enoch 1:9; the War Scroll; Rev. 19:11–20:3. Here I have grouped together references from late prophetic discourse and from apocalyptic discourse; for discussion of how the use of the combat myths in these two forms of prophecy differed from one another, see Forsyth, 142-46.

38. Cf. Levenson, 38.

place of God.[39] The Vulgate would translate the expression rendered in the NRSV as "Day Star" (Isa. 14:12) with the Latin *lucifer* ("light-bearer"), thereby giving the enemy one of his most enduring names.

Such application of the ancient Near Eastern myths of combat to a single spiritual adversary of God or the people of God reflected a fundamental shift in worldview: the shift from a world in which God's uncompromised ordering of the kingdom, cult, and community are taken for granted to a world in which the forces of good and the forces of evil are arrayed against each other, locked in an age-old (and escalating) struggle. In my view, the best explanation for this momentous shift in perspective is one that posits influence from Persian religion.[40] "Zoroastrianism" or "Mazdaism" (founded by Zarathustra [Gr. "Zoroaster"], thought to have lived and taught in the seventh and sixth centuries B.C.E.) asserted the existence of opposing cosmic adversaries, principles of good and evil, through whom all life and nonlife had come into being. The evil or "Destructive Spirit" ("Angra Mainyu," or "Ahriman") was linked to a host

39. For a discussion of the influence of Isaiah 14 and Ezekiel 28-32 on evolving ideas about Satan, see Collins, *Combat Myth*, 79-85; Forsyth, 134-42; S. R. Garrett, *The Demise of the Devil: Magic and the Demonic in Luke's Writings* (Minneapolis: Fortress Press, 1989), 135-36 n. 54; Garrett, "Exodus from Bondage." On the use of these traditions in 1 Enoch (where Satan is not a character), see P. D. Hanson, "Rebellion in Heaven, Azazel, and Euhemeristic Heroes in 1 Enoch 6–11," *Journal of Biblical Literature* 96 (1977): 195-233. More generally on the theme of the arrogance or self-exaltation of Satan and his emissaries, see Garrett, *Demise of the Devil*, 144 n. 32; S. R. Garrett, "Paul's Thorn and Cultural Models of Affliction," in *The Social World of the First Christians: Essays in Honor of Wayne A. Meeks*, ed. L. M. White and O. L. Yarbrough (Minneapolis: Fortress Press, 1995), 94-96.

40. Here I am dependent on J. J. Collins ("The Mythology of Holy War in Daniel and the Qumran War Scroll: A Point of Transition in Jewish Apocalyptic," *Vetus Testamentum* 25 [1975]: 596-612), who argues that the shift is illustrated by the difference between the biblical book of Daniel and the Qumran War Scroll. Although motifs in Daniel 7–8 derive from many sources, the *structure* of the vision still reflects the Ugaritic-type myth of conflict with the forces of chaos; the worldview presupposed by the Qumran War Scroll appears as more radically dualistic. Collins compares the content of the War Scroll with the description of Zoroastrianism by the late-first-century C.E. author Plutarch, in *Moralia* 369A-370C (*Isis and Osiris* 45-47), and concludes that — although the War Scroll certainly does incorporate traditional ancient Near Eastern combat motifs — the foundational structure of its depiction of the war "of the attack of the sons of light against the sons of darkness" was supplied by the Zoroastrian myth. Collins writes, "The War Scroll has in effect substituted for the Canaanite chaos myth another myth in which the world is divided equally between the antagonists, at least for a period. In this way the foundation is laid for a thorough-going dualism" (607).

of malevolent powers (Avestan: *daevas*), said to be worshipped by those who choose the Lie rather than Truth.[41] Familiarity with the Zoroastrian archfiend Ahriman and his entourage may well have been a decisive factor in the emergence in Judaism of a *singular* cosmic adversary — lord of the demons, lover of deceit, user of magic, source of affliction and death.[42]

But the radical dualism that we find in Zoroastrianism was not adopted uncritically by Jewish authors, who insisted that God remains sovereign over the archenemy. In underscoring God's sovereignty, authors sometimes used language from the book of Job, which reported that Satan could act to afflict Job *only after God had granted Satan authority to do so.* Perhaps the best evidence for the influence of the Job account on emerging views of Satan is simply the preeminence of the designations "Satan" and "the devil" in Christian discourse about the archenemy, over other designations such as "Belial" and "Mastema." "Satan" and "the devil" *[ho diabolos]* are the respective Hebrew and Greek terms for the adversary-figure in the Hebrew and Greek [LXX]) renditions of the Job account.[43] Job's picture of "Satan" as a servant of God, who must be *authorized by God* before carrying out his task of testing the righteous, profoundly affected Jewish and Christian thinking about Satan in the years around the turn of the millenium, as I shall now demonstrate.

---

41. R. C. Zaehner, *The Dawn and Twilight of Zoroastrianism* (New York: G. P. Putnam's Sons, 1961), 39, 154-72 and *passim*, contends that the *daevas* were pre-Zoroastrian deities who had been demoted to the status of demons. Zoroaster tried to eradicate the cult of the *daevas*, but the cult continued to exist alongside of the evolving Zoroastrian movement, which reabsorbed some aspects of it as early as the Achaemenid period (530–330 B.C.E.). In an earlier work (*Zurvan: A Zoroastrian Dilemma* [Oxford: Clarendon Press, 1955], 20), R. C. Zaehner notes that some of the Magians who emigrated from Persia during the Achaemenid and Hellenistic periods appear to have practiced occult-like worship of the *daevas*, or demons (and note Plutarch's indication in *Moralia*, 369E-F, that the *magoi* make offerings to Ahriman — a practice quite at odds with Zoroaster's teaching). Familiarity with such practices would help to account for the frequent association of the devil with "demons" and with "magic" in Jewish and early Christian writings (regarding this association, see Garrett, "Demise of the Devil").

42. So also Day, 63; Hamilton, 988.

43. Other evidence for the influence of Job on developing views of Satan is discussed below and in Garrett, "Paul's Thorn," 87-91.

The Book of Job and Ancient Views of Testing

Job 1–2 and Zechariah 3:1-7 both feature a figure called the *satan* — a celestial or angelic adversary — and provide glimpses into the workings of the divine council. In the prologue of Job, the council assembles before God one day, and the *satan* is among them. God commends Job's righteousness to the *satan,* who then challenges God, saying, "Stretch out your hand now, and touch all that he has, and he will curse you to your face." Next, the Lord tells the *satan* that Job is in the *satan's* power — "Only do not stretch out your hand against him!" (Job 1:7-12). Catastrophes befall Job, but he worships and blesses God rather than cursing God (as the *satan* had predicted). Consequently God points out Job's piety to the *satan* a second time; the *satan* then predicts that if God but stretch out God's hand "and touch his bone and his flesh," Job will curse God to God's face (2:5). God responds, "Very well, he is in your power; only spare his life" (2:6). The *satan* then inflicts loathsome sores on Job's body. But, even when Job's own wife tries to persuade him to "curse [lit. "bless"] God and die" (2:9), the righteous man refuses to "sin with his lips" (2:10).

A later Jewish document called the *Testament of Job* retells the Job story, offering a remarkable glimpse of how persons living close to the turn of the millenium interpreted the LXX version of Job.[44] In the *Testament of Job,* "Satan" (it is here a proper name) is given a motive for attacking the righteous man: Job has destroyed an idol's temple, wherein Satan was worshipped. A revealing angel makes it clear to Job at the outset that Satan is his combatant, and that if Job exhibits endurance he will receive eternal life. Because Job withstands Satan's attacks, at last the devil tearfully concedes that Job has become the victor in their "wrestling match." Thus, by his endurance Job actually *triumphs over* the adversary. Below, and also in Chapters 2 and 3, I shall have more to say about certain key scenes in

44. I am in agreement with B. Schaller, ed., *Das Testament Hiobs* (Gütersloh: Mohn, 1979), 311, that the *Testament of Job* was most likely written by a Hellenistic Jewish author sometime between the beginning of the first century B.C.E. and mid–second century C.E. A date of composition prior to the advent of Christianity seems reasonable, though it cannot be proven; see D. Rahnenführer, "Das Testament des Hiob und das Neue Testament," *Zeitschrift für die neutestamentliche Wissenschaft* 62 (1971): 93. (On date and provenance, see further Garrett, "God of This World," 106 n. 35; for more general remarks on the worldview presupposed by this document, see S. R. Garrett, "The 'Weaker Sex' in the *Testament of Job," Journal of Biblical Literature* 112 (1993): 55-70.)

the *Testament of Job*. Here it is sufficient to note that some of the most intriguing premises of this melodramatic account derive from a particular reading of canonical Job. These premises, which were shared by some Jewish and Christian writers around the time of the composition of the canonical Gospels, include the following:

(1) that human righteousness and service for God may prompt satanic attack;
(2) that Satan views his affliction of humans as a contest in which honor and authority are at stake;
(3) that because God gives Satan authority *only* over the righteous man's body, Satan cannot gain authority over that man's soul unless he himself forfeits the authority by cursing God;[45] and
(4) that Satan stands in an ambiguous relationship to God, authorized by God but seeking nonetheless to lead God's faithful astray.

The last assumption in particular is relevant to the question of *agency* in incidents of testing: if Satan tests persons, but does so only with God's permission, then are Satan and God jointly the "agents of testing"? I shall have more to say about this matter below.

Eschatological Testing

According to a widespread belief in ancient Judaism and early Christianity, the Day of the Lord will be characterized by affliction; these eschatological "woes" or "birthpangs" will commence in advance of the Day itself. Such beliefs were based in part on certain passages from the Hebrew Scriptures, including Daniel 12:1: "There shall be a time of anguish, such as has never occurred since nations first came into existence" (cf. Hab. 3:16; Zeph. 1:15). These birth pangs of the new age represent active resistance by the powers of the old age, who attempt to thwart God's saving action every step of the way (cf. Rev. 3:10; 12:10-12). Sometimes the hostile, satanic powers are expected to concentrate especially in one person or being, an "eschatological adversary." Such figures include the lawless one in 2 Thes-

---

45. See *T. Job* 16:7; 20:1-3; 26:3; cf. Job 1:11; 2:5, 6, 9. I enumerate a similar list and elaborate on some of the material in this discussion in Garrett, "Paul's Thorn."

salonians, the antichrist in 1 John, and the beast from the sea (with its counterpart "beast from the land") in Revelation. The eschatological adversaries manifest Satan's power and perform Satan's tasks: they afflict persons and use deception to lead them astray from right behavior and belief.[46]

In texts about eschatological testing, magicians and false prophets often figure as vehicles of satanic power. Magic, false prophecy, and satanic agency are intertwined in a number of Jewish and Jewish-influenced texts dating from the late second-temple period through the early second century c.e., including the synoptic Gospels, the fourth Gospel, and the book of Acts. The traditions about eschatological false prophets found throughout the New Testament have been influenced not only by the mythic (combat) traditions discussed above, but also by Deuteronomy 13:1-5 and 18:20-22. In these passages God tells the Israelites (through Moses) how to identify and avoid the seductive maneuvers of false prophets. Throughout the ancient world, many persons believed that magicians utilized spirits or "daemons" to achieve their desired results; in Jewish and Christian contexts, this datum was reformulated: Satan and the demons empower false prophets to perform "signs and wonders" so that they might persuade observers to follow them down the crooked path to idolatry.[47] False prophets conceal their true nature from most people, but a spiritually discerning person — an Isaiah, or a Peter, or a Paul — can instantly recognize the wicked nature of false prophets, and mobilize the power of God against them.[48] And, at the eschaton, the false prophets — who, as living

---

46. These various adversary-figures can be genetically traced to many of the same mythic traditions that shaped the evolving (and related) figure of Satan, including combat myths from the ancient Near East, Zoroastrian mythology, and historical traditions about Antiochus IV Epiphanes. On the contribution of such traditions to developing ideas about the "antichrist," see G. C. Jenks, *The Origins and Early Development of the Antichrist Myth* (Berlin: Walter de Gruyter, 1991). For another discussion of ancient beliefs about eschatological testing (and their relevance for interpretions of Mark), see R. E. Brown, *The Death of the Messiah: From Gethsemane to the Grave* (New York: Doubleday, 1994), 159-62.

47. For fuller discussion of the association among magic, false prophecy, and satanic agency, see Garrett, *Demise of the Devil*, 13-17; regarding Acts 13:4-12 in this connection, see 79-87. On magicians' use of demons or spirits, see n. 41 above. For analysis of the false prophet motif at Qumran and elsewhere, see W. A. Meeks, *The Prophet-King: Moses Traditions and the Johannine Christology* (Leiden: E. J. Brill, 1967), 47-57. Meeks discusses the centrality of Deuteronomy 13 and 18 in postbiblical traditions.

48. Regarding false prophets who conceal their identity, see *Mart. Isa.* 3:1, 11 (Belkira deceives Manasseh); Acts 8:9-11; 13:7-8, 10; cf. 2 Cor. 11:13-15. The servants of God

implements of God's supreme adversary, wield the very forces of chaos, or lawlessness — will be captured and punished eternally.[49]

The authors of the New Testament texts assume that Satan (himself served by false prophets and by other human and demonic characters) opposes God's work of converting persons to belief in Christ. And yet, it is scarcely the case that these authors believed Satan to be on an equal footing with God. Paul, for example, sometimes refers to Satan in a way that suggests that God could instruct Satan to do God's bidding (1 Cor. 5:5; cf. 2 Cor. 12:7). I have already suggested that the conflicting notions of Satan as opposed to God but nonetheless subordinate to God had their origins in distinct mythic or literary complexes: Satan's opposition to God, in the ancient Near Eastern combat myths and in Zoroastrianism; and Satan's subordination to God, in Job's account of the *satan* as a member of God's heavenly court. The question of how Jews and Christians around the turn of the millenium balanced or even reconciled these conflicting notions is a difficult but important one.

God and Satan as Partners in Testing?

Eventually, elaborate narratives would be devised to account for the relationship of Satan to God. One of the most enduring and influential of such schemata would identify Satan as the fallen "day star" (*lucifer* in the Vulgate) of Isaiah 14. According to the Latin version of *The Life of Adam and Eve*,[50] which preserves this schema, Satan explains to Adam and Eve why he pursues them "treacherously and enviously" and "with deceit." It seems that when God created Adam, Michael had instructed the angels

---

who see through such deceit respond by cursing the evil characters, or by otherwise consigning them (if only symbolically) to the place of perdition that is their true home of origin. See, for example, 2 Thess. 2:3 (the lawless one is designated a "son of perdition [Gk. *apōleia*]"); Rev. 19:20; 20:10; 2 Cor. 11:15; Acts 8:20; 13:10-11; *Mart. Isa.* 6:4-10. For further discussion of the cursing of evil characters by righteous persons, see Garrett, *Demise of the Devil*, 81-85.

49. On the eternal punishment of the enemies of God generally, see Matt. 8:12; 22:13; 25:30; 2 Pet. 2:17; 1QS 4:12-14; on the punishment of false-prophet-type figures in particular, see the citations in the preceding note.

50. M. D. Johnson's introduction to and translations of the Greek and Latin recensions of the text are found in *The Old Testament Pseudepigraph* (hereafter *OTP*), 2 vols., ed. J. H. Charlesworth (Garden City, N.Y.: Doubleday, 1983, 1985), 2.249-295.

to "worship the image of the Lord God, as the Lord God has instructed" (14:1). Satan refused, saying that he would not worship someone who was inferior and subsequent to him: "I am prior to him in creation; before he was made, I was already made. He ought to worship me" (*LAE/Vita* 14:3). Michael threatened Satan with God's wrath, to which Satan replied, "If he be wrathful with me, I will set my throne above the stars of heaven and will be like the Most High" (15:3; an allusion to Isa. 14:13). Then, Satan reports, he and his angels were cast from glory and onto the earth. Out of jealousy Satan assailed Eve and caused Adam to be expelled from the Garden, just as he himself had been expelled from heavenly glory (16:1-3).[51] There are good indications that some elements of this and related narratives were known already in the first century C.E.[52] Still, it seems unlikely that there was already by this time a *widely accepted, comprehensive master narrative* that could explain Satan's origin and nature. The best guess is that ideas about the relationship between Satan and God and about their respective roles in the testing of the righteous were still largely piecemeal and evolving during the first century.

N.B.

A sampling of pertinent texts from this era (including *Testament of Job, Jubilees,* and the writings of Paul) enables us to glimpse certain pieces in this "still-changing picture" of Satan's relationship to God. In *Testament of Job,* for example, Satan's and God's activities are closely identified with one another. Job knows from the outset that Satan is his antagonist (4:3-10; cf. 7:1-13; 18:5; 26:6–27:6), but when "Baldad" later asks Job about the

---

51. The document weaves together several distinct antecedent traditions: with the Genesis story of Adam and Eve serving as framework, Satan is identified with the tempter in the Garden; with the chief of the Watchers, cast out of heaven together with his angels (cf. *1 Enoch* 6–12, discussed in Hanson); with the rebel king of Isaiah 14; and with "Satan" (i.e., the *satan* of Job and Zechariah, now interpreted as archfiend).

52. The transmission history of the Adam-and-Eve literature is extremely complicated; the various recensions are, accordingly, difficult to date (see M. Stone, *A History of the Literature of Adam and Eve* [Atlanta: Scholars Press, 1992]). Some of the traditions contained in these variant accounts are known already in New Testament times: Paul, for example, knows the story of Satan's transforming of himself into an angel of light (2 Cor. 11:14), a story found also in *LAE (Vita)* 9–10. Though the narrative details found in *LAE* may be somewhat later, the interpretation of the lament in Isaiah 14 as an oracle concerning Satan is probably presupposed already in Luke 10:18 (see Garrett, *Demise of the Devil,* 135-36 n. 54; also the works cited in n. 39 above). I here express my thanks to Michael Stone for insights gained in his seminar on the Adam and Eve literature, given at Yale University in the fall of 1992.

source of his afflictions, Job claims that it is *God* who has destroyed his goods and inflicted these plagues on him. Baldad protests:

> "Do you hope upon God? Then how do you reckon him to be unfair by inflicting you with all these plagues or destroying your goods? If he were to give and then take away, it would actually be better for him not to have given anything. At no time does a king dishonor his own soldier who bears arms well for him. Or who will ever understand the deep things of the Lord and his wisdom? Who dares to ascribe to the Lord an injustice? Answer me this, Job. (*T. Job* 37:5-7)[53]

By ascribing the cause of his suffering to God, Job implicitly affirms that even satanic afflictions fall under divine control.[54] Satan opposes God, but nonetheless remains subordinate to him and is unable to grasp beyond the authority that God expressly delegates.

The book of *Jubilees* is characterized by similar ambiguity in its portrayal of the Satan-figure (called variously "Satan," "Belial," and "Prince Mastema").[55] Satan/Belial/Mastema is here depicted as an evil character who opposes God's will by leading God's people astray (10:20; 11:5). But, in at least one version of *Jubilees,* Mastema and the demons are said to have authority from God to "test humans for the purpose of proving each one," as the *satan* does in canonical Job.[56] Moreover, *Jubilees* 17:15-16 (the retelling of the story of the testing of Abraham) echoes the canonical Job account: when Abraham's uprightness is proclaimed in heaven, Mastema says, "Tell [Abraham] to offer [Isaac] (as) a burnt offering upon the altar. And you will see whether he will do this thing. And you will know whether he is faithful in everything in which you test him" (*Jub.*

---

53. Here and elsewhere in the book I follow R. P. Spittler's translation of *Testament of Job* (in *OTP* 1:829-68), occasionally with slight modifications.

54. This affirmation coheres with the narrator's earlier notice (20:2-3) that Satan had petitioned God for the authority to test Job (as in the canonical account). Compare Luke 22:31-32: here Satan "demanded to have" *(exaitēsai)* the apostles; i.e., demanded that God give them over into Satan's authority.

55. On the etymology of "Belial," see T. J. Lewis, "Belial," in *ABD,* vol. 1 (1992), 654-55. The Hebrew word *mastēmâ* occurs in Hos. 9:7, 8, with the meaning "hatred, hostility, enmity"; see Hamilton, 987-88.

56. Greek: *hōste peirazein tous anthrōpous pros dokimēn tēs hekastou.* This rendering follows the Greek fragment of this passage as given in A. M. Denis, *Fragmenta pseudepigraphorum quae supersunt graeca* (Leiden: E. J. Brill, 1970), 87.

17:16; cf. Job 1:9-11; 2:4-5). The command is issued, and Abraham obeys. When Abraham thus proves to be willing to sacrifice Isaac, *Jubilees* reports that "Prince Mastema was shamed" (18:12). Mastema here does God's bidding, but hopes for failure rather than endurance on Abraham's part.[57]

Paul's writings include diverse remarks about the devil. Some references are entirely negative in tone, and point to Satan's role as one who seeks to undermine God's purposes (1 Thess. 3:5 ["the Tester" or "the Tempter"]; 1 Cor. 7:5; 2 Cor. 2:11; and 11:13-15).[58] But in 1 Corinthians 5:5 Paul instructs the gathered community to turn a particular transgressor over to Satan "for the destruction of the flesh, so that his spirit may be saved in the day of our Lord" — almost as if Satan tended the fires of judgment, which would burn away this sinner's impurities (cf. 1 Cor. 3:13).[59] Moreover, in 2 Corinthians 12:7, Paul refers to a "thorn in the flesh, an angel [or messenger] of Satan" that had been sent to him, in order that he might learn not to exalt himself.[60] These latter passages suggest that Paul sometimes thought of Satan as the agent who did the work of administering God's saving chastisement or discipline (a most severe discipline in the case of the offender of 1 Cor. 5:5, and a less rigorous discipline in Paul's own case). Perhaps when Paul refers in 1 Corinthians 11:32 to the "chastising" or "disciplining" illness and death undergone by the Corinthians on account of their mishandling of the Lord's supper, he is assuming that Satan was the immediate agent behind the afflictions.

How could Paul suppose that Satan acted sometimes on his own and sometimes at God's bidding? I suggest that he and some of his contemporaries took it for granted that at some point in the past God had relinquished limited but real authority to Satan (cf. Luke 4:6). Hence Paul assumes that this age is an "evil age": evil powers have a measure of control over it (Gal. 1:4). The authority or control is not absolute. Satan's dominion in the present eon is like the rule of a client-king in the first century Roman empire: over such a one stands a higher power. This "higher power"

---

57. The motif of Satan's defeat and even shame occurs also at James 4:7 and *Hermas Mandate* 12.5.2 (cf. *Visions* 4.1.5-9).

58. For a fuller discussion of Paul's view of Satan, see Garrett, "God of This World," 104-9.

59. See Gundry-Volf, 113-20, for a recent discussion of this passage, with citations of earlier works. Gundry-Volf underestimates the extent to which Satan would be *serving the purposes of God* in the anticipated encounter with the transgressor.

60. I discuss this passage extensively in Garrett, "Paul's Thorn."

(be it Caesar or God) generally permits the client-king to act autonomously but can intervene at will; moreover, the one higher up can revoke the delegated authority at any time. Paul likely supposes that the partial transfer of authority from God to lesser powers took place at the time of Adam's transgression; the apostle refers to this momentous event as the occasion when "creation was subjected to futility" (*tē gar mataiotēti hē ktisis hypetagē;* Rom. 8:20; cf. 5:12-21).[61]

The passages from *Testament of Job, Jubilees,* and the writings of Paul that I have here surveyed may act as a corrective to modern popular assumptions about Satan and God as uncompromising enemies. Ancient Jewish and Christian authors insisted that Satan — despite his unrelenting efforts to turn persons away from serving God — himself remains subordinate to God. Satan exercises authority in the present age only because God (temporarily) bestowed it upon him, and God can still call upon Satan to serve God's own purposes. By assuming that *Satan's authority to test the righteous came from God,* ancient authors maintained continuity with the picture in Job, and also balanced conventional (scriptural) attestations about God as one who "tests" and "chastises" with apocalyptic notions about Satan as the "ruler of this world" and the "enemy of all righteousness."[62]

Conclusion

The conviction that the righteous will be put to the test pervades the Hebrew Scriptures, noncanonical Jewish writings from the late second-temple era, and the New Testament and other early Christian texts. These writings interpret the tests of the righteous in a variety of ways. In the Hebrew Scriptures and some intertestamental writings, *God* often figures as the agent of testing. God tests the Hebrews (as a whole people or as individuals) for different reasons, including to discern whether persons are unswerving in their obedience to God, to chastise or discipline them when

---

61. A number of commentators hold that in Romans 8:20 Paul is alluding to the curse of Genesis 3:17-19.

62. For brief but valuable reflections on God's and Satan's respective roles in testing, see R. S. Barbour, "Gethsemane in the Tradition of the Passion," *New Testament Studies* 16 (1969–1970): 247, 250.

they err, and to exact payment (including, in a few cases, vicarious payment) of a debt owed to God on account of sinful or lawless conduct. In intertestamental writings and in the New Testament, *Satan* is often assumed to fill the role of tester. Expressions about satanic testing vary from one text to another. But in general, it is supposed that Satan tests (or "tempts") the righteous through affliction by human or demonic servants and through deceptive promises of benefit or pleasure. When Satan tests the righteous, he hopes that they will fail the tests (by disobeying, or even cursing, God), and so lose their rightful place in God's realm. When the righteous endure Satan's tests, Satan is put to shame.

I have suggested that several distinct streams of tradition coalesced to form the figure of Satan as known from New Testament–era sources, including whole cycles of ancient Near Eastern "combat myths" together with Zoroastrian myths, and also traditions about the divine court as depicted in Job 1–2 and Zechariah 3. I briefly sketched these streams of tradition as a means of clarifying tensions or paradoxes in the New Testament's several references to Satan. The combat myths contributed to the image of Satan as commander of the forces of chaos — forces squelched by Yahweh at the time of the earth's creation, but reasserting themselves as the present age nears its end. Zoroastrian influence sharpened the dualistic aspect of the Lord's battle with hostile powers. On the other hand, the canonical story of Job checked an escalation in the power and authority that were ascribed to the Satan-figure, by the repeated and unambiguous assertions (in Job 1–2) that Satan had obtained the authority to test Job from none other than God. Similarly, later writers would insist that Satan's testing of the righteous ultimately lies within God's control. God remains sovereign over Satan and responsible for granting him (even if in times primeval) the authority he now exercises. Still and all, the purposes of Satan are not identical to the purposes of God. Whereas God anticipates the endurance and consequent salvation of the righteous, Satan works furiously to lead the righteous astray from the straight and narrow path of the Lord.

CHAPTER 2

A Straight and Narrow Path

The Way of the Lord

Mark opens his "good news of Jesus Christ, the Son of God" with a word from God, as written in the Scriptures:

"See, I am sending my messenger before your face, who will prepare your way; the voice of one crying out in the wilderness: 'Prepare the way of the Lord, make his paths straight.'" (Mark 1:2-3)

The speaker is God. "Your face" and "your way" refer to the face and the way of Jesus. The "messenger" is John the Baptist, who prepares Jesus' way — the "way of the Lord."[1] Mark attributes the prophetic oracle to Isaiah, but in fact the proclamation blends allusions to Isaiah, Exodus, and Mala-

---

1. On why the *kyrios* in v. 3 ought to be taken as a reference to Jesus, see U. Mauser, *Christ in the Wilderness: The Wilderness Theme in the Second Gospel and Its Basis in the Biblical Tradition* (Naperville, Ill.: Alec R. Allenson, 1963), 80; cf. J. D. Kingsbury, *The Christology of Mark's Gospel* (Philadelphia: Fortress Press, 1983), 59; W. L. Lane, *The Gospel of Mark* (Grand Rapids: William B. Eerdmans, 1974), 46. M. A. Tolbert, *Sowing the Gospel: Mark's World in Literary-Historical Perspective* (Philadelphia: Fortress Press, 1989), 239-48, argues that *kyrios* in v. 3 refers to God, not Jesus; that the "your" (2x; second person singular pronoun) in v. 2 refers to the Israelite people as a whole; and that the "messenger" who "cries out in the wilderness" is Jesus, not John the Baptist. But the use of the second person *singular* pronoun counts against Tolbert's revisionist reading and in favor of the more traditional one advocated here. Note also that in Mal. 3:1 and 4:5 (to which Mark 1:2-3 alludes) the messenger sent "to prepare the way" is identified as Elijah; in 9:13 Mark identifies John the Baptist with Elijah.

chi. The motif of *preparing the way* appears only once in each of the biblical passages; by conflating them, Mark reinforces this motif.[2] Mark's stress on this theme at the outset of his Gospel hints at its importance throughout the remainder of the work: "the way" or "the path" *(he hodos)* is the fundamental designation in Mark's Gospel for Jesus' journey to suffering and death in Jerusalem.[3]

For Mark's earliest readers, the "way" would have been a term rich with meanings. Texts of the Hebrew Scriptures and corresponding LXX texts ranging from Exodus to Isaiah, from Deuteronomy to Proverbs and Ben Sira, frequently use the words for "way" (MT: *ha derek;* LXX: *hē hodos*]. Sometimes those words refer literally to a physical path to follow, including the "path" or "way" opened by God in the Exodus (which literally means "way out"),[4] and sometimes they refer figuratively to a given course of action, belief, or behavior. Such figurative uses of "way" often remain very close to the literal. Consider, for example, Deuteronomy 5:32-33, in which Moses conveys God's commandments, statutes, and ordinances to the people:

> You must therefore be careful to do as the Lord your God has com-
> manded you; you shall not turn to the right or to the left. You must
> follow exactly *the way* that the Lord your God has commanded you, so
> that you may live, and that it may go well with you, and that you may
> live long in the land that you are to possess. (Deut. 5:32-33 [emphasis
> added]; compare Deut. 1:33; 11:28)

Here "way" (or "path") refers figuratively to a divinely ordained ethic or standard of behavior, but the language about turning "to the right or to the left" graphically evokes the image of travel along a straight road. Early Christians referred to the Christian movement as "the Way."[5] So, when Mark reported that God sent John the Baptist to "prepare the way," he was evoking Israel's rich ethical and historical heritage and also

---

2. For a redactional analysis of the conflated quotation, see Mauser, 80-82; also J. Marcus, *The Way of the Lord: Christological Exegesis of the Old Testament in the Gospel of Mark* (Louisville: Westminster/John Knox Press, 1992), 12-17.

3. See especially 8:27; 9:33; 10:17, 32, 46, 52.

4. See, for example, Exod. 13:17, 18, 21; 18:20; 23:20; Isa. 51:10.

5. In Acts, Luke uses the term "way" in an absolute sense to designate the Christian movement (9:2; 19:9, 23; 22:4; 24:14, 22).

pointing to the extension of that heritage into the Christians' own present.[6]

In this chapter and the next, I shall read Mark's Gospel as a story of Jesus' singleminded perseverance on the difficult "way" from bondage to freedom.[7] The "way" or "path" pursued by Jesus is, I shall argue, a "straight and narrow" path, with many temptations (or "tests") along its course, but with no room for deviation "to the right or to the left." Jesus' way ends on Golgotha, when he is crucified. By his perseverance on this path to its very end, Jesus in turn has opened a new way for others to follow (compare Heb. 5:7-10; 10:20).

Throughout the Hebrew Scriptures, to "follow straight paths" means to avoid idolatry and other wicked behaviors, but the "cry in the wilderness" that Mark associates with John the Baptist is not a cry to *follow* straight paths. Rather, it is an exhortation to *"make paths straight"* (Mark 1:3). To *prepare* a straight path is to assist ones who strive to walk in "the way of the Lord" — to ensure their unhindered travel. For example, in Isaiah 40:3-4, the prophet's command to "make straight in the desert a highway for our God" (Isa. 40:3) is quickly followed by the prophecy that "every valley shall be lifted up, and every mountain and hill be made low; the uneven ground shall become level, and the rough places a plain" (40:4). As Ulrich Mauser explains, "Everything in the nature of the desert which is troublesome for the journey of the redeemed will be transformed into

6. Regarding Mark's Gospel, Marcus, *Way of the Lord*, 47, writes, "It would be no exaggeration, then, to say that 'the way of Jesus/the way of the Lord' is not only the double theme of Mark's Gospel but also the controlling paradigm for his interpretation of the life of his community." Cf. E. Best, *Following Jesus: Discipleship in the Gospel of Mark* (Sheffield: JSNT Press, 1981), 15.

7. Mauser develops the theme of Jesus' "way through the desert" (or wilderness) as a new Exodus. I am in agreement with his work at many points; however, Marcus, *Way of the Lord*, 25 n. 49 rightly criticizes Mauser for construing the wilderness theme too broadly, so that in Mauser's reading most of Mark's references to the mountain and the sea are brought under this rubric. Scriptural passages referring to the "way" of the first Exodus include Exod. 13:18, 21; 18:8, 20; 23:20; 32:8; 33:3; Deut. 1:33. Passages referring to the "way" of the second Exodus include Isa. 43:18-19; cf. 35:8; 40:3; 42:16; 43:16; 45:13; 48:17; 49:11; 51:10; 57:14; 62:10. On the motif of an Exodus and return to the wilderness in the prophetic writings, see Mauser, 44-52; relevant scriptural passages include Hos. 2:14-15; Ezek. 20:33-38; Isa. 40:3; 48:20-21; 51:9-11. On Luke's use of the "second Exodus" as a model for understanding the salvation effected by Jesus, see S. R. Garrett, "Exodus from Bondage: Luke 9:31 and Acts 12:1-24," *Catholic Biblical Quarterly* 52 (1990): 656-80.

a condition ensuring an easy passage."[8] In Mark 1:3, the cry to "prepare the way of the Lord, make his paths straight" is, then, a call to the people to assist Jesus as he strives to walk on the way that leads from the Jordan to the cross — that is, to ensure Jesus' own unhindered travel on that way.

Joel Marcus discusses possible ways to construe the phrase "preparing the way," and whether or not any characters in Mark actually do so.[9] One of Marcus's suggestions — that characters pave the way by making physical preparations for Jesus' death — comes close to the one that I shall offer here but is not identical to it. "Preparing Jesus' way" involves not merely the making of physical preparations for death, but *the giving of encouragement to Jesus to persevere in his trials leading to death* (cf. Luke 22:28). In my reading of Mark's Gospel only two characters take up this command. The first such character is John the Baptist: he prepares the Lord's way by making the people ready to receive Jesus (Mark 1:4-8) and by showing through the example of his own death where Jesus' course will end (6:14-29).[10] The second such character is the woman at Bethany who "anoints Jesus beforehand for burying" (14:3-9). By anointing him for burial — rather than hindering him, as Peter has done (8:27-33) — the woman "prepares Jesus' way." On that account Jesus praises her: "Truly I tell you, wherever the good news is proclaimed in the whole world, what she has done will be told in remembrance of her" (14:9). But the major characters in Mark's story "make the Lord's paths crooked." One makes [straight] paths crooked by acting as a seducer, as an agent of temptation who leads others astray from the straight and narrow way (see Deut. 13:5, 10, 13). For example, when, in Acts 13, Bar Jesus tries to lead the proconsul, Sergius Paulus, astray from belief, Paul upbraids the false prophet, saying, "You son of the devil, you enemy of all righteousness, full of all deceit and villainy, will you not stop *making crooked the straight paths of the Lord?*" (Acts 13:10 [italics added]).[11] To "make

8. Mauser, 51. Compare Isa. 45:13.

9. Marcus, *Way of the Lord,* 41-45.

10. Cf. T. J. Geddert, *Watchwords: Mark 13 in Markan Eschatology* (Sheffield: JSOT Press, 1989), 156. Lane, 63 n. 85, thinks that the use of *paradothēnai* in 1:14 may already be intended to suggest the parallel between John's fate and the passion of Jesus.

11. For an analysis of the Acts passage, see S. R. Garrett, *The Demise of the Devil: Magic and the Demonic in Luke's Writings* (Minneapolis: Fortress Press, 1989), 79-87. Compare 2 Pet. 2:15; *Barn.* 20.1. OT passages that make reference to "crooked paths" include Ps. 125:5; Prov. 2:15; Isa. 59:8; Lam. 3:9.

paths crooked" is to tempt travelers so as to lead them astray from the straight and narrow way.

Three actors or groups of actors function as agents of temptation or testing in Mark's narrative. The first and most obvious such actor is Satan, who tests Jesus in the wilderness, and so I shall begin by studying Jesus' confrontation with the devil in the wilderness. Less obvious characters who put Jesus to the test in Mark's Gospel are Jesus' human adversaries (both Jewish adversaries and Roman ones) and also Jesus' own disciples. I shall treat all of these characters below, in this chapter and in the next.

The Testing by Satan in the Wilderness (Mark 1:12-13)

Mark's account of the testing of Jesus in the wilderness should be read together with the preceding story of his baptism:

> And just as he was coming up out of the water, he saw the heavens torn apart and the Spirit descending like a dove on him. And a voice came from heaven, "You are my Son, the Beloved; with you I am well pleased." And the Spirit immediately drove him out into the wilderness. He was in the wilderness forty days, tested by Satan; and he was with the wild beasts; and the angels waited on him. (Mark 1:10-13)

The baptism and the testing episode are linked in at least two ways: First, the spirit is active in both events. At the baptism, the spirit descends upon Jesus and the heavenly voice says, "You are my Son, the Beloved; with you I am well pleased" (1:11). It is then this same spirit that immediately "drives" Jesus or "casts him out" into the wilderness to confront Satan.[12] Second, the sequence of events corresponds to a traditional model, evi-

---

12. As many have noted, the word here translated as "to drive out" or "to cast out" (*ekballein*) is the same word that Mark elsewhere applies to Jesus' own casting out of demons. Used in this context, the word underscores the strength of the spirit's control over Christ's entry into the wilderness. Mauser, 97 n. 4, observes that, according to Mark, John's baptizing itself took place in the wilderness. Why, then, would Mark claim that the spirit *cast Jesus out into* the wilderness if he were already there? Mauser thinks that the inconsistency may show that the baptism and testing accounts were originally separate. In any case, Mark "is not interested in geographical precision. To him the wilderness is a theme full of theological implications, not primarily a locality." On the role of the spirit in the

denced in Job: declaration of divine approval, followed by satanic testing (Job 1:8-12; 2:3-6). Jubilees follows this same Joban pattern in its refashioning of the story of Abraham's near-sacrifice of Isaac (discussed above, pp. 46-47). In Job's case, and in Abraham's case according to Jubilees, God granted the Satan-figure authority to carry out the test. So also in Mark, God permitted Satan to test the righteous one: it is God who thrusts Jesus into confrontation with Satan, so that the devil may assess whether Jesus meets the standard of faithfulness expected of the Son of God. God and Satan both have a hand in the wilderness testing, though they may hope for different outcomes (see pp. 44-48 above).

Mark does not describe the nature of the test(s) that Jesus experienced in the wilderness. Were they tests of seduction? So supposed Matthew and Luke: in their versions of Jesus' testing (based on Q), the devil tries to lead Jesus astray by offering him physical sustenance and earthly dominion in exchange for Jesus' submission and by urging Jesus to use his power for self-aggrandizement.[13] Alternately, perhaps we should infer that Jesus' tests in Mark were tests of suffering, the result of hunger or other sorts of pain and deprivation. This reading coheres best with Mark's emphasis elsewhere on Jesus' suffering. But Mark leaves us to make up our own minds on this point. Mauser suggests that Mark is silent about the content of the testing because "the whole Gospel is an explanation of how Jesus was tempted."[14]

Mark's notice that the testing of Jesus lasted "forty days" recalls the

---

testing, especially on how the spirit's activity serves to connect the baptism and the testing, see E. Schweizer, *The Good News According to Mark,* trans. Donald H. Madvig (Atlanta: John Knox Press, 1970), 42-43.

13. Mark's story of the testing (Mark 1:12-13) must be read independently of the later versions in Matthew and Luke, although one can legitimately use the later accounts as commentary on Mark.

14. Mauser, 100 (cf. 102, 130, 132, 141); so also Lane, 60; R. S. Barbour, "Gethsemane in the Tradition of the Passion," *New Testament Studies* 16 (1969–1970): 244-45 (referring to all three Synoptics); J. H. Korn, ΠΕΙΡΑΣΜΟΣ, *Die Versuchung des Glaübigen in der gr. Bibel* (Stuttgart: W. Kohlhammer Verlag, 1937), 76-78 (referring to passages throughout the NT). The position I am taking is thus diametrically opposed to that of R. H. Gundry, *Mark: A Commentary on His Apology for the Cross* (Grand Rapids: William B. Eerdmans, 1993), 54-62, who refers to the "so-called temptation" in the wilderness (preferring instead to conceive of the episode as "acknowledgements of Jesus by Satan, wild beasts, and angels" (54). Gundry rejects most conventional readings of various aspects of the testing narrative, and argues further that Satan never tempts Jesus (or even confronts him) elsewhere in the Gospel.

"forty years" that the Israelites were tested. Thus the temporal notice underscores Mark's comparison of Jesus to the Israelites, implied also by the wilderness setting. On the other hand, there are biblical passages that do refer specifically to periods of forty *days,* including the account of Moses' abiding "forty days and forty nights" at the top of Mt. Sinai (Exod. 24:18), and especially the story of Elijah's being sustained by angels for "forty days" as he wandered to Mount Horeb (1 Kings 19:8; note the comparable reference to angels in Mark 1:13).[15] Thus, for some readers, Mark's mention of "forty days" would have called to mind two other servants of God, who likewise carried out God's work and were sustained by God (or the angels of God) in the wilderness (cf. Mark 9:2-8, where Moses and Elijah are expressly mentioned). William Lane observes that in the case of Moses and Elijah, "the time of the forty days concentrates into one crucial period the innermost quality of their mission." So also with Jesus in Mark: "The forty days do not describe a period whose significance is exhausted once Jesus begins his public ministry but sound the dominant note of his entire ministry."[16]

The mention of "wild beasts" in Mark's account of the testing is suggestive, but ambiguous. I suspect that Mark intended for the beasts to symbolize the dangers that Jesus faced and from which he was protected, in accordance with Psalm 91. This psalm promises that the one who trusts in God will receive angelic protection from beasts and other harmful things:

> Because you have made the Lord your refuge, the most High your dwelling place, no evil shall befall you, no scourge come near your tent. For he will command his angels concerning you to guard you in all your ways. On their hands they will bear you up, so that you will not dash your foot against a stone. *You will tread on the lion and the adder, the young lion and the serpent you will trample under foot.* Those who love me I will deliver, *I will protect those who know my name.* (Ps. 91:9-14 [emphasis added])

15. The allusion to Moses and/or Elijah is discussed in Mauser, 98-99; H. A. Kelly, "The Devil in the Desert," *Catholic Biblical Quarterly* 26 (1964): 196. For an excellent discussion of the forty-days motif, see B. Gerhardsson, *The Testing of God's Son* (Lund: C. W. K. Gleerup, 1966), 41-43.

16. Lane, 60.

Psalm 91 is the passage from which Satan quotes in the Q-account of the testing in the wilderness (Matt. 4:6; Luke 4:10-11), indicating that this psalm was linked to the tradition about Jesus' testing at a very early date.[17] Moreover, Jews of Mark's era interpreted Psalm 91 as a prayer for angelic protection from demonic powers; how better to illustrate Jesus' strength against the ruler of those powers than by an allusion to this psalm?[18] But even if Mark intended to allude to Psalm 91, early readers likely heard echoes of other biblical texts too. For some, the notice about the wild beasts would have recalled the story of Adam in the Garden of Eden (Gen. 2:19); such readers might have contrasted Jesus' (assumed) perseverance in trial with Adam's fateful disobedience.[19] Other readers would have linked the wild beasts to the animals mentioned in certain prophecies of Isaiah, thought to foretell "the eschatological age of salvation when humankind and wild animals will once again dwell in peace with one another (Isa. 11:6-9; 65:25; 2 Apoc. Bar. 73:6)."[20] These various possible

17. Here I assume that the Q-version of Jesus' testing (known to us from Matthew and Luke) was written independently of Mark, and so provides independent evidence for the link between Jesus' testing and Psalm 91 (LXX: Psalm 90). Other commentators who see a possible allusion to this psalm in Mark's account of the testing include J. Gibson, "Jesus' Wilderness Temptation According to Mark," *Journal for the Study of the New Testament* 53 (1994): 21-23; P. Pokorny, "The Temptation Stories and Their Intention," *New Testament Studies* 20 (1973–1974): 116-17; V. Taylor, *The Gospel According to St. Mark* (London: Macmillan and Co., 1957), 164. On the use of Psalm 91 (LXX: Psalm 90) in Luke, see Garrett, *Demise of the Devil,* 55-56, 137-38 n. 66.

18. On the use of Psalm 91 in rabbinic literature and at Qumran (as a prayer for protection from demonic powers), see Garrett, *Demise of the Devil,* 139 n. 71. See also *T. Levi* 18:12 and *T. Naph.* 8:4 (either or both of these verses may, however, have been subjected to Christian redaction). In the Q account, Satan's use of this particular psalm to dare Jesus is wickedly ironic.

19. In Romans 5, which probably predates Mark, Paul had written about Jesus as "the last Adam," who by his obedience reversed the effects of the first Adam's transgression: see Rom. 5:12-21; cf. 1 Cor. 15:45-49. Commentators who see an allusion to Adam or to the Garden in Mark 1:12-13 include R. Pesch, *Das Markusevangelium* (Freiburg: Herder, 1976), 95; E. Best, *The Temptation and the Passion: The Markan Soteriology* (Cambridge: Cambridge University Press, 1990), 6-7; Schweizer, *Good News,* 42-43; Pokorny, 120-21; W. Schulze, "Die Heilige und die wilden Tiere," *Zeitschrift für die neuetestamentliche Wissenschaft* 46 (1955): 280-83; for others, see Lane, 61 n. 79. Lane himself rejects any Markan association of the beasts with paradise, insisting that their affinity is not with paradise, but with the realm of Satan. I prefer Lane's reading, but recognize that some ancient readers may have made the connection with the beasts of the Garden.

20. Kingsbury, *Christology of Mark's Gospel,* 68.

readings of Mark's testing account reinforce one another: each views Jesus as the faithful and righteous servant of God, who obeys or trusts God and so is protected from harm.

Mark's account of Jesus' testing in the wilderness lacks a decisive ending. The remark about angelic aid, which implies divine favor, is as close as the evangelist comes to telling us that Jesus endured Satan's tests. I presume that early readers took it for granted that Jesus persevered through Satan's tests. By enduring, Jesus proved himself worthy of God's acclamation of him ("You are my Son, the Beloved; with you I am well pleased" [1:11]), thereby foiling Satan's effort to show Jesus as unworthy.[21]

Mark's testing narrative is so brief that we can easily pass by without stopping. The situation is much different than in Matthew and Luke, where scene changes and extensive dialogue force us to slow down and take notice. But Mark's placement of his testing episode at the outset of Jesus' ministry, his use of strong language (especially *ekballein*, "cast out"), and his integration of the testing narrative with the account of Jesus' baptism are like blinking red lights, warning us not to fly through this section of the story. At least two points deserve further consideration before we move on. The first concerns Mark's notice that it was (the spirit of) God who put Jesus into the wilderness to be tested. God has declared Jesus to be his son, and now God arranges for Satan to test Jesus to see whether he is worthy of that assessment. From this context, I infer that *the test was a real one*, in which Jesus was free to choose whether he would follow God's way or not, and in which his obedience could not simply be assumed. Otherwise the test would not have achieved its purpose of proving Jesus to be righteous. The second point deserving further mention is the cultural convention described in Chapter 1, that worthy figures are tested regularly and often. Job was tested more than one time; Abraham was tested more than one time (according to *Jubilees*); the Israelites in the

---

21. On the other hand, it is scarcely the case (as Best, *Temptation and Passion*, 15 insists) that in the wilderness Jesus accomplished the *decisive* victory over Satan, so that the entire rest of his ministry is but a mopping-up operation; see above, p. 8. Gibson, "Jesus' Wilderness Temptation," 30-32, argues that the ending of Mark's testing account is not ambiguous, inasmuch as Mark's references to Jesus' being "with" the wild beasts and to the angels' serving him both indicate that Jesus "successfully resisted the efforts of Satan to sway him from his divinely appointed path and had proven himself loyal and obedient to the commission he received at baptism." See also J. B. Gibson, *The Temptations of Jesus in Early Christianity* (Sheffield: Sheffield Academic Press, 1995), which I discovered too late to utilize in this work.

wilderness were tested more than one time. So also we may expect that Jesus will be tested again before the story is through.

Now I turn to consider Mark's depiction of the testing of Jesus by his enemies. In order to sustain my thesis that Mark portrayed Jesus as tested (or tempted) throughout his ministry, I do not need to prove that *all* Jesus' conflicts with his enemies were construed as tests or temptations by Mark or early readers. Mark writes in an episodic style; repetition is the key means by which he emphasizes the traits or social patterns that he views as characteristic of Jesus and those around him.[22] Thus, to make the case that testing is for Mark an important interpretive theme, I need only to show that in Mark's portrayal Jesus' enemies tested him *repeatedly* during the period of his itinerant ministry and his passion. This lesser point is easy to demonstrate: in Mark, three of Jesus' conflicts with Jewish leaders explicitly mention their "testing" of him (discussed below). Moreover, the accounts of Jesus' arrest, trials before authorities, and crucifixion include narrative details that ancient readers would have associated with "testing" or "temptation" (discussed below, in Chapter 3). Thus, Mark does show Jesus as repeatedly tested by his enemies.

And indeed, it may not be out of line to suppose that, for Mark and for some early readers, the notion of "testing" was the key to interpreting *all* of Jesus' interactions with his adversaries. I shall suggest below that Mark was influenced in his narration of Jesus' story by a passage in Wisdom of Solomon, which describes how certain evildoers scheme and plot against a righteous servant of God, resolving to put that servant to a shameful death. In this important passage, all of the evildoers' actions against the righteous one are categorized as "testing." The plans of these evildoers are summed up in their resolutions to "see if his words are true" and to "test what will happen at the end of his life," to "test him with insult and torture" and "make trial of his forbearance" (Wis. 2:17-20). Given such a precedent, it would not be surprising if Mark likewise saw *all* the actions of Jesus' enemies as just so many ways of "putting him to the test."

22. W. T. Shiner, *"Follow Me!" Disciples in Markan Rhetoric* (Atlanta: Scholars Press, 1995), effectively makes the point about Mark's episodic style; see especially 3, 7-9, 16-17, 29, 211-12.

Testing by Jesus' Enemies

In three passages Mark writes that Jesus' enemies[23] put him to the test:

(1) In 8:11-13 Mark reports that "the Pharisees came and began to argue with him, asking him for a sign from heaven, to test him *[peirazontes auton]*." In response Jesus sighs deeply and says, "'Why does this generation ask for a sign? Truly I tell you, no sign will be given to this generation.'"[24]

(2) In 10:2 the evangelist introduces Jesus' dispute with the Pharisees about divorce with the notice that the latter came "to test him" *[peirazontes auton]*.

(3) In 12:13-17 "some of the Pharisees and Herodians" ask him the question about taxes to Caesar, "in order to trap him in what he said" *(hina auton agreusōsin logō):*

And they came and said to him, "Teacher, we know that you are true [NRSV: "sincere"; Greek *alēthēs*], and show deference to no one; for you do not regard people with partiality, but teach the way of God *[hē hodos tou theou]* in accordance with truth. Is it lawful to pay taxes to the emperor, or not? . . . But knowing their hypocrisy *[hypokrisis]*, he said to them, "Why are you putting me to the test *[ti me peirazete]?*" (Mark 12:14-15)

---

23. On the various Jewish groups that oppose Jesus (chief priests, scribes, elders, Pharisees, Herodians, Sadducees), see J. D. Kingsbury, *Conflict in Mark: Jesus, Authorities, Disciples* (Minneapolis: Fortress Press, 1989), 64-65. I agree with Kingsbury's assessment that the authorities in Mark "form a united front in the relentless opposition they all mount against Jesus"; therefore "they can be treated as a single character" (65; cf. E. S. Malbon, "The Jewish Leaders in the Gospel of Mark: A Literary Study of Marcan Characterization," *Journal of Biblical Literature* 108 [1989]: 419-41, which presents a nuanced argument and also reviews some important earlier literature on the subject). For the argument that the "scribes" are the chief adversaries in Mark (possibly reflecting Mark's own historical situation), see D. Lührmann, *Das Markusevangelium* (Tübingen: Mohr [Siebeck], 1987), 50-51.

24. On how Jesus' rebuke of "this generation" connects the ones who tested him to the "generation" that opposed Moses, see above, pp. 22-23. J. Gibson, "Jesus' Refusal to Produce a 'Sign' (MK 8.11-13)," *Journal for the Study of the New Testament* 38 (1990): 37-66, misses the symbolic, allusive character of Jesus' references to "this generation," and therefore also the way in which these references underscore the faithlessness of the ones whom Jesus so addresses.

Mark and other early readers would likely have interpreted such notices about *the testing of Jesus* in light of biblical conventions about *the testing of God*. As discussed above (pp. 22-23), the Hebrew Scriptures and other ancient Jewish writings consistently portray the testing of God by humans as a sin. Especially pertinent to Jesus' situation are the accounts of the Israelites' testing of God during the wilderness sojourn, for these acts of testing took the form of complaints against God's servant, Moses. So also in Mark's story, the Jewish leaders are in effect *testing God* whenever they test God's servant, Jesus — seeking signs, even after he has already done signs (cf. Num. 14:11, 22). In the Israelites' case, the testing of God had a most serious consequence: God refused to permit those delivered out of Egypt to enter the promised land (Num. 14:20-24).[25]

Cultural convention in Mark's day held that the testing of God or the seeking of signs from God gives evidence of a divided heart — of less than full commitment to God. Luke, for example, builds on this convention in 11:33-36, a passage in which Jesus admonishes the crowd because they are seeking a sign. In his admonition, Jesus speaks about the need for "single(minded)ness" or "simplicity." He employs a metaphor of vision or sight: persons whose "eye" is "single" *(haplous)* have wholly committed themselves to the Lord, whereas persons whose "eye" is "evil" are divided in their loyalties or intentions, and so do not truly "see the things of God." In other words, in Luke, Jesus interprets the crowd's testing of him — its request for a sign — as showing that their commitment to God and knowledge of God are *less than whole*.[26] So also in Mark, the adversaries who test Jesus are not "single"/"singleminded," but duplicitous or hypocritical. The enemies' testing of Jesus reveals their hypocrisy and suggests that they do not trust God fully or know God truly; they are divided in heart, and hence do not share in the higher knowledge of God.[27]

25. Note that, in 1 Cor. 10:9 (according to some manuscripts, including P[46] D F G Ψ 𝔐 latt sy co; Ir[lat] Epiph), the Israelites' behavior is used as the basis for an exhortation not to put *Christ* to the test.

26. See further S. R. Garrett, "'Lest the Light in You Be Darkness': Luke 11.33-36 and the Question of Commitment," *Journal of Biblical Literature* 110 (1991): 93-105.

27. Lane, 275 n. 19 (also 277) regards Deuteronomy 18:18-22 (on the testing of false prophets) as relevant background to the authorities' testing of Jesus in Mark 8:11. He shows how the testing in 8:11-13 harks back to the Beelzebul controversy in 3:22-30. Lane suggests, as I do here, that the demand for a sign is to be interpreted as an expression of unbelief (278).

Mark's Apocalyptic Epistemology

In Mark (as in Luke), the metaphor of vision functions as an element in an "apocalyptic epistemology."[28] Such an epistemology, or theory of knowledge (though the word "theory" is perhaps too formal in its implications), reflects the esteem for esoteric knowledge found not only in apocalyptic contexts but throughout the ancient Mediterranean world. *In the apocalyptic view, events transpiring on the earthly plane are merely the reflection or outworking of events happening on a higher, unseen plane.* Thus, according to Daniel 10:20, victory over Persia and Greece will come when the archangel Gabriel conquers the patron angels of those states. Mark makes similar assumptions, as Joel Marcus points out, by having Jesus refer to *hoi dokountes archein tōn ethnōn* ("those who are thought to rule over the Gentiles" [Mark 10:42]). The implication here is that the *apparent* rulers of the Gentiles are acting out the intentions of unseen beings, who are the *authentic* rulers of the cosmos. These

28. I have borrowed the expression from J. Marcus, "Mark 4:10-12 and Marcan Epistemology," *Journal of Biblical Literature* 103 (1984): 557-74. In this helpful article, Marcus identifies seven features of apocalyptic epistemology, offering analogies from Jewish apocalyptic writings. See also J. L. Martyn, "Epistemology at the Turn of the Ages: 2 Corinthians 5:16," in *Christian History and Interpretation: Studies Presented to John Knox,* ed. W. R. Farmer et al. (Cambridge: Cambridge University Press, 1967); J. Marcus, *The Mystery of the Kingdom of God* (Atlanta: Scholars Press, 1986), 63, 104, 112, 121, 156, and 161; S. Freyne, "The Disciples in Mark and the *maskilim* in Daniel. A Comparison," *Journal for the Study of the New Testament* 16 (1982): 7-23; Shiner, 212-16; Geddert, 59-87; M. A. Beavis, *Mark's Audience: The Literary and Social Setting of Mark 4.11-12* (Sheffield: JSOT Press, 1989), 41-42; L. T. Johnson, *The Letter of James* (New York: Doubleday, 1995), 182-83, 191, 265, 272, 287, 340; M. Hengel, *Judaism and Hellenism: Studies in Their Encounter in Palestine during the Early Hellenistic Period,* trans. John Bowden (Philadelphia: Fortress Press, 1974), 1.210-18 (on the widespread esteem for esoteric knowledge in the ancient Mediterranean world). In S. R. Garrett, "The God of This World and the Affliction of Paul: 2 Cor 4:1-12," in *Greeks, Romans, and Christians: Essays in Honor of Abraham J. Malherbe,* ed. David L. Balch et al. (Minneapolis: Fortress Press, 1990), 99-117, I explicate 2 Cor. 4:4-6 as an example of "apocalyptic epistemology" (without using that expression): because Paul's opponents are "blinded by the god of this world," when they look to Paul they see only a devastated and decomposing "outer nature" (4:16), and so regard Paul's afflicted condition as a disgrace. Paul, by contrast, is the recipient of divine knowledge: knowledge of things unseen and eternal (4:6, 18). In S. R. Garrett, "The 'Weaker Sex' in the *Testament of Job,*" *Journal of Biblical Literature* 112 (1993): 55-70, I argue that *Testament of Job* also trades on an assumed contrast between "lower" and "higher" knowledge. Job is portrayed as able to perceive heavenly realities, whereas his wife and his "friends" are locked in the realm of the perishing, lower world.

authentic rulers are, namely, "God and Satan, each with a host of servants."[29] An apocalyptic epistemology posits that some enlightened humans can penetrate surface appearances to "see" the true meaning of events — but only because this knowledge has first been revealed to them. (*Apokalypsis* means, literally, "revelation" or "unveiling," referring to "the revelation of heavenly events, which provide the key for understanding earthly events.")[30] Other persons, who have not been so enlightened, are held to be "blind" to the true meaning of events. One can here paraphrase Luke: such persons' "eyes" are "evil."

Sometimes authors write as if it is God who gives and withholds higher knowledge; in other texts, authors indicate that Satan is the one who imprisons humans in the darkness of ignorance and idolatry.[31] Satan does

29. Marcus, "Mark 4:10-12," 558; cf. Shiner, 214. On the view of Satan as a ruler or *archōn* of this world, see Marcus, "Mark 4:10-12," 558 n. 5; also Garrett, *Demise of the Devil*, 38, 43, 51, and 128 n. 7 (citing John 12:31; 2 Cor. 4:4; *Mart. Isa.* 1:3); Garrett, "God of This World," 104-5.

30. Marcus, "Mark 4:10-12," 557-58. Marcus points out (559) that the Dead Sea Scrolls (especially the Community Rule, the Damascus Rule, and the Hymns) emphasize "that God is a God of knowledge and that all knowledge comes from him." Marcus quotes 1QH 1:21: "These things I know by the wisdom which comes from thee, for thou hast unstopped my ears to marvellous mysteries" (quoted from G. Vermes, ed., *The Dead Sea Scrolls in English* [Middlesex: Penguin, 1975]).

31. Marcus, "Mark 4:10-12," 561-63, stresses *God's* role in apocalyptic epistemology as source of knowledge and agent of blinding (citing 1QH 1:19-20; CD 2:13; 1QH 2:9-10; 1QS 3:18-21; cf. Shiner, 221; F. J. Matera, "The Incomprehension of the Disciples and Peter's Confession [Mark 6,14–8,30]," *Biblica* 70 [1989]: 157-59). Marcus does, however, acknowledge the role of Satan in Peter's failure to understand Jesus at Caesarea Philippi, and sees the parallel to 1QS 3:20-22, where even the children of righteousness have their minds darkened by the angel of darkness (Marcus, "Mark 4:10-12," 562, 568-69; cf. Beavis, 151: "Thus the dichotomy of 'divine hardening' *vs* human 'hardness of heart' may have been less relevant to Mark and his audience than it is to us; the more prominent, and less irreconcilable, opposition is between succumbing to or resisting the influence of Satan"). Ancient Jewish authors who address the topic seem to have presupposed that God is ultimately sovereign over Satan (or Belial, or Mastema, etc.), no matter how much autonomy the latter may seem to possess in "the present evil age"; hence, even satanically induced blindness can at some higher level be traced to God. In the Community Rule, for example, the "spirits of truth and of falsehood" govern the two classes of human beings, but these spirits have themselves been appointed by the one sovereign God (1QS 3:18-21). To cite a second example, in 2 Thess. 2:9-11, Satan is said to use all sorts of means to deceive the perishing, but God is also said "to send them a powerful delusion, leading them to believe what is false so that all who have not believed in the truth but took pleasure in unrighteousness will be condemned." See the fuller discussion of ancient views on the relationship between Satan and God in acts of testing, above, pp. 44-48.

this so as to keep the blinded under his dominion: were their eyes ever to be opened, they would know and do what God requires of them, and so serve God rather than Satan.[32] In Mark's Gospel, Satan is blamed for the failure of some to receive and hold Jesus' word: "When they hear, Satan immediately comes and takes away the word that is sown in them" (Mark 4:14). In this Gospel, Jesus is the only human character with full access to higher knowledge, which for Mark encompasses the secret of Jesus' identity.[33] The enemies of Jesus do not have such knowledge: they are the "outsiders" who "look, but do not perceive," who "listen, but do not understand." I shall argue below that even the twelve disciples are denied access to higher knowledge for the duration of Jesus' earthly ministry.

As James M. Robinson noted some years ago, there are similarities between Jesus' debates with opponents (and disciples) in Mark and his exorcisms. Robinson argued that the debates are presented by Mark as "a continuation of the cosmic struggle initiated at the baptism and temptation and carried into the narrative of Jesus' public ministry first by the exorcisms."[34] The debates, like the exorcisms, are the action of Satan. As evidence, Robinson remarked on various similarities of form between the exorcisms and the debates.[35] While I share Robinson's perception that

32. See Acts 26:18; 2 Cor. 4:4; *T. Dan.* 6:3-4. Regarding 2 Cor. 4:4, see Garrett, "God of This World."

33. As Marcus, "Mark 4:10-12," 559, points out, the spiritual beings who are privy to this knowledge include God (1:11; 9:7), the demons (1:24, 34; 3:11; 5:7; 9:20), and (by implication) Satan. Marcus's argument (against Wrede and others) that the secret of Jesus' identity is distinct from the "mystery of the kingdom of God" (565) seems overly nuanced; as Marcus later concedes, "the two secrets are closely intertwined" (567 n. 36; on the Markan theme of "mystery" see M. Boucher, *The Mysterious Parable: A Literary Study* [Washington: Catholic Biblical Quarterly, 1977], 64-85; Marcus, *Mystery of Kingdom of God;* for a survey of scholarly opinions on the content of the mystery in Mark, see Beavis, 75-78; also Kingsbury, *Conflict in Mark,* 135-36 n. 15). Although the word *mysterion* is not mentioned, Luke 10:21-22 seems pertinent: the special knowledge that God/the Son reveals pertains to the identity of the Son (on this passage, see Garrett, *Demise of the Devil,* 48-49). Useful comments on the Greek and Jewish overtones of the word *mysterion* may be found in Beavis, 143-46.

34. J. M. Robinson, *The Problem of History in Mark* (Philadelphia: Fortress Press, 1982), 94. Cf. Shiner, 241: "In the Markan world, the divine reality overlaps the mundane world through the person of Jesus, but the divine remains hidden. The miracles are unexpected flashes that point to that reality."

35. Robinson, 92-94. Robinson conceded that the dualistic cosmic struggle between the spirit and Satan "has here reached a more subtle form and is stated in more immanent language than was the case in the exorcisms" (93). But the debates, like the exorcisms, do

there are parallels in Mark between Jesus' exorcisms and his debates with opponents and disciples, still, I do not want to overlook the differences between the exorcisms and the debates. One striking difference concerns the *knowledge* displayed by Jesus' spiritual adversaries versus the *ignorance* or *blindness* of his human ones. In the exorcisms, the demons perceive instantly and accurately who Jesus is, and they comprehend the finality of his word of command (Mark 1:24, 34; 3:11; 5:7). In contrast to the demonic host, Jesus' human opponents are unable to perceive the truth about Jesus. Indeed, the accounts of Jesus' debates with human enemies serve to underscore the prevalent human condition of spiritual blindness: by putting Jesus to the test, his opponents demonstrate that they cannot "see" Jesus as God sees him.

The Righteous Sufferer

Wisdom of Solomon 2 illuminates ancient Jewish ideas about the testing of a righteous one by persons who do not share in divine knowledge, who are blinded by their own wickedness. The drama that unfolds through this first-person discourse and the narrator's comment is highly evocative of the Mark's portrayal of Jesus. The passage begins with the plotting of the wicked:

"Let us lie in wait for the righteous man, because he is inconvenient to us *[enedreuein]* and opposes our actions; he reproaches us for sins against the law, and accuses us of sins against our training. He professes to have knowledge of God, and calls himself a child [or "servant": Greek *pais*] of the Lord. He became to us a reproof of our thoughts; the very sight of him is a burden to us, because his manner of life is unlike that of others, and his ways are strange. We are considered by him as something base, and he avoids our ways as unclean; he calls the last end of the righteous happy, and boasts that God is his father. *Let us see if his words are true [aletheis]* and *let us test [peirazein] what will happen at the end of his life;* for if the righteous man is God's son *[huios]*, he will help him, and will deliver him from the hand of his adversaries. *Let us test [etazein] him with insult and torture, so that we may find out how gentle he is, and make trial [dokimazein] of his forbearance [anexikakia].* Let us condemn him to a shameful death,

attest to Mark's notion of "'trials' instigated by Satan and consisting in a historical encounter in a specific situation" (94).

for, according to what he says, he will be protected." Thus they reasoned, but they were led astray, *for their wickedness blinded them,* and they did not know the mysteries *[mysteria]* of God, nor hoped for the wages of holiness, nor discerned the prize for blameless souls; for God created us for incorruption, and made us in the image of his own eternity, but through the devil's envy death entered the world, and those who belong to his company test [the righteous one]. (Wis. 2:12-24 [emphasis added])[36]

This account of the confrontation between ungodly persons and God's righteous sufferer draws on the psalms of individual lament (sometimes called the "psalms of the righteous sufferer"), as well as the Deutero-Isaian "songs of the suffering servant."[37] To a certain extent, the similarities between the Wisdom passage and Mark's account of Jesus' testing may be due to their common use of these scriptural traditions. But in my opinion, the correspondences of plot and even of vocabulary are sufficient to suggest that Mark had read Wisdom of Solomon's portrait of the afflicting of the righteous man and was directly influenced by it.[38] Especially striking

---

36. On the translation of v. 24, see Garrett, " 'Lest the Light,' " 102 n. 26; also Kelly, 207 n. 46.

37. See the careful and illuminating discussion of Mark's use of the psalms of the righteous sufferer and of the Isaian servant songs (which may themselves have been influenced by the aforementioned psalms) in Marcus, *Way of the Lord,* 172-96. Marcus discusses (191) the influence of Isa. 52:13–53:12 on Wis. 2:12-20 and 5:1-7; cf. S. K. Williams, *Jesus' Death as Saving Event: The Background and Origin of a Concept* (Missoula, Mont.: Scholars Press, 1975), 115-16.

38. C. Maurer, "Knecht Gottes und Sohn Gottes im Passionsbericht des Marcusevangelium," *Zeitschrift für Theologie und Kirche* 50 (1953): 1-38, argues for the importance of the Isaianic model of the "suffering servant" for the Markan passion account, especially as that model has been adapted by the author of Wisdom 2:13-20. My own query is about the possible influence of Wisdom 2:12-24 on Mark's accounts of the *testing* of Jesus by Jewish authorities (rather than on the passion narrative per se, as in Maurer's study). The testing motif is more explicit in Wisdom than in the Isaianic servant-songs. Others who see a possible influence of Wisdom's accounts of the righteous sufferer on Mark's christology include L. Ruppert, *Jesus als der leidende Gerechte? Der Weg Jesu im Lichte eines alt-und zwischentestamentlichen Motivs* (Stuttgart: KBW Verlag, 1972) (who postulates that Wis. 2:12-20 and 5:1-7 incorporate an apocalyptic Palestinian source), 23-24, 46, 53-56, 68-69, 72, 75; K. Berger, "Die Königlichen Messiastraditionen des Neuen Testaments," *New Testament Studies* 20 (1974): 1-44 (esp. 16-17, 28-37); E. Schweizer, "The Son of Man Again," *New Testament Studies* 10 (1962–63): 256-61, esp. 261; J. R. Donahue, "Temple, Trial, and Royal Christology (Mark 14:53-65)," in *The Passion in Mark: Studies on Mark 14–16,* ed. W. H. Kelber (Philadelphia: Fortress Press, 1976), 66. See Lührmann, 42-44 for an interesting discussion of Wisdom 2:12-20 and the genre of Mark.

correspondences of plot include: (1) the basis for the evildoers' opposition (namely, that the righteous man opposes and reproaches them, and claims to know God); (2) their plotting to try him with insult and torture and to put him to a shameful death; and (3) their own condition of blindness, and hence their inability to participate in the higher knowledge of God. Specific verbal correspondences to Mark's accounts of the authorities' testing of Jesus include: (1) the use of *peirazein,* "test" (Wis. 2:17; cf. vv. 19, 24; Mark 8:11; 10:2; 12:15); (2) the enemies' interest in knowing whether his words are *aletheis,* "true" (Wis. 2:17; cf. Mark 12:14); and (3) the reference to their wicked "ways" (Wis. 2:16; cf. 5:7) versus the "way of the Lord" or "of God" (Wis. 5:7; cf. Mark 12:13). Further, Wisdom's reference to the enemies' not knowing the "mysteries" of God is striking, as it evokes Mark's reference to the "mystery of the Kingdom of God," which is not given to outsiders (Wis. 2:22; Mark 9:11). Finally, though linguistic correspondence is not exact, it is significant that the enemies in Wisdom are said to "lie in wait for" or "plot against" *(enedreuein)* the righteous man; this reminds one of Mark's notice in 12:13 that Pharisees and Herodians were sent "to trap" *(agreuein)* Jesus in what he said. (Luke uses *enedreuein* in a very similar context). Again, all of these correspondences make it seem likely that Wisdom influenced Mark's portrayal of the authorities' testing of Jesus.[39]

But even if Mark had not himself read the Wisdom of Solomon, the plot line shared by the two accounts of righteous sufferers was conventional, and presumably evident to Mark's earliest flesh-and-blood readers. Elsewhere I have argued that the *Testament of Job* and 2 Corinthians employ such a plot about a righteous sufferer, whose adversaries are blind to God's higher truths.[40] So also in Mark, *Jesus and his human enemies play*

---

39. Berger, 16, argues for a parallel between the challenge beginning "if you are the son of God" in Matthew 27:40 (cf. Luke 23:35, 37, 39) and Wisdom 2:18: these traditions imply the demand for a sign, itself a form of testing. Cf. Mark 15:29-30, which does not, however, use the term "Son of God" in this context.

40. Garrett, "God of This World." Berger, 10-13, 18, also interprets the testing motif against a conventional story or plotline of ancient Judaism. This plot pits prophet against false prophet: the latter "tests" the true prophet, but through the process of testing the true prophet demonstrates his own legitimacy. Berger sees this conventional story continued and extended in the traditions about legitimate versus illegitimate claims to wisdom and divine power, as in Wisdom 2:12-20 and 5:1-7. It is central to these stories as Berger constructs them that there is a tension raised by the wise one's claims to divine wisdom and power and his temporary refusal or incapacity to "prove" these claims by performing

stock roles in a stereotyped story: Jesus is the righteous sufferer who patiently endures affliction, knowing that he will inherit life. Jesus' adversaries, meanwhile, are blinded by their own wickedness. "They did not know the mysteries *[mysteria]* of God, nor hoped for the wages of holiness." Because the adversaries are not wholly and unreservedly committed to God, they cannot accurately perceive God's truth. They do not comprehend that the righteous sufferer is God's "child." Instead they view him as "mad,"[41] and put him to the test. Familiarity with this plot line would have helped Mark's readers to fit the pieces of his story together in a coherent and meaningful way. Such readers would likely have recognized that the testing of Jesus by his enemies gave evidence of those enemies' own blindness and that Jesus' endurance of such testing would lead to his own vindication before God.

Testing by Jesus' Disciples

The enemies of Jesus seek to impede his work and to "test" him by setting verbal traps and seeking heavenly signs. By their actions they hint at their own alliance with the cosmic adversary and tester, Satan. But what sense are we to make of the opposition to Jesus' work posed by his so-called allies, the disciples? I designate them the "so-called" allies because the

---

miraculous signs. M. Hengel, *The Atonement: The Origins of the Doctrine in the New Testament,* trans. John Bowden (Philadelphia: Fortress Press, 1981), 3-4, 41-43, argues (against Ruppert and others) that the pattern of the humiliation and exaltation of the innocent (such as is found in Wisdom 2–5) is so general and imprecise that it could not have been formative for Mark's more nuanced theological reflection. Hengel contends that the only psalms that Mark uses to illuminate specific aspects of Jesus' suffering are exclusively *messianic* psalms; moreover, where Mark has integrated features from the suffering of the righteous man (for example, in the mocking of Jesus), these features are in "a messianic key." Hengel holds, in sum, that Mark has completely integrated the theme of the suffering of the righteous into his predominant theme of the suffering of the messiah (41). Later, Hengel adds the further comment that Wisdom 2–5 cannot have influenced Mark because in Wisdom "the righteous sufferer first achieves salvation only for himself; for others he acts as a model, or is an accuser of his enemies" (42-43). But Hengel has not really *disproved* the influence of Wisdom on Mark; he has merely asserted the subordination of the righteous sufferer model to other models.

41. Wis. 5:4; cf. Mark 3:21-22; also 2 Cor. 5:13. On Paul's reference to himself as "beside himself" in 2 Cor. 5:13, and on how Job's friends perceive him to be mad in *Testament of Job,* see Garrett, "God of This World," 113 (including n. 54).

disciples in Mark are as much a hindrance to Jesus as they are a help. They are forever failing to understand Jesus' words or to support him in his mission. Judas betrays him; Peter denies him; in Gethsemane the disciples fall asleep; at Jesus' arrest they all flee. To say that the disciples "try Jesus' patience" would be accurate, although something of an understatement. But does this "trying of patience" constitute a trying or testing of Jesus in any stronger sense of the term? One passage in particular suggests that the answer is "yes": Jesus' rebuke of Peter at Caesarea Philippi. In this incident, Peter confesses Jesus to be the Christ, but then rebukes Jesus when he predicts the suffering and death of the Son of Man. In turn Jesus rebukes Peter, saying, "Get behind me, Satan! For you are setting your mind not on divine things but on human things" (Mark 8:33). In some way, Peter's refusal to accept the necessity of Jesus' passion is linked to (or likened unto) the activity of Satan. But how? Moreover, if in this passage Peter's opposition to Jesus is satanic, are the disciples' other failings and misunderstandings in the Gospel also to be viewed as diabolical?[42]

The Incomprehension of the Disciples

The disciples' repeated failures to comprehend Jesus' words and deeds are occasions for profound narrative irony, for early on in Mark, Jesus identified the disciples as initiates into "the mystery of the kingdom of God."[43] After recounting the parable of the sower to a large crowd

42. Shiner, 8-9, argues that the disciples do not really interest Mark in their own right, but only insofar as their words or actions can say something *about Jesus* at any given point in Mark's presentation. Indeed, Shiner doubts whether it is accurate even to insist that Mark *has* a coherent picture of the disciples (29-30). My own argument that the disciples serve as "agents of trial" for Jesus is consistent with Shiner's view that these characters function primarily to further the portrayal of Jesus; I do, however, think that Mark's portrait of the twelve is (at least loosely) coherent, and that the twelve characters would have held at least some interest in their own right for Mark and his early readers (see further my discussion of the disciples in Chap. 4). Shiner's argument is a helpful corrective to analyses such as R. C. Tannehill, "The Disciples in Mark: The Function of a Narrative Role," in *The Interpretation of Mark*, ed. W. Telford (Philadelphia: Fortress Press, 1977), 134-57; and E. S. Malbon's "Fallible Followers: Women and Men in the Gospel of Mark," *Semeia* 28 (1983): 29-48, which ascribe a very linear and coherent (rather than a more episodic) character to Mark's narrative.

43. See R. M. Fowler, *Let the Reader Understand: Reader-Response Criticism and the Gospel of Mark* (Minneapolis: Fortress Press, 1991), 167-75.

gathered near the edge of the sea, Jesus says to a smaller group, including the twelve, "To you has been given the mystery of the kingdom of God, but for those outside, everything comes in parables; in order that 'they may indeed look, but not perceive, and may indeed listen, but not understand; so that they may not turn again and be forgiven'" (Mark 4:11-12, here quoting Isa. 6:9). But immediately Jesus discerns that the disciples still do not grasp his meaning. He asks, "Do you not understand this parable? Then how will you understand all the parables?" (4:13). The answer is, they will not. Again and again throughout the narrative, Jesus chides the disciples for their hardness of heart, their inability to comprehend. The disciples lack faith during a storm on the sea (4:40). They fail to understand Jesus' first and even his second miraculous feeding of the multitudes (6:52; cf. 8:4). They are frightened when he comes to them on the water, and then don't understand Jesus' teaching about the yeast (or "leaven") of the Pharisees and of Herod (8:14-21). When Jesus offers this teaching, they say to one another, "It is because we have no bread" (8:16), at which point Jesus chides,

> "Why are you talking about having no bread? Do you still not perceive or understand? *Are your hearts hardened? Do you have eyes, and fail to see? Do you have ears, and fail to hear?* And do you not remember? When I broke the five loaves for the five thousand, how many baskets full of broken pieces did you collect?" They said to him, "Twelve." "And the seven for the four thousand, how many baskets full of broken pieces did you collect?" And they said to him, "Seven." Then he said to them, "Do you not yet understand?" (8:17-21 [italics added])

Here the disciples prove themselves to be as obtuse as outsiders. They are as incapable of perceiving the truth as those to whom Jesus speaks in parables so that "they may indeed look, but not perceive, and may indeed listen, but not understand."[44] Their blindness amazes Jesus. He has tried to give them eyes to see, but still they look and do not perceive. *Despite Jesus' effort to enlighten the disciples, they do not have access to higher knowledge.*[45] Jesus' apparent inability to enlighten the disciples during his earthly

---

44. Beavis argues that v. 18 "is not, as many commentators hold, a quotation of Jer. 5.21 or Ezek. 12.2, but a paraphrase of Isa. 6.10a, a section of the oracle not quoted in 4.12" (157; see also 90-91).

45. For various remarks regarding the blindness of the disciples, see Beavis, 109-10 (she

mission drives the plot of Mark's story by raising questions that demand an answer. Will Jesus succeed, finally, in opening the eyes of the twelve? When? How? In the meantime, what is the reason for his failure?

The principal stumbling block to understanding on the part of the disciples is the necessity of Jesus' suffering. To them, this necessity is offensive. Its offensiveness becomes especially apparent in the second half of Mark's narrative, but is implied already in the first half, particularly in Mark's reports of the disciples' two failures to comprehend the miracles of loaves and fishes.[46] In these feeding miracles (Mark 6:30-44; 8:1-9), Jesus "gave thanks, broke the loaves, and gave them to his disciples to distribute," thereby foreshadowing both the breaking of bread at the Last Supper and the imminent breaking of his body on the cross. The feeding miracles are *acted parables:* that is, figurative expressions that point beyond the immediate context to a higher meaning, a meaning discernible to those with eyes to see and ears to hear.[47] The "parables of the loaves" point beyond the deserted places where Jesus, the disciples, and the crowds gathered, to the upper room and, in turn, to the cross. The disciples in Mark see these "parables" being enacted, but do not comprehend their meaning. Jesus later reprimands them for their hardness of heart and their blindness/deafness with respect to the feeding events (6:52; 8:17-21).

To be sure, Mark never states what aspect or feature of the feeding miracles has been misunderstood. The disciples' incomprehension first

---

reads the disciples' blindness against the background of the blind *douloi theou* of Isaiah [LXX 42.18-20]); Kingsbury, *Conflict in Mark,* 95-103; Lane, 281; Marcus, "Mark 4:10-12," 567-70; Marcus, *Mystery of Kingdom of God,* 99-103; Shiner, 251-53 and *passim* ("incomprehension"); D. Rhoads and D. Michie, *Mark as Story: An Introduction to the Narrative of a Gospel* (Philadelphia: Fortress Press, 1982), 124-25; J. B. Tyson, "The Blindness of the Disciples in Mark," *Journal of Biblical Literature* 80 (1961): 261-68; Lane, 177; and W. H. Kelber, *Mark's Story of Jesus* (Philadelphia: Fortress Press, 1979), 30-42. Gundry, 409, 410, 414, 415, deemphasizes their incomprehension.

46. Cf. E. S. Johnson, "Mark viii.22-26: The Blind Man from Bethsaida," *New Testament Studies* 25 (1979): 382, who writes that 8:27ff. "is not a turning-point in the gospel because Peter confesses Jesus as the Christ or because the mystery is first revealed there. It is important because Peter's faulty confession and Jesus' open proclamation make clear what has been implied all along: spiritual blindness consists in the failure to understand Jesus' word and follow him on the road to suffering" (cf. E. S. Johnson, "Mark 10:46-52: Blind Bartimaeus," *Catholic Biblical Quarterly* 40 [1978]: 203).

47. For similar views on the feeding miracles as "parabolic" in Mark, see J. M. Bassler, "The Parable of the Loaves," *Journal of Religion* 66 (1986): 157-72; Boucher, 69-80; Lane, 237-38; Shiner, 199-253.

comes to the fore after the walking-on-water miracle (which is itself reported in 6:45-52, immediately after the first feeding-story). Mark reports that when Jesus got into the boat with the disciples and the wind ceased, they "did not understand about the loaves, but their hearts were hardened" (6:52). The reader is left puzzled: what links the first feeding-miracle to Jesus' walking on water? Madeleine Boucher argues that Mark's readers are intended to see, from their post-Easter perspective, that the pair of miracles alludes to the passion and resurrection of Jesus:

> The miracles tie together the first and the final redemptive events; for Christians Jesus' death and resurrection is the moment in history which is the point of departure for the new Exodus. If the miracle of the loaves points to the Last Supper (6:41; 14:22), a Passover meal, it is not unreasonable to infer that it suggests also its context, the passion. Christians know that at both meals the bread which is broken and distributed that those who partake may have life is Jesus' body. That the sea miracle suggests the resurrection is clear enough from the biblical symbolism of water, the motifs which recur in the resurrection stories, and the glorious appearance of Jesus. The passion-resurrection foreshadowing provides the most satisfactory explanation for the joining of these two miracles in Mark. What the readers are urged to understand is the relation between the two miracles: the breaking of the bread, symbol of Jesus' death, precedes the victory over waters, symbol of the resurrection.[48]

After the second feeding-miracle, Jesus' disciples misunderstand his teaching about the "yeast" or "leaven" of the Pharisees. Jesus' reaction to their misunderstanding, which certainly comes from the hand of Mark (8:17-21), suggests that in some way the teaching about leaven is intended to draw still further meaning out of the feeding miracles. But neither is this "further meaning" obvious. Boucher tentatively concurs with the suggestion (made by various scholars) that the teaching about leaven may be intended to show that the two feeding-miracles signify salvation to Jews

---

48. Boucher, 74-75. Q. Quesnell, *The Mind of Mark: Interpretation and Method through the Exegesis of Mark 6,52* (Rome: Pontifical Biblical Institute, 1969), is a classic exposition of the feeding miracles as alluding to the Eucharist, itself understood as a symbol or shorthand for "the full meaning of Christianity" (276); for lists of other scholars who think that the feeding stories would have been read as pointing typologically to the Eucharist, see Boucher, 70 n. 17; Shiner, 221 n. 35; scholars who reject such a reading are noted in Beavis, 219 n. 76.

and Gentiles respectively. In the passage about leaven, the readers and disciples are invited to comprehend that the Gospel is universal in its application. "Jesus' death is the sacrifice of the new covenant (14:24), by which a community is instituted composed of Jews and Gentiles whose fellowship is realized in their breaking of bread together."[49] On the other hand, Whitney Shiner has made the interesting suggestion that the bouts of incomprehension triggered by the walking-on-water miracle and the warning about leaven function for Mark chiefly as narrative pretexts to exhort readers to ponder the meaning of the loaves. In other words, the descriptions of incomprehension in 6:52 and again in 8:16 offer Jesus/Mark two additional occasions to bring the feeding miracles before the disciples/the readers. In these accounts of misunderstanding, Mark has sacrificed coherence at the narrative level, so as to stress the centrality of the feeding miracles for comprehending Jesus' identity and mission as a hidden and suffering messiah.[50]

In the second half of the narrative — beginning with the confession and rebukes at Caesarea Philippi (8:27-33) — it becomes even more apparent that the necessity of Jesus' suffering is what causes the disciples to stumble. Three times Jesus predicts his own passion; all three times, the response of the disciples shows that that they are completely unable to accept his teaching. At Caesarea Philippi Peter rebukes Jesus when he foretells his suffering and death (8:32). On the way to Capernaum, Jesus for the second time prophesies his betrayal, death, and resurrection; immediately afterward he learns that the disciples had been arguing with one

---

49. Boucher, 78-79. For arguments against interpretations of the first and second feeding miracles as "Jewish" and "Gentile" feedings that make a point about the inclusion of Gentiles in the church (an argument found also in, e.g., W. H. Kelber, *The Kingdom in Mark: A New Place and a New Time* [Philadelphia: Fortress Press, 1974], 45-65; Kelber, *Mark's Story*, 40-41; D. J. Hawkin, "The Incomprehension of the Disciples in the Markan Redaction," *Journal of Biblical Literature* 91 [1972]: 491-500; D. Senior, *The Passion of Jesus in the Gospel of Mark* [Collegeville, Minn.: Liturgical Press, 1984], 54-50), see Shiner, 228-29 n.62; here Shiner argues that it is the theme of *Jesus' identity* that links the three boat scenes in 4:35–8:21. Beavis, 112, argues against insistence on one and only one meaning for the feeding miracles; several different interpretations *are congruent with themes and motifs developed elsewhere in Mark, and it is unnecessary to try to choose among them* (italics original).

50. Shiner, 224-25; cf. Lührmann, 122, 138-39; and R. A. Culpepper, *Anatomy of the Fourth Gospel: A Study in Literary Design* (Philadelphia: Fortress Press, 1983), 165, who argues that the chief function of misunderstandings in the Fourth Gospel "is to teach readers how to read the Gospel."

another about who was the greatest (9:34). On the road up to Jerusalem Jesus again predicts his passion, at which point James and John, the sons of Zebedee, ask Jesus to grant that they may sit at his right and left hand in glory (10:35-37). In all these scenes, the disciples give evidence of their blindness. They do not yet grasp the divine necessity that Jesus suffer, nor perceive that they will be called upon to partake from the same cup as Jesus. The climax of the motif of incomprehension occurs in Peter's denials of Jesus ("But he began to curse, and he swore an oath, 'I do not know this man you are talking about'" [14:71; cf. v. 68]).[51] The denials are ironic: the reader recognizes that Peter is lying, for on one level Peter does indeed know Jesus. But on another level Peter speaks the truth: he does not "know" Jesus as the suffering Christ.

How is one to explain the disciples' persistent blindness, given Jesus' stated intent to enlighten them? Is it God who withholds understanding, as in the case of Pharaoh?[52] This proposal wouldn't make very much sense within the context of the narrative, because it implies that Jesus and God were working at cross purposes with one another (Jesus wants to enlighten the disciples, but God does not).[53] Rather, one achieves a more consistent and coherent reading by viewing Satan as the cause of the disciples' incomprehension (compare 4:15).[54] Satan's grip on the world continues for the duration of Jesus' earthly ministry. Jesus *wants* to open the disciples' eyes, but he cannot, because Satan prevents the scales from falling away. Hence, the disciples — much like the opponents of Jesus — have eyes that "seeing, do not perceive." As I noted earlier, the notion that Satan (or sin) renders people blind to divine truths can be found elsewhere in Jewish

51. So also Marcus, "Mark 4:10-12," 569.

52. Shiner, 238 and 251 (cf. Matera, 157-59), makes the comparison to the hardening of Pharaoh in the Exodus account. Shiner's comments on the narrative functions of the disciples' incomprehension (comments made in light of other ancient depictions of master/disciple relationships) are well worth reading (in Shiner, 243-51). Elsewhere Shiner contends that "through Jesus' persistence they [the disciples] receive insight as a gift" (218); I do not see sufficient evidence that the disciples ever actually receive this insight within the context of the narrative. True, Peter confesses Jesus to be the Christ, but the subsequent rebukes show that Peter is still partially blind; that is why Satan can still use him to try to lead Jesus astray.

53. On Jesus' amazement at his own inability to enlighten the disciples see Shiner, 237-38 (he compares this inability with the situation in ancient philosophical biographies, where philosophers can reveal themselves at will); also Kingsbury, *Conflict in Mark, 7, 97.*

54. Cf. Freyne, 16, 19-20; cf. Beavis, 151; Marcus, "Mark 4:10-12," 568-69.

and Christian writings from this period. In Mark's gospel, the strongest evidence for an assumed link between the disciples' incomprehension and the activity of Satan is Jesus' rebuke of Peter at Caesarea Philippi ("Get behind me, Satan!"). This is an electrifying scene — an instant in which the disciples' routine trying of Jesus' patience is transmogrified into satanic presence. As I have noted, the disciples will fail yet again in scenes to follow, but few scenes surpass this one for sheer high drama or for relevance to the theme of Jesus' trials. The incident repays careful consideration.

The Rebukes at Caesarea Philippi (Mark 8:27-33)

Jesus is here traveling with his disciples to Caesarea Philippi. He asks his disciples who people say that he is. The story proceeds:

> And they answered him, "John the Baptist; and others Elijah; and still others, one of the prophets." He asked them, "But who do you say that I am?" Peter answered him, "You are the Messiah." And he sternly ordered them not to tell anyone about him.
>
> Then he began to teach them that the Son of Man must undergo great suffering, and be rejected by the elders, the chief priests, and the scribes, and be killed, and after three days rise again. He said all this quite openly. And Peter took him aside and began to rebuke him. But turning and looking at his disciples, he rebuked Peter and said, "Get behind me, Satan! For you are setting your mind not on divine things but on human things." (Mark 8:28-33)

Why does Jesus address Peter as "Satan"? Because Peter told Jesus he needn't suffer. According to Mark, although God is able to move mountains (Mark 11:23), sometimes God wills that one suffer for one's faith.[55] To deny this truth is to oppose the will of God. Mark's use of the Greek verb *dei* ("the Son of Man *must* suffer") indicates that Jesus is here describing *God's will for him.* Therefore, when Peter rebukes Jesus, he is blocking the path that God wills for Jesus to follow. Peter is a *satan* in the root sense of the word — he is an adversary, an opponent, one

---

55. This point is explored very effectively in S. E. Dowd, *Prayer, Power, and the Problem of Suffering: Mark 11:22-25 in the Context of Markan Theology* (Atlanta: Scholars Press, 1988).

standing in the way. Jesus responds, "Get behind me" — in other words, "stop blocking my path."

But there is more to Jesus' address of Peter as "Satan." Influenced in part by the story of Job, many ancient Jews (and Christians in their turn) assumed that Satan inflicts suffering *so as to cause the righteous to stumble on the path of righteousness* (see above, pp. 41-48). In Dietrich Bonhoeffer's words, "Satan knows that the flesh is afraid of suffering."[56] Paul makes such an assumption when he mentions his past fear for the Thessalonians, that somehow the Tempter, Satan, had tempted (or "tested") them, and Paul's work would prove to have been in vain. In other words, Paul fears that Satan had successfully used affliction — the devil's tool of choice — to coerce the Thessalonians into abandoning their faith in the living God (1 Thess. 3:1-5). The author of 1 Peter makes similar assumptions about Satan's use of affliction as a tool to provoke apostasy. This author writes, "Like a roaring lion your adversary the devil prowls around, looking for someone to devour. Resist him, steadfast in your faith, for you know that your brothers and sisters in all the world are undergoing the same kinds of suffering" (1 Pet. 5:8-9).[57] But the *Testament of Job* is the text that best illuminates the influence of the story of Job on portrayals of Satan in this era. This melodramatic retelling of Job's story expands the roles both of Satan and of Job's wife, here named "Sitidos." In the canonical account, Job's wife tells Job to "curse God and die." The *Testament of Job* elaborates the wife's role as Satan's mouthpiece. The narrator reports that when Sitidos approached Job to tell him to curse God and die, "Satan followed her along the road, walking stealthily, and leading her heart astray" (23:11). Sitidos beseeches Job,

> "Job, Job! Although many things have been said in general, I speak to you in brief: In the weakness of my heart, my bones are crushed. Rise, take the loaves, be satisfied. And then *speak some word against the Lord and die.* Then I too shall be freed from weariness that issues from the

56. D. Bonhoeffer, *Creation and Fall, and Temptation: Two Biblical Studies* (New York: Macmillan, 1959), 104.

57. For a discussion of how this passage echoes the scriptural account of Job's testing, see S. R. Garrett, "Paul's Thorn and Cultural Models of Affliction," in *The Social World of the First Christians: Essays in Honor of Wayne A. Meeks,* ed. L. M. White and O. L. Yarbrough (Minneapolis: Fortress Press, 1995), 89.

pain of your body." So I answered her, "Look, I have lived seventeen years in these plagues submitting to the worms in my body, and my soul has never been depressed by my pains so much as by your statement, *'Speak some word against the Lord and die.'* I do indeed suffer these things, and you suffer them too: the loss both of our children and our goods. Do you suggest that we should *say something against the Lord,* and thus be alienated from the truly great wealth? . . . Do you not see the devil standing behind you and unsettling your reasoning so that he might deceive me too? For he seeks to make an exhibit of you *as one of the senseless women* who lead their husbands astray from their single-mindedness." (*T. Job* 25:9–26:6 [italics original, to designate LXX quotations])[58]

Sitidos was blind to the devil's presence. *She could not perceive that in prompting Job to give up the fight she was acting as Satan's proxy.* Next, Job commands Satan to "come up front!" and to "stop hiding yourself!" Satan comes out from behind Sitidos, and tearfully concedes that Job has defeated him by his patient endurance (27:1-7). The similarity to the Caesarea Philippi incident in Mark is remarkable. To be sure, the spatial metaphors are different: in Mark, Satan is blocking the path, and commanded to "get behind," whereas in *Testament of Job* Satan is behind, and commanded to "come forth." But in both texts, *the righteous person discerns Satan's agency in a human denial of the need to suffer.* In *Testament of Job,* when Sitidos exhorts Job to curse God and die (so as to end his own suffering), Job discerns the satanic attempt at seduction, and declares that Sitidos is like "one of the senseless women who lead their husbands astray from their singlemindedness." So also in Mark, Jesus identifies Satan as the agent behind Peter's resistance to Jesus' passion. By opposing Jesus, Peter threatens to lead Jesus astray from his singleminded devotion to following the will of God.[59]

---

58. The translation and punctuation generally follow R. P. Spittler's translation in *OTP* 1.829-868, though I have modified Spittler's rendering of the last sentence, to communicate the use in the Greek text of the term *haplotes,* "singlemindedness" (on which see S. R. Garrett, "'Lest the Light in You Be Darkness': Luke 11:33-36 and the Question of Commitment," *Journal of Biblical Literature* 110 [1991]: 93-105).

59. Gundry, 432-33, 451, reads Jesus' rebuke of Peter ("Get behind me") as an admonition to "go back where he belongs," i.e., to a subordinate position behind Jesus; in order to sustain this reading Gundry must trivialize Jesus' addressing of Peter as "Satan" to the point that it becomes virtually meaningless. Best, *Temptation and Passion,* 28-31, similarly trivializes this addressing of Peter. By contrast, J. Gnilka, *Das Evangelium nach*

Jesus says to Peter, "You are not thinking the thoughts of God but of humans." In other words, Peter's perspective on Jesus' impending passion is strictly a human one. He has been blinded, and so is unable to discern the higher purposes of God that the passion will accomplish.[60] He does not yet share in "the mystery of the kingdom of God." Peter unwittingly serves as Satan's tool to lead Jesus astray, because Satan has first prevented Peter from seeing the light of the gospel of the glory of the suffering Christ, who is the image of God. Hence, Peter is much like the blind man whose two-stage healing has just been recounted (8:22-26). After Jesus' first laying on of hands, the blind man could see persons, but said that "they look like trees, walking" (8:24). Similarly, Jesus has partially succeeded in enlightening Peter: he can see that Jesus is the Christ. But his vision is still blurred.[61] He does not yet understand that Jesus is to be a *suffering* messiah.

Markus, 3rd ed. (Zürich: Benziger; Neukirchen-Vluyn: Neukircher Verlag, 1989), 2.17; D. E. Garland, *Mark* (Grand Rapids: Zondervan, 1996), 326-27; Gibson, "Jesus' Wilderness Temptation," 14 n. 37; and Shiner, 271-72, all (like myself) interpret Peter's rebuke as a new temptation for Jesus. Shiner compares Jesus' "Get behind me" to Jesus' command for Satan to depart in the Matthean account of the temptation (Matt. 4:10) and notes how in Matthew's version of the confession at Caesarea Philippi, Matthew makes explicit Peter's role as a *skandalon* (a stumbling block in the path [Matt. 16:23]). Gnilka (2.17) cites Gen r 56 (35c) in which Satan tries to warn Isaac away from the sacrifice. Mauser, 117-18, sees Peter's intention to build booths for Jesus, Moses, and Elijah at the transfiguration (Mark 9:5) as an analogous failure: Peter thinks that "the way through the wilderness" has already ended, but it has not. This reading of the transfiguration account is similar to the view of Origen that Peter's offer to build tabernacles was an attempt to keep Jesus from the passion (noted in Kelly, 217).

60. The implication of Jesus' charge is not that "human things" equal "satanic things." Rather, Peter focuses on a mundane and earthly matter (Jesus' bodily suffering). This focus on the "human" level keeps Peter blind to truths on a higher plane, and so enables Satan to use him for his own evil purposes. Cf. Kingsbury, *Conflict in Mark,* 14, 44, 106; and compare my arguments about Sitidos's focus on mundane affairs (esp. the preservation of Job's flesh), in *Testament of Job,* in Garrett, "'Weaker Sex,'" 63-66; see also L. T. Johnson, *James,* 272 and 287 (on the dualism of heavenly wisdom versus earthbound, demonic wisdom, and the relation of both to "doublemindedness").

61. Here my position is fundamentally in agreement with that of E. S. Johnson, "Blind Man from Bethsaida," 382-83 (see also 374-75, 380). Johnson also reviews and critiques several scholarly theories about the relationship between the two-stage healing on the one hand and Peter's confession together with the subsequent rebuke by Jesus on the other (381-82). Cf. Lane, 286-87, 291-92; Marcus, "Mark 4:10-12," 569; Best, *Following Jesus,* 135-37. Notice that the two-stage healing is also preceded by an account of the disciples' incomprehension (8:14-21). Against a reading of Peter's confession as defective, see Shiner, 229-30 n. 63.

Jesus' rebuke of Peter indicates that Satan is responsible for this incomprehension or blindness.[62]

My argument that Satan used Peter to test Jesus does not imply that Mark thought of Peter as momentarily "possessed." Again, the parallel with the role of Sitidos in *Testament of Job* is instructive. The author portrays Sitidos not as "possessed," but rather as *focused on the human realm* and therefore *ignorant of higher truths*. Because of her blinding preoccupation with "the things of humans" — specifically, because of her desire to keep Job from suffering — Satan can use Sitidos in his endeavor to lead Job astray from the patient endurance of affliction. Similarly in Mark, Peter is blind to the divine necessity of Jesus' suffering; therefore, Satan can use Peter to try to dissuade Jesus from traveling the straight and narrow path set before him.

Does the *good intent* of Peter and the other disciples counterbalance their blindness? Yet again, comparison with Sitidos in *Testament of Job* may supply an answer. Like the disciples in Mark, Sitidos meant well. She wanted to help Job (and herself) by caring for Job's body. But her very concern for Job's *fleshly well-being* attested to her preoccupation with the mundane realm and blocked her access to revealed wisdom.[63] Sitidos and Peter may be compared with a character from a contemporaneous Jewish narrative: the mother of the seven martyred sons in 4 Maccabees. In distinction from the blind Sitidos and from Peter in Mark's Gospel, the mother of the seven perceived that her tortured loved ones were struggling against a tyrant, and she urged each of them to face their persecutor boldly. Thus she demonstrated that she shared fully in "devout reason" (*eusebēs logismos* [16:1]) or "piety" (*eusebeia* [16:23]). Without denying their differences, I wish to underscore the similarities among Mark, *Testament of Job,* and 4 Maccabees: in all three accounts, righteous sufferers are privy to a higher knowledge, which informs them that their affliction is temporary and in accordance with God's purposes. In all three, those who would lead the righteous ones astray from perseverance do so out of ignorance, and with good intent, but they are held to be culpable nonetheless.[64] Based on these comparisons, I infer that the

---

62. Scholars who read Jesus' rebuke of Peter as indicating satanic intervention include D. H. Juel, *A Master of Surprise: Mark Interpreted* (Minneapolis: Fortress Press, 1994), 73-74; Kingsbury, *Conflict in Mark,* 106; Mauser, 131-32. See also n. 59 above.

63. On this point, see further Garrett, " 'Weaker Sex.' "

64. See 4 Macc. 16:5-11, where the author speculates on what the mother of seven sons *might* have said, had she been fainthearted. The monologue sounds like the mourning

Markan disciples' good intent to help Jesus does not alter their role as *agents of testing.*

To be sure, the disciples are not as reprehensible as Jesus' opponents, who *deliberately* scheme to trap him and put him to death.[65] The opponents are completely blind; the disciples, only partially so. But their partial blindness is severe enough that they not only fail to urge Jesus forward on the path he must follow, but they even act to lead him astray from that path. Thus they threaten Jesus' singleminded commitment to pursuing "the way of the Lord." Never in Mark's Gospel do Jesus' disciples cheer him on as he runs the race that is set before him. In Luke's account of the last supper, Jesus says to the disciples, "You are those who have stood by me in my trials" (Luke 22:28). But Mark's Jesus could not have made such a statement. At best the disciples in Mark are a dead weight that Jesus must carry along the way as it leads up to Jerusalem; at worst they are a satanic obstacle in his path. They do not stand by Jesus or support him in his trials.

The disciples' testing of Jesus may be contrasted with the act of the woman who anoints Jesus at Bethany (Mark 14:3-9). Jesus commends her "beautiful" deed, which he interprets as an anointing of his body beforehand for burial. This unnamed woman helped *to prepare Jesus' way to suffering and death,* much as the mother in 4 Maccabees prepared the way for her sons. The woman at Bethany is virtually the only character in Mark besides John the Baptist who "makes the Lord's paths straight" as Jesus moves toward the cross. In this incident, some of those present with Jesus are distracted by a worldly concern: the monetary value of the ointment, which could have been sold and the money given to the poor (14:4-5). One may here compare *Testament of Job,* where Job's wife is likewise distracted by a worldly concern, namely her devotion to feeding Job — a concern which seems, on the face of it, just as laudable as concern for the poor. But, such concerns serve (in the particular circumstances) to trap people in a human way of thinking, to keep them from perceiving God's higher truth. In the anointing story in Mark, the woman does not "think the things of humans," and so she is able to assist Jesus on his path. Hence Jesus' response to her: "She has performed a good service for me. . . . She

---

of Sitidos for her children in *T. Job* 24:2; 39:10. For further discussion of the character of the mother of the seven, see Garrett, " 'Weaker Sex,' " 64-65.

65. Cf. Kingsbury, *Conflict in Mark,* 7-8.

has done what she could; she has anointed my body beforehand for its burial. Truly I tell you, wherever the good news is proclaimed in the whole world, what she has done will be told in rememberance of her" (14:6, 8-9).[66]

In sum, in the Caesarea Philippi episode, Mark permits us to glimpse the power of the forces that seek to lead Jesus astray, and the massive effort required to overcome them. The severity of Jesus' rebuke of Peter in Mark 8:33 corresponds to the magnitude of Jesus' temptation here: the rebuke is sharp because the temptation is profound. Although Jesus knows where God's path for him leads — through suffering, rejection, death, and resurrection (8:31) — he is sorely tempted to follow Peter in departing from this path. Jesus perseveres on the straight and narrow in spite of the temptation, but one senses that his endurance is hard-won.

"Blessed Are the Eyes"

In Mark's Gospel those who are closest to Jesus fail to comprehend that he must be a *suffering* Christ, and hence they fail to "prepare his way" and also to follow him all the way to the cross. I have suggested one way to make sense of this portrayal: by construing the twelve as pawns in the struggle between Satan and Christ. Satan, the knowledge-broker, has kept the disciples (with many others) in darkness. Jesus tries to open the disciples' eyes to a higher truth, but he is not entirely successful: not until *after* the resurrection will they fully understand. But in addition to John the Baptist and the woman at Bethany, there is one other minor character in the narrative who — at least on a symbolic level — seems to violate Mark's "schedule of concealment and disclosure."[67] This is the character

66. Mark doesn't say explicitly whether the woman understands her deed in this way, but by ascribing to Jesus the interpretation of her deed as an anointing for burial, Mark makes this the *authoritative* interpretation. Thus, against Malbon, "Fallible Followers," 40, it is not the woman's "self-denial" that Jesus praises, but her positive act of anointing him, i.e., of preparing his way. For a reading of this passage as a messianic anointing (as well as an anointing for burial), see M. D. Hooker, *The Message of Mark* (London: Epworth Press, 1983), 98. On the portrayal of Job's wife in *Testament of Job* as obsessed with the mundane realm, see Garrett, " 'Weaker Sex.' "

67. I have borrowed this phrase from R. J. Dillon, "Easter Revelation and Mission Program in Luke 24:46-48," in *Sin, Salvation, and the Spirit*, ed. D. Durken (Collegeville, Minn.: Liturgical Press, 1979), 244.

of blind Bartimaeus, whose sight Jesus restores (10:46-52). The nature of this healing (a restoration of sight) and the freighted language at the conclusion of the episode (Bartimaeus "followed Jesus on the way") invite an interpretation of the episode as symbolic. I suggest that this episode anticipates the time after the resurrection (the time of Mark's own readers), when people would at last see with clear vision.[68]

The account of the healing concludes what is widely regarded as the "central section" of Mark's Gospel. This section begins, significantly, with the two-stage healing of the blind man at Bethsaida (8:22-26). I have already suggested (following other commentators) that this earlier healing is to be read alongside Peter's confession and subsequent rebuke of Jesus at Caesarea Philippi (8:27-33): at first the blind man sees, but only indistinctly; at first Peter perceives that Jesus is the Christ, but does not see that Jesus must suffer. In the next several chapters, Jesus repeatedly prophesies the imminent suffering of the Son of Man. Then comes the healing of Bartimaeus:

> They came to Jericho. As he and his disciples and a large crowd were leaving Jericho, Bartimaeus son of Timaeus, a blind beggar, was sitting by the roadside. When he heard that it was Jesus of Nazareth, he began to shout out and say, "Jesus, Son of David, have mercy on me!" Many sternly ordered him to be quiet, but he cried out even more loudly, "Son of David, have mercy on me!" Jesus stood still and said, "Call him here." And they called the blind man, saying to him, "Take heart; get up, he is calling you." So throwing off his cloak, he sprang up and came to Jesus. Then Jesus said to him, "What do you want me to do for you?" The blind man said to him, "My teacher, let me see again." Jesus said to him, "Go; your faith has made you well." Immediately he regained his sight and followed him on the way. (10:46-52)

68. On Mark as a two-level narrative (that is, one that depicts events that transpired in the past, but overlays the account with an address to persons reading at a later time and place), see Marcus, "Mark 4:10-12," 566 n. 34. On John as such a two-level narrative see J. L. Martyn, *History and Theology in the Fourth Gospel,* rev. and enlarged ed. (Nashville: Abingdon Press, 1979); D. Rensberger, *Johannine Faith and Liberating Community* (Philadelphia: Westminster Press, 1988). In the literary critical terminology of Fowler, the historical depiction is the "story-level," whereas the address to later readers is the "discourse-level." But Fowler writes as if certain verses of Mark could be classified as "story," whereas other verses could be classified as "discourse"; in practice, both "levels" often operate within the very same stretch of text (see further in Introduction n. 19).

The persistence of Bartimaeus is impressive, as is the efficiency of Jesus' healing effort. Here Jesus achieves a complete and perfect "giving of sight," such as he has not yet been able to impart to the disciples. Thus the story serves as a counterpoint both to the two-stage healing of the blind man at Bethsaida and to the corollary episode with Peter at Caesarea Philippi. Whereas the blind man at Bethsaida had not seen clearly (at least not at first), Bartimaeus *immediately regains his sight.* Whereas Peter had obstructed Jesus on his way, Bartimaeus *follows him on it.*

The title of this subsection ("Blessed Are the Eyes") alludes to Luke 10:23-24. Here Jesus addresses not the twelve but the "seventy other" disciples (see Luke 10:1):

> Then turning to the [seventy] disciples, Jesus said to them privately, "*Blessed are the eyes that see what you see!* For I tell you that many prophets and kings desired to see what you see, but did not see it, and to hear what you hear, but did not hear it." (Luke 10:21-24 [emphasis added]; see also vv. 21-22)

Elsewhere I have argued that the episode of the seventy — recounted by Luke alone — is modeled after Moses' appointment of seventy helpers, upon whom God bestowed some of the spirit that was on Moses (see Num. 11:16-25).[69] I have suggested that Luke inserts the account of the seventy so as to foreshadow the time after Jesus' resurrection, when Christians would receive the spirit of Jesus. Jesus' blessing of the eyes (like the larger episode of the seventy, of which it is a part) is prefigurative, for according to Luke's timeline, at this point in the narrative the eyes of the twelve have not yet been opened. Such an opening will not occur until after the resurrection (Luke 24:31, 45). Thus, Jesus' "blessing of the eyes" in Luke 10:21-24 anticipates a later epoch — beyond the framework of the Gospel narrative, reaching into the time span depicted in Acts and even into the time of Luke's own audience. In this later epoch, Jesus' spirit will have been poured out and the eyes of many will have been opened. I am now suggesting that Mark's account of the healing of blind Bartimaeus functions in an analogous way, to anticipate the "clear sight" enjoyed by Mark's own readers, who stand on the far side

---

69. See Garrett, *Demise of the Devil,* 46-57, esp. 46-49.

of the resurrection.[70] Other episodes in Mark about "little people" who exhibit faith may serve a similar narrative purpose, although the blindness/sight motif makes the Bartimaeus episode more pointed than these others.[71]

Interpreted in this way, the Bartimaeus episode supplies a counterweight to Mark's portrayal of the disciples as uncomprehending. In painting this negative picture of the twelve, Mark appears to have been observing a division of holy history into the period before the resurrection and the period after it (see especially 8:30; 9:9). Prior to the resurrection, no humans — not even the twelve — could fully perceive the higher wisdom pertaining to Jesus. But after the resurrection, persons who (like Bartimaeus) come to Jesus in faith are "healed." They are made to see "what many kings and prophets desired to see." The blind disciples and seeing Bartimaeus serve as paired models for readers to make sense of their own pre- and post-conversion experiences: prior to faith, readers fail to perceive what afterward they recognize as divine truth. "I once was lost but now am found, was blind, but now I see."[72]

The so-called messianic secret in Mark coheres with this Markan division of history into the periods before and after the resurrection. The notion of a

---

70. Cf. Best, *Following Jesus*, 137, 141-43; E. S. Johnson, "Blind Bartimaeus," esp. 198-204; Lührmann, 183; Gnilka, vol. 2, 111-12; Marcus, "Mark 4:10-12," 572. Marcus, *Way of the Lord*, 34, argues that the Bartimaeus episode confirms the link between the Markan *hodos* ("Way") and the Deutero-Isaian picture of eschatological triumph. I do not disagree with Marcus's positing of a Deutero-Isaian background for the imagery of blindness/sight (cf. Garrett, "Exodus from Bondage"), but only with the function Marcus posits for that imagery in the Bartimaeus story: in my reading, the story is not related so as to prove Jesus' historical ministry as a triumphal march through the wilderness (as Marcus claims), but to anticipate Jesus' healing of (spiritual) blindness after the resurrection.

71. I have taken the term "little people" (cf. Mark 9:42) from Rhoads and Michie, 129-36 (a very helpful discussion). Some of the passages that might be included as describing "the little people" include 2:3-5 (the friends who bring the paralytic to Jesus); 5:21-24, 35-43 (Jairus); 5:25-34 (the woman with the flow of blood); 7:25-30 (the Syrophoenician woman); 9:14-29 (the man whose boy had a convulsing spirit); 10:46-52 (Bartimaeus); 12:41-44 (the poor widow); 14:3-9 (the woman who anoints Jesus at Bethany).

72. Cf. E. S. Johnson, "Blind Bartimaeus," 200-201, who argues that in this pericope Mark speaks to the problem of unbelief and doubt in his own church: "Bartimaeus serves as a prototype of the true disciple and provides a model for the Christian who needs to know what it means to see and be saved" (201); see also E. S. Johnson, "Blind Man from Bethsaida," 380, 383. I will have more to say about this hypothesis for how Mark was read by the Gospel's earliest flesh-and-blood readers below, in Chap. 4.

"messianic secret" goes back to William Wrede, who identified various features of the Markan narrative that exhibit a secrecy motif, including especially Jesus' injunctions to silence after certain of his healings.[73] There has been tremendous debate in the decades since Wrede's work about whether these motifs have a basis in the historical ministry of Jesus, and whether it is even legitimate to view them as part of a single phenomenon ("the" messianic secret). Here I do not wish to enter into this debate, but only to suggest (along with a number of other scholars) that several of the "secrecy" motifs in this Gospel may be read as variations on the theme that the humans around Jesus were blind to the *suffering nature* of his messiahship. In my reading, Jesus enjoins silence because he recognizes that outsiders *cannot understand the mystery of his identity as the suffering messiah/son of God until after the veil has been parted at the cross and resurrection* (9:9).[74]

The messianic-secret passages ought to be read in conjunction with the so-called parable theory in Mark — that is, Jesus' explanation that he teaches in parables "in order that 'they may indeed look, but not perceive, and may indeed listen, but not understand; so that they may not turn again and be forgiven'" (Mark 4:12).[75] Both the messianic-secret passages and the parable theory suggest that during Jesus' earthly ministry the time for full disclosure had not yet arrived. Although Jesus intended to enlighten the insiders (the disciples) and to obscure matters for outsiders, for the duration of his earthly life he was hindered from achieving his stated intention. That is, he was prevented from revealing the mystery of the

---

73. W. Wrede, *The Messianic Secret* (Cambridge: James Clark, 1971 [repr.; orig. 1901]). The features identified by Wrede include: (1) Jesus' commands to the demons to keep silent (Mark 1:23ff, 34; 3:11ff.; 5:6f.; 9:20); (2) Jesus' admonitions to certain persons whom he healed to remain silent (Mark 1:44; 5:43; 7:36; 8:26); (3) Jesus' order to the disciples not to disclose that he was the Christ (8:30); (4) Jesus' instruction that the disciples not discuss the transfiguration until after the resurrection (9:9); and (5) Jesus' withdrawals from the crowd with the disciples and his giving of private instruction. For a recent summary of research on the messianic secret, see Gnilka, vol. 1, 167-70.

74. Cf. the works cited in n. 70 above; also Chap. 4, n. 15 below.

75. For history of research on the parable theory in Mark, see Gnilka, vol. 1, 170-72; Beavis, 69-86. Beavis's own research seriously undermines the theory of H. Räisänen, *Die Parabeltheorie im Markusevangelium* (Helsinki: Finnish Exegetical Society, 1973), and others that Mark did not originate the parable theory and did not approve of it: on the contrary, as Beavis demonstrates (87-130), elements similar to Mark 4:11-12 are to be found throughout the Markan Gospel, suggesting that Mark approved and thoroughly integrated the theory into his work. Boucher also sees the parable theory as fully consistent with the rest of the Markan narrative.

kingdom of God even to insiders: like the outsiders, they could not see (or could see only in part) how God was acting through Jesus. After the resurrection, however, Jesus' healing of his disciples would be brought to completion. Henceforward the twelve — and *all* Jesus' followers — would be true insiders, ones who do indeed see and comprehend the mystery of the kingdom of God. For outsiders, on the other hand, even after the resurrection the parables (and Jesus himself) will still confound. Not until the coming of the Son of Man will the things that are hidden finally come to light (4:22), and only then will those who opposed Jesus finally behold him in his glory (14:62).[76]

Conclusion

In Mark's Gospel Jesus embarks on the "way of the Lord," which is a straight and narrow path to the cross. This way is fraught with tests or temptations — occasions with potential for Jesus to go astray from the course that God has ordained for him. The agents of testing that line Jesus' path are many: Satan, the Jewish authorities, and even the twelve disciples. To be sure, John the Baptist "prepares Jesus' way," through preaching and especially through his own death. Moreover, the woman who anoints Jesus at Bethany prepares his way, by readying his body beforehand for burial. But others fail to prepare Jesus' way — at least during Jesus' earthly ministry. They do not encourage him to persevere in the way. Instead of "making his paths straight," they make them crooked — in other words, they act in ways that threaten to seduce Jesus away from "the straight and narrow path," or to obstruct him on it.

The motif of Jesus as tested is intertwined with the motif of blindness and sight. Foe and friend alike put Jesus to the test because their minds have been blinded to keep them from perceiving the mystery of the Kingdom of God. This blinding will last for the duration of Jesus' earthly ministry. The use in Mark of the motifs of lower and higher knowledge,

---

76. Cf. Lane, 173: "There was *veiling* (or very partial disclosure) before the multitude and *disclosure* (but only partial understanding) to the disciples. . . . Only through revelation does the enigma become partially resolved; not until the consummation . . . will it become resolved for all men" (italics original). In Lane's opinion, Mark 9:9 makes it clear that the enigma will be resolved for the disciples after Jesus' resurrection (Lane, n. 85).

blindness and sight, is consistent with what we see in some other authors from the first-century Mediterranean world. Such an emphasis typified especially the apocalypticism that was Mark's cultural home. In this setting, it could be assumed that Satan tries to keep persons thinking in a mundane, "human" way, in which they place excessive value on human affairs, including especially the preservation or gratification of the flesh. Such a mindset assisted Satan in controlling his domain, for (it was supposed) those who esteem the flesh will do whatever Satan desires in order to stop his afflicting of them or in order to satisfy the fleshly desires that Satan arouses. On the other hand, there are those whom Satan cannot blind, who have been gifted with sight: they discern the satanic character of their trials and know that their endurance will be rewarded in the afterlife. Hence Satan cannot lead them astray with his deceptive offers to cease his afflictions or to fulfill his promises of benefit or pleasure. By enduring Satan's tests, such persons prove that they are stronger than he.

In Mark's Gospel, prior to Jesus' crucifixion, Jesus himself is the only human character who possesses divine wisdom. The Jewish authorities are utterly blind, and so test Jesus. The disciples glimpse aspects of the truth, but even Jesus cannot rip the veil that has been placed over their eyes. Failing to grasp the mystery, they, too, put Jesus to the test. To be sure, after Jesus' healing of Bartimaeus, the healed man does "see" with clear and unobstructed vision and make the appropriate response; moreover, John the Baptist and the woman who anoints Jesus at Bethany both "prepare Jesus' way" to the cross. But these are not major characters in the narrative. Possibly they are best viewed as symbolic: as anticipating the time after the resurrection, when *all* Jesus' followers would see him clearly, follow him on the way, and proclaim the good news of his suffering, death, and resurrection to the world.

The leitmotif of testing begins with Mark's portrayal of Jesus' testing in the wilderness and runs through Mark's portrayal of Jesus' earthly ministry of healing and teaching, as I have shown. In Mark's passion account — when Jesus is "given over into the hands of sinners" for the final testing of his flesh — this motif will reach its stunning climax.

CHAPTER 3

Into the Hands of Sinners

Jesus in Gethsemane (Mark 14:32-42)

Three times now Jesus has predicted his own passion (8:31; 9:31; 10:32-34). Clearly he knows that it is God's will for him to suffer and die. He has repeatedly been tested, and thus far has persevered along the straight and narrow path: he emerged victorious from the testing in the wilderness, withstood the tests of his earthly adversaries, and silenced Satan when he spoke through Peter at Caesarea Philippi. Especially in the Caesarea Philippi account, Mark has hinted at the great effort required for Jesus to endure these tests: they are *real tests,* and at no time was Jesus' victory in them to be taken for granted.[1] If Mark has been subtle in making this point before, in his account of Jesus in Gethsemane the evangelist abandons all such subtlety and lays the point out with shocking clarity:

> They went to a place called Gethsemane; and he said to his disciples, "Sit here while I pray." He took with him Peter and James and John, and *began to be distressed and agitated. And he said to them, "I am deeply grieved, even to death;* remain here, and keep awake." And going a little farther, he threw himself on the ground and prayed that, if it were possible, the hour might pass from him. He said, "Abba, Father, for you all things are possible; remove this cup from me; yet, not what I want, but what you want." He came and found them sleeping; and he said

1. For a similar argument, also made in discussion of the Gethsemane episode, see R. S. Barbour, "Gethsemane in the Tradition of the Passion," *New Testament Studies* 16 (1969-70): 247.

to Peter, "Simon, are you asleep? Could you not keep awake one hour? Keep awake and pray that you may not come into the time of trial; *the spirit indeed is willing, but the flesh is weak.*" And again he went away and prayed, saying the same words. And once more he came and found them sleeping, for their eyes were very heavy; and they did not know what to say to him. He came a third time and said to them, "Are you still sleeping and taking your rest? Enough! The hour has come; the Son of Man is given over [or "betrayed"] into the hands of sinners. Get up, let us be going. See, the one who gives me over [or "my betrayer"] is at hand." (Mark 14:32-42 [italics added])

The evangelist employs unusually strong language to describe Jesus' emotional struggle to come to grips with what lies ahead: Jesus begins to be "distressed" *(ekthambeisthai)* and "agitated" *(adēmonein)* (14:33), and says to the inner circle of disciples, "I am deeply grieved, even to death" (*perilypos estin hē psychē mou heōs thanatou* [v. 34]).[2] This picture of distress and sorrow evokes the sentiments expressed by the figure of the "righteous sufferer" in some of the psalms of lament:

> My heart is in anguish within me, the terrors of death have fallen upon me. Fear and trembling come upon me, and horror [LXX: darkness] overwhelms me. (Ps. 55:4-5 [LXX 54:4-5])

> Why are you cast down [LXX: *perilypos*], O my soul, and why are you disquieted *[syntarassein]* within me? (Ps. 42:5 [LXX 41:5])[3]

Sharyn Dowd points out that Jesus' lack of detachment as he looks into his own future startles readers. The element of surprise makes the scene all the more wrenching. "The audience is completely unprepared for Jesus'

---

2. See the discussion of the terms *ekthambeisthai* and *adēmonein* in R. E. Brown, *The Death of the Messiah: From Gethsemane to the Grave* (New York: Doubleday, 1994), 153. See the discussion of possible translations of the clause *perilypos estin hē psychē mou heōs thanatou* in R. E. Brown, 155-56; also S. E. Dowd, *Prayer, Power, and the Problem of Suffering: Mark 11:22-25 in the Context of Markan Theology* (Atlanta: Scholars Press, 1988), 153 (incl. n. 9).

3. See the discussion of these psalms and their relevance for the Gethsemane account in R. E. Brown, 153-54; J. Marcus, *The Way of the Lord: Christological Exegesis of the Old Testament in the Gospel of Mark* (Louisville: Westminster/John Knox Press, 1992), 172-86 (on the psalms of lament throughout the passion narrative); D. Senior, *The Passion of Jesus in the Gospel of Mark* (Collegeville, Minn.: Liturgical Press, 1984), 70-73.

extreme distress and for his request that God intervene to prevent his death (14:36)."[4]

Is Jesus being tested here? Is he himself enmeshed in a "time of trial," *peirasmos,* even as he exhorts the disciples to pray to avoid such a moment? It certainly is the case that in this scene Jesus struggles to choose God's way rather than another, easier path. And yet, I shall argue below, Mark indicates that Jesus' time in Gethsemane is primarily to be viewed as a time of intense *preparation* for the hour of satanic testing, which still lies ahead. While he is in Gethsemane, Jesus remains in communion with God, whom he addresses as "Abba" (Father); the actual confrontation with satanic powers begins at the conclusion of this episode, when he is "given over (or "betrayed") into the hands of sinners" (14:41).[5] The confrontation will reach its climax as Jesus hangs on the cross, forsaken by God. Thus, all the trials that Jesus has faced up till and including this time in Gethsemane are but the prelude to the final, most severe time of trial that he will undergo in his suffering and death at the hands of sinners.

Eschatological Testing

Mark's Gethsemane account is packed with vocabulary and imagery that signal the onset of eschatological testing.[6] The first red flag is the word "watch," or "keep awake" *(gregorein)* (vv. 34, 37, 38). Mark had Jesus use this word three times in the conclusion to the apocalyptic discourse in chapter 13:

> "But about that day or hour no one knows, neither the angels in heaven, nor the Son, but only the Father. Beware, keep alert; for you do not

4. Dowd, 153. On the shocking character of Mark's portrayal of Jesus in Gethsemane, cf. M. D. Hooker, *The Message of Mark* (London: Epworth Press, 1983), 98-100.

5. On Jesus' continuing communion with God while in Gethsemane, see Senior, 73-75. On Jesus' passion as a time of trial, see Senior, 78; R. E. Brown, 196. For an especially nuanced discussion of whether God was testing Jesus in the incident related in Mark 14:32-42, see Barbour, 244-46. Barbour finally determines that such a conclusion is warranted, but adds that the tradition can also be read as a temptation of Jesus by Satan.

6. Jesus' immediately preceding quotation (in Mark 14:27) of Zechariah 13:7 already sets the scene for a time of eschatological testing: note the pointed references to testing in the rest of the prophetic oracle (Zech. 13:8-9). See also below, pp. 144-45; in general on eschatological testing, see above, pp. 42-44.

know when the time will come. It is like a man going on a journey, when he leaves home and puts his slaves in charge, each with his work, and commands the doorkeeper to be on the watch *[gregorein]*. Therefore, keep awake *[gregorein]* — for you do not know when the master of the house will come, in the evening, or at midnight, or at cockcrow, or at dawn, or else he may find you asleep when he comes suddenly. And what I say to you I say to all: Keep awake *[gregorein]*." (Mark 13:32-37)

The parable concerns the time in which Mark's readers find themselves: for the master to come and find them sleeping would mean that they had failed to prepare themselves for the hour of eschatological trial (cf. Matt. 25:12, 13). Similarly in most of its other New Testament occurrences, the word *gregorein* means to be vigilant and watchful, to behave as a "child of the day" in a time when the powers of darkness press down on all sides (1 Thess. 5:6; cf. v. 10), when like a roaring lion the devil "prowls around, looking for someone to devour" (1 Pet. 5:8).[7]

The second clue that the events in Gethsemane mark the onset of eschatological testing is the word "hour" *(hōra)* in 14:35, 37, 41. Mark has also used this term in Jesus' apocalyptic discourse, to designate the moment when the Son of Man will return (13:32; cf. Rev. 3:3). Other New Testament authors use the word "hour" to designate the advent of salvation (Rom. 13:11), or to tag specific eschatological events, such as the coming of the antichrist (1 John 2:18), the hour of judgment (Rev. 14:7), and the eschatological "harvest" (Rev. 14:15). Especially noteworthy is Revelation 3:10, in which the risen Christ promises the angel of the Philadelphian church, "Because you have kept my word of patient endurance *[hypomonē]*, I will keep you from the hour of trial *[hōra tou peirasmou]* that is coming on the whole world to test *[peirasai]* the inhabitants of the earth."[8]

---

7. Other New Testament uses of *gregorein* are in Matthew 24:42 (par. Mark 13:35); 24:43; 25:13; 26:38, 40, 41 (Gethsemane); Luke 12:37; Acts 20:31; 1 Cor. 16:13; Rev. 3:2, 3; 16:15. On the eschatological import of the word in Mark's Gethsemane account, see R. E. Brown, 156-57, 195-96.

8. R. E. Brown, 167-68, argues against some other commentators in favor of the "preMarcan absolute (eschatological) use of 'the hour.'" He refers to some of the passages cited here, and also notes "John's *wide* use of 'the hour,'" which can hardly be derivative from Mark's three uses (167; italics his). Brown's position that the use of "hour" and "cup" indicates that Mark sees Jesus as entering into a time of eschatological trial is consistent with the one I am developing here (R. E. Brown, 165-72; also the discussion at 157-62, which primarily concerns Luke but also makes reference to Mark).

The third detail signaling the onset in Gethsemane of eschatological events is Jesus' prayer that God take away the cup (*potērion* [v. 36]). In the Hebrew Scriptures, *potērion* (so also the corresponding Hebrew term *kôs*) regularly describes God's wrath or punishment, which the guilty are to "drink."[9] Accordingly, some have suggested that Jesus here anticipates that he will himself drink the cup of God's wrath against sin. Others find this significance for "cup" implausible within the Markan context, citing instead evidence that "cup" can refer to any negative destiny or fate.[10] If one accepts the latter evidence as decisive, then Jesus is not the object of God's anger; but he is, as Raymond Brown suggests, required to partake of "a cup of suffering that will culminate in an anguished death as a condemned criminal."[11] Though Brown prefers this latter interpretation, he concedes that the wide usage in the ancient Near East of "cup" to signify wrath or judgment "may be preserved in Mark, not in the sense that Jesus is the object of wrath, but inasmuch as his death will take place in the apocalyptic context of the great struggle of last times when God's kingdom overcomes evil."[12] (Below I shall say more about the import of Jesus' reference to the "cup" that he must drink.)

Jesus exhorts the disciples, saying, "Keep awake *[gregorein]* and *pray that you may not come into testing [peirasmos]*" (Mark 14:38). This is the fourth and most significant clue that Mark construes the Gethsemane episode as initiating the time of eschatological trial. Jesus is here admonishing his followers to *do as he has done*. In other words, Jesus' just-concluded petitions that the hour may pass and that God remove the cup were likewise prayers to escape *peirasmos*. Jesus has beseeched God in order that he might himself avoid entry into the time of trial; now he exhorts the disciples to do likewise.[13] When Jesus says, at the conclusion to the Gethsemane episode, "The hour has come; the Son of Man is given over into the hands of sinners" (14:41), he is acknowledging that his prayer to

9. R. E. Brown, 168-69, citing A. T. Hanson, *The Wrath of the Lamb* (London: SPCK, 1957), 27-36. See Rev. 14:10 and 16:19 for examples of such usage in an apocalyptic context.

10. For bibliography of literature supporting the wrath-interpretation of the "cup" that Jesus drinks, see the works cited in n. 41.

11. R. E. Brown, 170.

12. R. E. Brown, 170.

13. Cf. R. E. Brown, 161.

God to take away the cup has not been granted. The hour of eschatological *peirasmos* has arrived.[14]

Jesus' remark to the disciples that "the spirit indeed is willing, but the flesh is weak" (v. 38) similarly applies to himself as much as to his disciples. Mark and other early readers would not likely have supposed that Jesus was here drawing a contrast between evil "flesh," or "matter," and good "spirit," or "nonmatter."[15] Nor was he making an oblique reference to the Holy Spirit. Rather, "spirit" and "flesh" would most likely have been understood as representing two distinct but inseparable aspects of human selves (in keeping with usage of the terms in the Hebrew Scriptures and in Jewish intertestamental literature). The "spirit" designates humans insofar as they are thinking, willing beings. "Flesh" symbolizes their earthly, mortal, creaturely aspect: it is the flesh that experiences desire and pain while alive, and that decays after death.[16] Earlier in the Markan narrative, Jesus and the disciples offered ample proof that their spirits are willing: James and John insisted that they are able to drink from the very cup that God extends to Jesus (10:39); Peter vowed that he will die with Jesus if need be (14:31); Jesus himself took a "cup," and declared it to be his blood, "poured out for many" (14:23-24). But here in Gethsemane the disciples and Jesus alike give evidence of their weak flesh: Jesus falls into deep distress over his impending passion, thereby revealing the desire of his flesh for self-preservation. And the disciples fail to "watch" or "keep awake," repeatedly falling asleep on account of their "heavy" or "burdened" eyes.[17]

14. Cf. R. E. Brown, 161, 209; also Barbour, 234, 236.

15. The "matter/nonmatter" dichotomy is a modern bifurcation, which can be traced to René Descartes; for most ancient theorists, "spirit" *(pneuma)* was itself "a kind of 'stuff' that is the agent of perception, motion, and life itself; it pervades other forms of stuff and, together with those other forms, constitutes the self" (D. B. Martin, *The Corinthian Body* [New Haven: Yale University Press, 1995], 21; see in its entirety the important discussion of "the body" in Greco-Roman culture, Martin, 3-37).

16. Here I am borrowing from the helpful discussion of the spirit/flesh dichotomy in R. E. Brown, 198-200; cf. Senior, 79.

17. On whether Jesus' comment about willing spirit and weak flesh applies also to himself, cf. Barbour, 244. On the disciples' sleep as evidence of unreadiness to face trials, see R. E. Brown, 174; cf. 206. R. E. Brown, 203, argues that in enumerating Jesus' movements in Gethsemane, Mark stresses the failure of the disciples. R. E. Brown, 206, suggests that 14:40 ("they did not know how to answer him") highlights their human frailty and misunderstanding (on analogy with the misunderstanding at the transfiguration: see Mark 9:5-6). T. J. Geddert, *Watchwords: Mark 13 in Markan Eschatology* (Sheffield:

Jesus' comment about willing spirit and weak flesh presumes that human "flesh" — though not inherently evil — is nonetheless a prime target for Satan's tests. In this instance, *tests of affliction* are in view: the flesh can be made to feel pain, which in turn may prompt persons to act against their own good resolutions. This notion that Satan afflicts the flesh so as to coerce the righteous to disobedience or apostasy finds its most important antecedent in canonical Job. In the prologue of Job, when the devil approaches God the second time, God points out that Job "still persists in his integrity" (2:3). Then Satan answers the Lord, "Skin for skin! All that people have they will give to save their lives. But stretch out your hand now and *touch his bone and his flesh* [LXX: *sarx*], and he will curse you to your face" (Job 2:4-5). In the period after the composition of canonical Job, persons began to take it for granted that Satan afflicts persons (i.e., afflicts their *flesh*).[18] Some held that he did so in the service of God, to test persons or to chastise them when they err. Paul, for example, presumes that Satan may afflict human flesh while acting as an agent of divine chastisement: Paul instructs the Corinthians to hand over *(paradidonai)* a certain transgressor to Satan "for the destruction of the *flesh [eis holethron tēs sarkos],* so that his *spirit* may be saved in the day of the Lord" (1 Cor. 5:5; note that "spirit" and "flesh" are here paired as opposites, just as in the Gethsemane account). And Paul's enigmatic reference to an "angel of Satan," sent to "torment" or "buffet" him, to keep him from becoming "too elated," may refer to some sort of physical ailment that Paul endured.[19]

JSOT Press, 1989), 104, argues that the disciples' problem in Gethsemane is "not that spiritual senses are in need of sharpening," but that "the flesh is too weak." The dichotomy is a false one, however: it is only when one's eyes have been opened to "divine things" that one is able to perceive how satanic forces exploit the weak flesh, and therefore that one is able to triumph over those forces by persevering in trial. Once the disciples' eyes have been opened, they (like Bartimaeus) *will* be able faithfully to follow Jesus in the way.

18. On Satan's use of affliction see *T. Job* 16:2-4; 20:1-2; 38:2; 1 Thess. 3:4-5; 1 Pet. 5:8-9. In the Qumran context, flesh (though not inherently evil or sinful) "is often the channel through which the Spirit of Wickedness attacks, tests, tempts, or takes over the individual" (R. E. Brown, 199, citing 1QS 11:12). For fuller discussion of first-century views of Satan's use of affliction, see S. R. Garrett, "The God of This World and the Affliction of Paul: 2 Cor 4:1-12," in *Greeks, Romans, and Christians: Essays in Honor of Abraham J. Malherbe,* ed. David L. Balch et al. (Minneapolis: Fortress Press, 1990); S. R. Garrett, "Paul's Thorn and Cultural Models of Affliction," in *The Social World of the First Christians: Essays in Honor of Wayne A. Meeks,* ed. M. White and L. Yarborough (Minneapolis: Fortress Press, 1995), 87-91.

19. On this passage, see Garrett, "Paul's Thorn." See also the discussion of first-century views of satanic testing, above pp. 32-48.

Jesus Chooses the Will of God

By describing Jesus as "distressed," "agitated," and "grieving," Mark indicates that during his vigil in Gethsemane Jesus experienced passions of the flesh.[20] Although *in his spirit* Jesus desired to obey God, his *fleshly desire* was to avoid treading the path that he knew God had laid out for him. Thus, with respect to his resolve Jesus was momentarily divided.[21] Ancient Jewish and Christian authors held that "divided," or "doubleminded," persons seek to serve God while simultaneously serving another. The "other" may be a different god, an inanimate object (such as "mammon"), or oneself and one's own interests.[22] In Luke Johnson's formulation, those

20. Philosophers in Mark's day were greatly concerned about the problem of the passions (that is, the problem of how to achieve "self-mastery," which referred to mastery over the passions). The four chief or cardinal passions in most ancient accounts were pain (which encompassed various types of emotional distress, including grief or sorrow), fear, pleasure, and desire. Recent secondary treatments of the topic include M. C. Nussbaum, *The Therapy of Desire: Theory and Practice in Hellenistic Ethics* (Princeton: Princeton University Press, 1994); and S. K. Stowers, *A Rereading of Romans: Justice, Jews, and Gentiles* (New Haven: Yale University Press, 1994).

21. Cf. Senior, 72: "The evangelist presents Jesus as an example of biblical faith, a tormented child of God in love with life and fearful of death, without support except for the bedrock of God's fidelity"; also D. E. Garland, *Mark* (Grand Rapids: Zondervan, 1996), 539. W. L. Lane, *The Gospel of Mark* (Grand Rapids: William B. Eerdmans, 1974), 516, argues that Jesus experienced horror specifically at the prospect of the alienation from God that God's judgment on sin would entail; thus the Gethsemane account anticipates the cry of dereliction.

22. Cf. Matthew 6:24, where the placement of the pericope immediately after Jesus' teaching about the "single eye" (6:22-23) suggests that in the mammon-saying also, Matthew is thinking of the problem of doublemindedness, or division of the heart. See S. R. Garrett, " 'Lest the Light in You Be Darkness': Luke 11:33-36 and the Question of Commitment," *Journal of Biblical Literature* 110 (1991): 93-105, on the saying about the "single eye" in Luke's Gospel. For citations of early Jewish and Christian texts that refer to "singleness" or "doubleness" of self (using various terms), see H. W. Hollander and M. de Jonge, *The Testaments of the Twelve Patriarchs: A Commentary* (Leiden: E. J. Brill, 1985), 340-41. Such texts include, for example, *Testament of Issachar* (regarding which, see the discussion "*Haplotēs* as central theme," in Hollander and de Jonge, 233-34); *Testament of Asher;* Philo *Quaest. in Gen.* 4.165; James 1:8; 4:8; *1 Clem.* 23.1-2; *Herm. Sim.* 9.21.1; *Vis.* 2.2.4. Secondary discussions include J. Amstutz, ΑΠΛΟΤΗΣ: *Eine begriffsgeschichtliche Studie zum jüdischchristlichen Griechisch* (Bonn: Peter Hanstein, 1968); Hollander and de Jonge, 233-34; O. J. F. Seitz, "Antecedents and Signification of the Term ΔΙΨΥΧΟΣ," *Journal of Biblical Literature* 66 (1947): 211-19; O. J. F. Seitz, "Afterthoughts on the Term 'Dipsychos,' " *New Testament Studies* 4 (1957/-58): 327-34; Garrett, " 'Lest the Light' "; J. Marcus, "The Evil Inclination in the Epistle of James," *Catholic Biblical Quarterly* 44 (1982): 606-21 (on James). There are important antecedents to the notion of double-

who are doubleminded attempt "to live simultaneously by the measure of faith (the wisdom from above) and the measure of the world (the wisdom that is earth-bound, unspiritual, demonic)."[23] Mark has already indicated that, according to "the wisdom from above," it is necessary for Jesus to suffer. Jesus has accepted this heavenly wisdom, as his earlier passion predictions made clear. But "the wisdom from below" dictates that one avoid suffering, and Jesus' "grief," "distress," and "agitation" reveal that he desires to live by this measure also. In other words, though in his spirit Jesus is willing to do what God requires, the desire of his weak flesh is for mortal life, rather than for suffering, alienation from God, and death. If only for an instant, Jesus is caught between two ways; he must make a choice. How remarkable that Mark should permit us to glimpse this dreadful moment of Jesus' inner conflict!

In order to resolve his own opposing desires, Jesus turns to God in prayer. It is God who gives the wisdom from above, and who thereby empowers believers to forsake earthly measures of goodness or success. Moreover, it is God who gives confidence in God's own power to save. Hence, when persons are doubleminded, or when they doubt, it is fitting for them to ask God to intervene (cf. Mark 9:24, discussed on pp. 166-67 below). As Johnson observes (in connection with James 1:2-8), "Prayer is the essential conversion for one unable to 'perceive' or 'calculate' life's testings in the appropriate way."[24] Because Jesus turns to God in his moment of grief and distress, he moves beyond his brief encounter with doublemindedness to a place of singleminded obedience to God. Prayer is his means of victory over the division of spirit and flesh. As soon as Jesus turns to God in prayer, God's will supercedes the will of Jesus' flesh. Having now conquered doublemindedness, Jesus will be able to stand firm throughout the trials ahead.[25]

---

mindedness already in the Hebrew scriptures; see Seitz, "Antecedents and Signification." On notions of doublemindedness and hypocrisy in the Dead Sea Scrolls, see Marcus "Evil Inclination"; U. Wilckens, "ὑποκρίνομαι κτλ.," in *The Theological Dictionary of the New Testament*, vol. 8 (Grand Rapids: William B. Eerdmans, 1972), 565-66. For provocative and well-informed theological reflection on the notion of doublemindedness, see L. T. Johnson, *The Letter of James* (New York: Doubleday, 1995), 184, 191, 192, 254, 264-65, 274-75, 285, 287-89, 340.

23. Johnson, 340.

24. Johnson, 184.

25. Cf. Senior, 80: Jesus' praying steels him for the impending crisis; the disciples, who failed to pray, "are overwhelmed with fear and will flee."

The division that Mark has portrayed, between Jesus' spiritual readiness and his state of fleshly desire (14:34), is not itself to be understood as an actual instance of temptation, and certainly not as a failure to persevere in temptation, but rather as a *conflicted state of being* — "doublemindedness." Doublemindedness puts persons who enter into it *at risk* of failing to endure trials. As the author of the epistle of James writes, those who are doubleminded are "like a wave of the sea, driven and tossed by the wind" (James 1:6). When tested, such persons — lacking the firm anchor of a singular set of commitments — are caught in indecision, propelled now this way and now that. Only when they have conquered doublemindedness, by renouncing worldly desires and by choosing obedience to God, do they set onto a steady course and find themselves able to endure trials. Prayer is the means by which persons put doublemindedness behind them, as Jesus demonstrates in his move from distress and grief (14:33-34) to confident obedience (vv. 35-36). In prayer, Jesus asks God to spare him from the hour of eschatological trial, but then immediately he chooses God's will over his own: "Yet, not what I want, but what you want" (v. 36). The notice concluding the pericope, that "the hour has come," signals that Jesus' request to avoid trial has not been granted.

As I have noted, it is remarkable that Mark should have portrayed Jesus as experiencing doublemindedness, even if only for a brief moment, and even if Jesus quickly passes beyond his division of self to resolute single-mindedness. Apparently Luke was offended by the portrayal: in taking over Mark's account, Luke omitted any mention of Jesus' grief and distress. So also John, if he knew Mark's form of the tradition, eliminated any hint of reluctance by Jesus: in the Fourth Gospel, Jesus' will and God's are one and the same (10:30; 17:11, 22). The third and fourth evangelists soften the offense of Mark's portrayal, but in doing so they detract from Jesus' humanity. For if there is any trait characteristic of human existence, it is surely a desire for life such as Mark ascribes to Jesus. Moreover, apart from such desire, the laying down of one's life would not be a genuine sacrifice — it would not express the limit of human love (John 15:13). By showing that Jesus' desire for life was very real, Mark conveys to us the magnitude of Jesus' suffering and of his sacrifice. Then, by showing us how prayer enabled Jesus to put God's desire ahead of his own, Mark shows us, too, how to dispel doublemindedness and prepare for trial.

Sharyn Dowd takes note of Mark's emphasis on the *twofold nature* of Jesus' repeated supplication to God (14:35-36). In Jesus' prayer, submission to God's will does not replace but *accompanies* a request that God take away the cup:

> And going a little farther, he threw himself on the ground and prayed that, if it were possible, the hour might pass from him. He said, "Abba, Father, for you all things are possible; remove this cup from me; yet, not what I want, but what you want." (14:35-36; cf. v. 39)[26]

The first line sounds tentative — "he prayed, if it were possible, that the hour might pass from him." But this apparent tentativeness is strongly countered by Jesus' next affirmation, "Abba, Father, for you all things are possible." Mark has Jesus echo his own earlier teaching about the omnipotence of God: Jesus' Father is one who can take up mountains and throw them into the sea (11:23-24; cf. 10:27).[27] Here in the Gethsemane account, Jesus' emphasis on God's omnipotence ups the ante in the prayer, for if "all things" are possible to God, then God could still intervene to change Jesus' destiny. As Dowd observes, "The scene is terrible, not because Jesus must suffer, but because his suffering is the will of the God who is powerful enough to prevent it, and who has eliminated so much suffering in the narrative prior to this scene."[28] Jesus knows full well that it is the divine will for him to drink the cup; nonetheless, he prays for divine intervention by the all-powerful God. Here Mark models for his readers the appropriate content of prayer in preparation for trial: one should pray that God prevent or remove the testing.[29] But in making such a request one acknowledges — whether expressly (like Jesus) or implicitly — that God may choose not to take away the cup, and one vows obedience to God either way.

---

26. On the narrative and theological significance of Jesus' twofold prayer (supplication to remove the cup, combined with submission to God's will), see Dowd, 157; R. E. Brown, 165-67. Brown observes, "John has both a form of Jesus' prayer about the hour (12:27-28) and a reference to the cup (18:11, in the context of the arrest). Unless one thinks John used Mark and divided the Marcan material in such a strange manner, one should reckon with the possibility that the content of both Marcan verses came from the preGospel tradition, even if Mark reshaped the material to the present indirect/direct pattern" (166). On p. 167, Brown gives examples to demonstrate that "in the biblical outlook, it is not irreverent to ask God for a change of mind."

27. Regarding Greco-Roman parallels to Jesus' statements about God's potentiality, see Dowd, 78-92; also R. E. Brown, 175.

28. Dowd, 158.

29. Cf. Matthew 6:13 (par. Luke 11:4); on whether Mark knew the Lord's prayer, see the works cited in Senior, 76 n. 38.

Into the Hands of Sinners

Jesus' prayer on the Mount of Olives indicates that here he is still in communion with God. In other words, while he prays, he continues as the beloved Son, bestowed with divine authority and power. But the conclusion of the Gethsemane scene marks the transition to Jesus' own time of trial: "The hour has come; the Son of Man is given over into the hands of sinners" (14:41). The word here translated as "given over into" is *paradidonai;* it is the same word used repeatedly to describe Judas as the one who "gave Jesus over" (or, more traditionally, who "betrayed" him). Literally the word designates the act of delivering someone or something over to another authority. It is used with great frequency in the LXX, often to designate God's delivering of persons over into their enemies' hands.[30] For example, Deuteronomy 7:2 (LXX) foretells how the Lord will bring the Hebrew people into the land and will remove great nations from before them: "And the Lord your God will give them over *[paradōsei autous]* into your hands, and you will destroy them." The verb *paradidonai* is also used in Isaiah 53, in one of the so-called songs of the suffering servant. Here it is written that the Lord "gave him [the servant] up for our sins" (53:12) and that "he bore the sins of many, and was delivered *[paredothē]* because of their iniquities." Joel Marcus cautiously asserts that the Markan references to Jesus as "given over" or "delivered up" (Mark 14:10-11, 18, 21, 41-42, 44; 15:1, 10, 15) were "probably intended to awaken echoes of Isaiah 53."[31]

Marcus may be correct, but Isaiah 53 is not by itself *sufficient* to explain how first-century readers would have interpreted Mark's descriptions of Jesus as "given over." In apocalyptic contexts, *paradidonai* probably would have evoked images of persons being *delivered to the authority of Satan for the purposes of testing or chastisement by affliction.* Such usage derives from Job 2:4-6 (LXX), in which Satan appears before God a second time, following God's report that Job persists in his integrity even after Satan initially afflicted him:

---

30. In the LXX, *paradidonai* translates the Hebrew *masar.* Other examples of such usage in the LXX include Deuteronomy 7:23; Joshua 2:24; Judges 13:1; Psalms 26[27]:12; 87[88]:8; 117[118]:18.

31. Marcus, *Way of the Lord,* 188.

Then the devil answered the Lord, "Skin for Skin! All that people have they will give to save their lives. But stretch out your hand now and touch his bones and his flesh, and he will curse [lit. "bless," as a euphenism for "curse"] you to your face." And the Lord said to the devil, "Behold, I give him over *[paradidonai]* to you; only preserve his life *[tēn psychēn autou]*." (Job 2:4-6 [LXX] [emphasis added])[32]

When the author of *Testament of Job* retells Job's story, he retains the use of *paradidonai:*

So when all my goods were gone, Satan concluded that he was unable to provoke me to contempt *[eis oligōrian trepsai]*. When he left he asked *[aitēsai]* my body from the Lord so he might inflict the plague on me. Then the Lord gave me over *[paradidonai]* into his hand to be used as he wished with respect to the body; but he did not give him authority over my soul *[psychē]*. (*T. Job* 20:1-3)

A similar scenario is presupposed at Luke 22:31-32: here Jesus says that Satan "requested to have" *(exaitēsai)* the apostles; that is, requested that God give them over into Satan's authority. Jesus then concedes that some sort of testing ("sifting") will occur, implying that God complied with Satan's request. In 1 Corinthians 5:5, Paul uses the term *paradidonai* in his instruction to the Corinthians to act in concert with the Lord Jesus in "giving over" a certain transgressor to Satan "for the destruction of the flesh."[33] In 1 Timothy 1:20, "Paul" refers to Hymenaeus and Alexander,

32. Compare the use of *didōmi* in the parallel verse at Job 1:12. Interestingly, R. E. Brown, 212-13 (cf. 802) discusses Old Testament/New Testament usage of the term *paradidonai,* but doesn't discuss these examples from Job. W. Popkes, *Christus Traditus: Eine Untersuchung zum Begriff der Dahingabe im Neuen Testament* (Zürich: Zwingli Verlag, 1967), 229 nn. 646, 647, rejects the notion that the account of the "giving over" of Job to Satan had any significant influence on the Gospels' picture of the giving over of Jesus; Popkes rejects also the corollary notion that Jesus was viewed as given over to evil powers (239). For Popkes's own theory about sources of influence on traditions about Jesus as "given over," see Popkes, 238-239.

33. Moreover, Paul uses *paradidonai* three times in Romans 1, to describe how God expresses divine wrath upon those who perversely suppress the truth, by giving them over to the power of their own debaucheries — almost as if the latter were punishing (i.e., satanic) agents (Rom. 1:24, 26, 28). Paul also uses the term *paradidonai* to describe himself as "given up to death for Jesus' sake" (2 Cor. 4:11). I discuss this usage in Garrett, "God of This World," 116. Simplifying, my argument there is that Paul may think of himself as handed over to *the power of death,* or Satan.

"whom I have given over *[paradidonai]* to Satan, so that they may learn not to blaspheme." In *Shepherd of Hermas* (early second century), when the Shepherd appears to Hermas, Hermas mistakes the Shepherd for one come to test him (i.e., for an angel of Satan?). Hermas writes, "I thought he was coming to test me *(parestin ekpeirazōn me)*, and I said to him. . . . 'I know to whom I was given over *[paradidesthai]'* " (*Herm. Vis.* 5.3).[34] When in Mark Jesus says, "The hour has come; the Son of Man is *given over* into the hands of sinners" (14:41), *he indicates that God has relinquished control over Jesus, remanding him to the authority of sinners (and of Satan) for the testing of his flesh.*[35]

If God "gave Jesus over" to sinners for the testing of his flesh, how great was the implied estrangement between Jesus and God? Was this "forsaking" viewed as absolute, or was it, rather, limited in some way? Was God genuinely absent from Jesus, or only seemingly so? How would Mark's earliest readers have understood the estrangement? Though we shall never answer such questions definitively, other sources from this era help us to delineate the issues. The Job passage and parallels discussed above (Job 2:6 [LXX]; *T. Job* 20:1-3; cf. *Jub.* 17:15-16) suggest a belief in Mark's era that God's "giving over" of righteous persons to Satan for testing does not mean that Satan gains total and/or abiding control over them. The passage from canonical Job already indicates that the authority that God delegates to Satan is limited: "Behold, I give him over to you; *only preserve his life [psychē]*" (Job 2:6 [LXX]). The author of *Testament of Job* assumes that Satan could do whatever he wanted to Job's body, but could gain authority over Job's *psychē* (soul? life?) only if Job relinquished it by "showing contempt for" (i.e., cursing) God (*T. Job* 20:1-3). This author presupposes a dualism of a body/soul (or body/"heart"): though Job's flesh is afflicted, his "heart" resides in the heavenly realm (36:4-5). Similarly, according to the *Martyrdom of Isaiah,* when Isaiah is being murdered by a satanically inspired false prophet, Isaiah proclaims, "If it is within my power to say, 'Condemned and cursed be you, and all your hosts, and all your house!' For there is nothing further you can take except the skin of my body" (*Mart. Isa.* 5:9-10). The author adds that as Isaiah was sawed in half, "he

34. The text of the quoted passage may be found in *The Apostolic Fathers,* LCL 2.68; the translation is my own.

35. Thus God is implicated in Jesus' trial, even if others ("sinners," Satan) carry it out. Cf. Senior, 17-18; and W. H. Kelber, *Mark's Story of Jesus* (Philadelphia: Fortress Press, 1979), 81. See also the discussion of "God and Satan as Partners in Testing," in Chap. 1 above.

did not cry out, or weep, but his mouth spoke with the Holy Spirit until he was sawed in two" (5:14). The assumption here is that so long as the righteous sufferer "speaks with the Holy Spirit" (that is, blesses and does not curse God), the satanic forces can do no worse than inflict physical death.[36] Mark does *not* portray Jesus as suffering in body only, while his spirit or soul remains firmly and obviously in God's grasp. Rather, during Jesus' hour of testing, the sinners and associated satanic powers appear to exercise complete authority over Jesus. The powers will be able to harm Jesus' weak flesh, and even to kill him. Jesus' cry from the cross will show the extremity of their power and the depth of Jesus' estrangement from God. In "giving Jesus over" to satanic powers, Mark seems to imply, God permits these powers to have their way with Jesus.

Does Mark imply that God is genuinely absent from Jesus during his passion? This is how Bonhoeffer reads Jesus' story: on the cross, as in Jesus' first temptation, he "is robbed of all his own strength, he is left alone by God and man, in anguish he must suffer Satan's robbery, he has fallen into the deepest darkness."[37] Second Chronicles already offers evidence for a view that God may withdraw from a person so as to test the content of the heart (2 Chron. 32:31),[38] and such a view is reflected also in the *Testament of Joseph:*

> For the Lord does not abandon those who fear him, neither in darkness, or chains, or tribulation or direst need. . . . In all these matters he takes

---

36. The translation of *Martyrdom of Isaiah* is by M. A. Knibb, in *OTP* 2.164. Cf. Garrett, "God of This World," 116-17. Luke may be thinking in such terms when he has Jesus tell Peter that Satan will sift the disciples but that Jesus has prayed for Peter "that your own faith may not fail" (Luke 22:32). This provision by Jesus (unique to Luke) ensures that later, Peter can be restored as leader of the flock. Even though Peter denies that he knows Jesus, in Luke's account (different from that in Mark's Gospel) Peter never *curses* Jesus (see Luke 22:60; cf. Mark 14:7: Luke eliminates the verb *anathematizein,* which the RSV apologetically translates as "invoke a curse on himself," but which is in the active voice and so could more plausibly be taken as a reference to Peter's cursing *of Jesus* [see n. 96 below]). Hence Peter can be restored, whereas Judas (who was possessed by Satan [Luke 22:3]) cannot. On the taboo against cursing Jesus, see also 1 Corinthians 12:3.

37. D. Bonhoeffer, *Creation and Fall, and Temptation: Two Biblical Studies* (New York: Macmillan, 1959), 106.

38. Cited in R. E. Brown, 1050 n. 53; cf. Barbour, 245; J. H. Korn, ΠΕΙΡΑΣΜΟΣ, *Die Versuchung des Gläubigen in der gr. Bibel* (Stuttgart: W. Kohlhammer Verlag, 1937), 83-84. The passage from 2 Chronicles figures importantly in Bonhoeffer's analysis of the temptations of Jesus (Bonhoeffer).

his stand, and in various ways he offers assistance, *even though for a brief time he may stand aside in order to test the disposition of the soul.* (*T. Jos.* 2:4-7)[39]

So also in Mark, God "stands aside" to test Jesus.[40] As he hangs on the cross, Jesus — who has enjoyed perfect "vision" — can no longer see God. Jesus has entered into the ultimate test of faithfulness and obedience. The earth and its inhabitants, including even Jesus, find themselves in darkness. In his cry of dereliction Jesus voices his anguish at this estrangement, as I shall argue below. But (Mark and early readers may have assumed) Jesus' alienation from God would become *permanent* only if he failed to continue acting as the faithful and obedient Son.

A Sacrifice for Sin?

I am now in a position again to consider the scholarly debate as to whether "cup" should be understood as referring to a "cup of wrath" or "cup of suffering." But first, it may be helpful to review what is at stake in the two theories. The wrath theory is consistent with a view of Jesus' death as a vicarious expiatory sacrifice that atoned for sin by appeasing the wrath of God. In other words, according to this theory Jesus "became sin" — that is, took the sin of the people upon himself, and then bore the wrath of God for it, thereby appeasing God.[41] Other textual clues sometimes invoked to support such a model of atonement for Mark include especially Jesus' references to his death as a ransom for many (*lytron:* Mark 10:45) and to his blood as establishing a new covenant (14:24).[42] On the other

---

39. Trans. H. C. Kee, in *OTP* 1.819.

40. Alternately, we might think in terms of satanic deception of Jesus — symbolized, perhaps, by the shroud of darkness (15:33) — which makes God *seem* to be absent. Whether we think in terms of God's absence or in terms of a satanic obscuring of God's presence, the consequence for Jesus is the same: God is no longer present to him.

41. Scholars who defend the wrath-interpretation of the cup are listed in R. E. Brown, 169 n. 6; see also E. Best, *The Temptation and the Passion: The Markan Soteriology,* 2nd ed. (Cambridge: Cambridge University Press, 1990), lxv-lxviii, and the works cited in Best, lxv n. 1 (cf. also 152-59).

42. See, for example, the discussions in Best, *Temptation and Passion,* 153, 156-57; and M. Hengel, *The Atonement: The Origins of the Doctrine in the New Testament,* trans. John Bowden (Philadelphia: Fortress Press, 1981), 47-55.

hand, the theory that the "cup" was a "cup of suffering" correlates with a supposed Markan portrayal of Jesus as *approved* by God, and of Jesus' *enemies* as the sole targets of God's wrath. Arguing for the latter ("cup of suffering") theory, Raymond Brown suggests that at the moment of Jesus' death, God rends the temple veil "not only to vindicate Jesus, whom God has *not* forsaken, but also to express anger at the chief priests and Sanhedrin who decreed such a death for God's Son."[43]

Brown's insistence that Mark presents Jesus as the righteous sufferer, who is *approved* by God, rather than as the object of God's wrath, seems sensible enough. And yet, Brown's effort to rule the connotations of wrath (as well as the connotations of God-forsakenness) out of Mark's account seem forced. For early readers of Mark's Gospel, the "cup" that Jesus mentions in 14:36 would have evoked a whole range of recollections from Scripture. Surely Jesus' saying about the cup would have jarred at least *some* early readers to think of the wrath of God, and to ponder whether and how God's wrath might have been related to Jesus' death. Indeed, in writing the word "cup," could Mark himself have completely excluded such notions? I do not think so. As I shall seek to demonstrate below, there are important points of correspondence between the wrath theory and my reading of Mark's story of Jesus as an account of one tested by Satan/by God.

I shall begin my consideration of this question by looking at the picture in Hebrews of Jesus as faithful when tested. The Epistle to the Hebrews assumes that Jesus' *endurance of testing* was the cause or proof of his perfection, and hence of his suitability as an atoning sacrifice. I shall then consider passages from three other Jewish texts from this era (Wisdom of Solomon, 4 Maccabees, and Pseudo-Philo) that likewise presume a connection between the testing of righteous persons by affliction and God's acceptance of their deaths as sacrificial. I shall contend that these four documents help to clarify the structure of Mark's argument: *in Mark, as in these other texts, the righteous one's endurance of testing exhibits his perfect obedience and faith, and results in God's acceptance of his death as a sacrifice.* In this reading of Mark, God does not vent divine wrath at Jesus. So one can legitimately say, as Brown does, that the "cup" is not

---

43. R. E. Brown, 1100 (italics original); for discussion of "the cup," see R. E. Brown, 168-72. Brown rejects a wrath/atonement theory for Mark (in addition to the passages just cited, see R. E. Brown, 1045 n. 38, 1049, 1100).

a "cup of wrath." But in another way the "cup" is *also* a cup of wrath, for by drinking the cup — that is, by enduring the tests of affliction — Jesus *averts God's wrath* against those who are deserving of it. That is to say, having seen Jesus' perfect endurance, God chooses to *regard* or *interpret* Jesus' faithfulness unto death as sufficient to atone for the sin of many.

Jesus in the Epistle to the Hebrews — "Tested as We Are"

There are various parallels between Hebrews and Mark that are pertinent to the theme of testing: both authors describe how previous generations put the Lord to the test; both associate Jesus with biblical traditions about a new Exodus, in which persons will not put the Lord to the test; both depict Jesus as opening a straight and narrow "way" in which others must follow.[44] But the most significant parallel for this study is the common portrayal in Hebrews and Mark of *Jesus as tested through what he suffered.* The epistle to the Hebrews includes several references to the testing of Jesus, and suggests that it was Jesus' endurance of suffering that made him "perfect":

> It was fitting that God, for whom and through whom all things exist, in bringing many children to glory, *should make the pioneer of their salvation perfect through sufferings.* . . . Since, therefore, the children share flesh and blood, he himself likewise shared the same things, so that *through death he might destroy the one who has the power of death, that is, the devil, and free those who all their lives were held in slavery by*

44. My wording in the description of the first parallel is deliberately ambiguous: in Hebrews, the "previous generation" was made up of the Hebrews of the wilderness era, who put *the Lord God* to the test; in Mark, the "previous generation" was (from the perspective of Mark's readers) made up of the enemies and the disciples of Jesus, who put *the Lord Jesus* to the test. Mark may be implicitly comparing the ones who tested Jesus to the wilderness generation. Regarding the use of *hodos* ("way") in Mark and in Hebrews (see Heb. 3:10; 9:8; 10:20): both authors present Jesus as opening a "way" into a new "temple," but they have developed this common element in rather different ways. Mark does not include a parallel to Hebrews' view of Jesus as opening a "way" into the heavenly sanctuary "through the curtain (that is, through his flesh)" (Heb. 10:20; for a similar argument about the difference between Mark and Hebrews, cf. R. E. Brown, 1109). Rather, as I shall argue below, Mark implies that Jesus' "way" leads to new life in the sanctified community, which replaces the earthly temple.

the fear of death. For it is clear that he did not come to help angels, but the descendants of Abraham. Therefore he had to become like his brothers and sisters in every respect, so that he might be a merciful and faithful high priest in the service of God, *to make a sacrifice of atonement for the sins of the people.* Because he himself was *tested by what he suffered,* he is able to help those who are being tested. (Heb. 2:10, 14-18 [italics added]; cf. 5:8-10)

The passage makes two points that are relevant to the interpretation of Mark. First is the notion that Jesus' suffering *made him perfect.* The author of Hebrews seems here to be presuming a traditional notion of testing as divine *paideia,* or chastisement performed out of parental love: affliction was God's way to discipline Jesus as a parent lovingly disciplines a child (compare Heb. 12:1-13, esp. vv. 3, 7-11).[45] Later in the epistle, Jesus' "perfection" is said to be the reason why his self-offering was able to atone for sin once and for all (7:27-28; 9:13-14, 24-26). A second point that is relevant for this study is the assumption of the author of Hebrews that Jesus' works of salvation encompassed both his making a sacrifice of atonement for the sins of the people and also his freeing of persons from

45. On the notion of divine *paideia* (chastisement or discipline), see above, pp. 24-28. R. E. Brown, 232 (cf. 1109) equates Jesus' "perfection" in Hebrews with his entry into the heavenly sanctuary, and compares this to the Synoptics' vindication of Jesus after his death by the tearing of the sanctuary veil of the Temple (Mark/Matthew) and the centurion's confession (all three synoptic Gospels). But the reference in Heb. 5:8 to Jesus' "learning of obedience" and the seeming equation of this with his "having been made perfect" in 5:9 suggest that the author of Hebrews interprets Jesus' suffering in traditional terms of *paideia,* that is, chastisement or discipline that *educates morally.* So also in Mark, I have argued, Jesus makes a kind of moral progress as he moves from doublemindedness to a singleminded commitment to doing God's will. The excursus in H. W. Attridge, *The Epistle to the Hebrews* (Philadelphia: Fortress Press, 1989), 83-87, on Jewish and Greco-Roman usages of "the language of 'perfection'" is very informative, though I disagree with Attridge's conclusion that Hebrews' language about the "perfecting" of Jesus cannot refer to a moral perfecting, inasmuch as (Attridge argues) the author of the epistle elsewhere presumes Christ to have been sinless. On the contrary: the "loud cries and tears" of Jesus as he faced death (Heb. 5:7) show that Jesus' own desire for life was at variance with God's plan and that Jesus *needed* to learn what it meant to be obedient, i.e., to choose the will of God instead of his own will (Heb. 10:5-10 notwithstanding). But, just as I argued for Mark's Gethsemane account (above, pp. 96-99), a conflicted mental state (one in which there is division between God's will and one's own desires) is equivalent neither to temptation nor to sin. In other words, in Hebrews Jesus is *sinless* prior to his suffering, but not yet *perfect.*

bondage to the devil (Heb. 2:14-15). Somehow the author regards these works of Jesus as parallel, or even identical.[46]

In 4:14-16 the author of Hebrews again refers to Jesus as tested: "For we do not have a high priest who is unable to sympathize with our weaknesses, but we have one who in every respect has been tested as we are, yet without sin" (v. 15). A few verses later the author returns to this theme. As many have observed, the passage offers a striking parallel to Mark's account of Jesus' struggle in Gethsemane:

> In the days of his flesh, Jesus offered up prayers and supplications, with loud cries and tears, to the one who was able to save him from [or "out of"] death, and he was heard because of his reverent submission. *Although he was a Son, he learned obedience through what he suffered; and having been made perfect, he became the source of eternal salvation for all who obey him,* having been designated by God a high priest according to the order of Melchizedek. (Heb. 5:7-10 [italics added])[47]

There are several points of similarity between this passage and Mark's Gethsemane account.[48] First, both Mark and the author of Hebrews portray Jesus as engaged in genuine struggle to come to grips with the suffering that

46. As Attridge, 92-93, recognizes, Heb. 2:14-15 employs a set of mythic images that has its background in Jewish apocalyptic tradition; this complex of images is distinct from the high-priestly imagery used by the author of Hebrews only a few verses later (in 2:17). For theoretical reflection on how authors can conjoin seemingly incommensurate mythic complexes, see Garrett, "Paul's Thorn," 84-85, and *passim*.

47. As R. E. Brown, 227, argues, linguistic variances between this passage and the Markan account of Jesus in Gethsemane cast doubt on any proposal that either author used the other's work as a written source. There may, however, be a more indirect link between the two passages. After studying Hebrews 5:7-10 at length, Brown suggests that the passage may offer an *independent* witness to Jesus' prayer in Gethsemane, and probably to his cry from the cross (Mark 15:34 [cf. v. 37]). In Brown's opinion, Hebrews, Mark, and also the Gospel of John are "three independent witnesses to a tradition that in the last period of his life Jesus struggled with and prayed to God about his impending death" (224; see also 225, 227, 233-34). On pp. 224-27, Brown offers his analysis of the elements common to John's Gospel and the Markan Gethsemane account (see, e.g., John 12:23, 27, 28, 29; 18:11). On pp. 228-29, Brown explicates his view that the author of Hebrews may have been heavily influenced by certain psalms (of the righteous sufferer), including especially Psalm 116, in the composition of 5:7-10.

48. R. E. Brown, 231-33, gives a fuller and somewhat different analysis of both similarities and differences between the Gospel accounts of Jesus' final prayer(s) and Hebrews 5:7-10.

lay ahead. Hebrews makes this point by referring to "the days of Jesus' flesh," thereby reminding the reader that Jesus was subject to the same tests/temptations as other fleshly creatures (see also Heb. 2:14-18). Jesus' struggles were acute enough to provoke "loud cries and tears" (5:7). Mark makes the same point by portraying Jesus as "distressed," "agitated," and "deeply grieved" (Mark 14:33-34) and by having Jesus refer to the weakness of the flesh (v. 38).[49] Second, both authors indicate that Jesus was finally obedient to God. Hebrews makes this point by mentioning both Jesus' "learning of obedience" and his "reverent submission" (Heb. 5:7, 8; cf. 10:9). Mark makes the point by depicting Jesus as praying to avoid testing, but then subordinating his own will to the will of God (Mark 14:36).[50] Third, both authors suggest that Jesus' struggle effected a significant change in him. The author of Hebrews writes that Jesus "learned obedience by what he suffered" (*emathen aph' hōn epathen tēn hypakoēn* [Heb. 5:8; cf. 2:9, 10]) and was "made perfect" (*teleiotheis* [Heb. 5:9; cf. 2:10]). Elsewhere this author gives further clues about Jesus' new and perfected condition: it is one in which he fully comprehends what it means to be tested (cf. 2:17; 4:15), and in which he stands as the paradigm of faithful obedience (12:3).[51] As I argued above (pp. 96-99), in Mark's Gethsemane account Jesus moves from division between his own desire for life and a desire to obey God to an unqualified choice to do God's will.

In Hebrews, it is Jesus' faithful endurance when tested that has made him able to save others.[52] "Although he was a Son, he learned obedience through what he suffered; and having been made perfect, he became the source of eternal salvation for all who obey him" (5:8-9). Jesus' obedient death was the perfect atoning sacrifice (7:27-28; 9:12-14, 26, 28; 10:12-14). I suggest that Jesus' endurance when tested plays a similar role in

49. Regarding Mark 14:38 ("the spirit indeed is willing, but the flesh is weak"), R. E. Brown, 200, writes, "We are very close here to the atmosphere of Heb 5:7, where 'in the days of his flesh' Jesus prays with a strong cry and tears to be saved from death — a situation that Heb 4:15 identifies as sharing our weaknesses *(astheneia)* and being put on trial *(peirazein)*."

50. Jesus' "perfection" (mentioned in Hebrews and assumed in later Christian theology) was not a presupposition to the testing, but rather, an attribute that could only come about *through* Jesus' endurance of genuine trials. Presumably Jesus could have failed his tests; otherwise, they would not have been real tests.

51. On the meaning of Jesus' "being perfected" in Hebrews, see nn. 45, 50 above.

52. On the importance of the motif of endurance in Hebrews, and on how this motif links Hebrews to 4 Maccabees, see S. K. Williams, *Jesus' Death as Saving Event: The Background and Origin of a Concept* (Missoula, Mont.: Scholars Press, 1975), 239-41 (cf. 167).

Mark's depiction of Jesus as savior. The two most direct soteriological statements in Mark (10:45, concerning the "ransom for many"; and 14:24, concerning Jesus' blood as the "blood of the new covenant") are parallel to views expressed in Hebrews, and may well be the traces of a shared tradition (see, e.g., Heb. 8:1-13). As in Hebrews, so in Mark, Jesus' blood establishes a new covenant and ransoms persons for God *because Jesus had first endured his tests of utmost affliction.*

Testing and Sacrificial Death in Other Ancient Jewish Texts

Wisdom of Solomon, Pseudo-Philo, and especially 4 Maccabees all depict righteous persons who were tested, who died unjustly, and whose deaths were regarded by God as sacrificial. The first passage I shall discuss is Wisdom of Solomon 3. This passage describes how certain foolish persons suppose that the death of certain righteous persons was a disaster, a form of punishment, whereas in truth the "hope [of the righteous] is full of immortality" (Wis. 3:1-4). The passage continues:

> Having been disciplined a little *[oliga paideuthentes],* they will receive great good, because God tested *[peirasai]* them and found them worthy of himself; like gold in the furnace he tried *[dokimasai]* them, and like a sacrificial burnt offering *[hōs holokarpōma thysias]*[53] he accepted them. (Wis. 3:5-6)

Here the images of "discipline" *(paideia)* and of the "refiner's fire" serve to underscore the perfection of the ones tested. Because of their obedient endurance of testing, God chooses to look upon their deaths as "like" or "equivalent to" a "sacrificial burnt offering" *(hos holokarpoma thysias).* (The passage does not, however, indicate in any way that the death of the righteous ones is beneficial or effective for others.)[54]

---

53. The word *holokarpōma* ("whole burnt offering") occurs in the LXX at Leviticus 5:10 (with reference to sin offerings); 16:24 (with reference to the offering on the Day of Atonement); Numbers 15:3; Judith 16:16; and Wisdom of Solomon 3:6 (with variation to *holokautōma,* the more common term for "whole burnt offering" in the LXX [occurring more than 175 times] at some of these passages in some manuscripts). The etymologically related form *holokarpōsis* occurs twelve times in the LXX.

54. On the language of sacrifice in Wisdom, see Williams, 181. For a discussion of other texts showing that in Diaspora Judaism, devotion to God could be described in cultic terms, see Williams, 180-82.

Pseudo-Philo's *Biblical Antiquities* (40:1-9) also depicts a sacrificial death by a blameless but willing victim.[55] This passage retells the biblical story of the sacrifice of Jephthah's daughter (see Judg. 11:29-40). The story is narrated in such a way as to emphasize the daughter's willingness to fulfill her father's vow by being offered as a "holocaust" (a whole burnt offering) to the Lord. The virgin daughter, here named Seila, compares herself to Isaac:

> And who is there who would be sad in death, seeing the people freed? Or do you not remember what happened in the days of our fathers when the father placed the son as a holocaust, and he did not refuse him but gladly gave consent to him, and the one being offered was ready and the one who was offering was rejoicing? And now do not annul everything you have vowed, but carry it out. (*Bib. Ant.* 40:2)[56]

Cheryl Anne Brown remarks, "Just as Isaac's readiness to be offered gave his offering meaning and value, so her [Seila's] readiness is crucial to the value of her own offering."[57] Because of Seila's great wisdom, demonstrated through her readiness, God declares, "Her death will be precious before me always" (40:4). Before the sacrifice is carried out, Seila spends time pouring out her tears and mourning her youth. She addresses the mountains, hills, and rocks:

> *Behold how I am put to the test!* But not in vain will my life be taken away. May my words go forth in the heavens, and my tears be written in the firmament! That a father did not subdue by force his daughter whom he had devoted to sacrifice, *so that her ruler approve of the only-begotten, promised as a sacrifice.* (*Bib. Ant.* 40:5-6 [italics added])[58]

---

55. Pseudo-Philo's *Biblical Antiquities (Liber Antiquitatum Biblicarum)* is probably to be dated around 100 C.E. (see the secondary studies cited in *OTP* 1.170-171; to these should be added C. A. Brown, *No Longer Be Silent: First Century Jewish Portraits of Biblical Women* [Louisville: Westminster/John Knox Press, 1992], 20-22); it is likely that the author lived in Palestine and wrote in Hebrew.

56. The translation is that of D. J. Harrington in *OTP* 2.353.

57. C. A. Brown, 103. Brown's treatment of Pseudo-Philo on Jepthah's daughter (in C. A. Brown, 95-117) is highly illuminating. She sees Pseudo-Philo's portrayal of Seila's sacrifice as paralleling in important respects the doctrine of the Akedah (on the Akedah see n. 61 in this chapter; the parallels posited by Brown are discussed in C. A. Brown, 94-95, 98, 101, 103, 127, 129).

58. Translation from *OTP* 2.354, with modifications by C. A. Brown, in part to take account of manuscript variants that she argues are to be preferred (see C. A. Brown, 134 n. 51).

The sacrifice is carried out, and an annual four-day feast is established on which the children of Israel should come together and weep for Jephthah's daughter (40:8). Pseudo-Philo does not indicate that Seila's sacrifice atones for the sin of the people (rather, God shows mercy because of Israel's prayer: see 39:11). Still, the account's emphasis on the death as a sacrifice, on the testing of Seila, and on God's approval of her obedience are significant parallels to the other passages discussed here and also to Mark's Gospel.

In 4 Maccabees (discussed also in Chapter 1 above) we find the themes of testing through affliction, perfect endurance, God's acceptance of un-merited deaths as a sacrifice, and (differently than in Wisdom and *Biblical Antiquities*) the vicarious benefit of those sacrifices. In this document, an elder Jewish man and seven Jewish brothers and their mother are martyred by the tyrant Antiochus IV Epiphanes. The victims' astonishing endurance is stressed. "All people, even their torturers, marveled at their courage and endurance, and they became the cause of the downfall of tyranny over their nation. By their endurance they conquered the tyrant, and thus their native land was purified through them" (1:11). By their endurance of Antiochus's tortures, the martyrs thwarted his intentions against Israel (1:11; 9:30; 11:24-25). Moreover, by their endurance they obtained God's favor. At the start of their tortures the seven sons say to Antiochus,

> Therefore, tyrant, put us to the test *[peiraze garoun tyranne]* and if you take our lives because of our religion, do not suppose that you can injure us by torturing us. For we, through this severe suffering and endurance, shall have the prize of virtue and shall be with God, on whose account we suffer; but you, because of your bloodthirstiness toward us, will deservedly undergo from the divine justice eternal torment by fire. (4 Macc. 9:7-9)

After the deaths, the author declares that "the tyrant was punished, and the homeland purified — they having become, as it were, a ransom *[an-tipsychon]* for the sin of our nation. And through the blood of those devout ones and their death as an atoning sacrifice *[tou hilastēriou thanatou autōn]*, divine Providence preserved Israel that previously had been mistreated" (17:21-22).[59] Here God's wrath is not directed at the martyrs, and yet out

---

59. On the cultic terminology in this and other passages in 4 Maccabees, see Chap. 1, n. 23. Regarding 17:21-22, S. K. Stowers (*A Rereading of Romans: Justice, Jews, and Gentiles* [New Haven: Yale University Press, 1994], 933) writes, "The combination of language and concepts here are most closely paralleled in early Christian texts about the effects of

of graciousness God accepts or "interprets" the deaths of these proven righteous ones as atonement for the sins of those who genuinely *are* guilty and hence deserving of God's wrath.

The three texts discussed above are important, first, because all three use the motif of *testing* to accentuate the perfect endurance of their protagonists and their willingness to die, and second, because all presume that this perfect endurance and willingness made the deaths worthy to be regarded as *sacrifices to God*. In all three documents, it is clear that God is not angry with the sacrificial victims, but rather with those around them; indeed it is precisely because God *approves* of the victims' faithfulness that God accepts the deaths as sacrifices. Fourth Maccabees specifically refers to the "blood" of the executed as efficacious in "ransoming" and "preserving" Israel from the tyrant and in atoning for the sin of the people.[60] The

---

Jesus' death, especially Rom. 3:21-26." Cf. N. A. Dahl, "The Atonement — An Adequate Reward for the Akedah? (Ro 8:32)," in *Neotestamentica et Semitica: Studies in Honor of Matthew Black,* ed. E. E. Ellis and M. Wilcox (Edinburgh: T. and T. Clark, 1969), 24, who makes the further argument that in 4 Maccabees 17:21-22, "The vicarious death of the Maccabean martyrs is seen as an imitation of Isaac" (see specifically 4 Macc. 7:14; 13:12; 16:20; 18:11). On how 4 Maccabees goes beyond 2 Maccabees in expressing the notion of the vicarious expiation effected by the martyrs' deaths, see Williams, 196 (discussed above, pp. 31-32); also H.-J. Klauck, *Unterweisung in lehrhafter Form: 4. Makkabäerbuch,* (Gütersloh: Gütersloher Verlagshaus Gerd Mohn, 1989), 670-72, who notes that 4 Maccabees identifies Eleazar as a priest (5:4; 7:11f.) and emphasizes the blamelessness of all the victims (which, Klauck remarks, reminds one of the OT instructions that sacrificial animals be without blemish).

60. The origins of the notion of vicarious expiatory sacrifice have been much debated by scholars. A traditional view is that Isaiah 53 attests to this doctrine and was so interpreted by Mark and other first-century readers. Williams argues that there is little or no evidence for such interpretation of Isaiah 53 in first-century Judaism; he argues that 4 Maccabees is the earliest unequivocal reference to the doctrine and may have been the inspiration for early Christians' conviction that Jesus' death vicariously atoned for sin (see Williams, 107-35 and *passim*). Williams thinks that the author of 4 Maccabees drew upon "the concept of effective death that is most clearly expressed in the Greek funeral orations and in the dramas of the tragic poets, especially Euripides" (196). Whatever the origin of the doctrine, I myself think it likely that Isaiah 53 was one among several influences on Mark's depiction of Jesus' death at the hands of the unrighteous. Even if Isaiah 53 was not intended by its author to express a doctrine of vicarious atoning sacrifice, it seems likely to me that it would have been read that way by persons already inclined to interpret Jesus' death as having an expiatory effect. The motif of *testing* is not made as explicit in Isaiah 53 as it is in the other texts I have discussed here (including Wisdom of Solomon 2, which was probably influenced by Isaiah 53; see Chap. 2 n. 37). For other comments on Isaiah 53, see n. 91 below.

examples suggest how the motif of Jesus' testing fits into Mark's view of Jesus' death as a saving death. As one who was tested even unto death and yet persevered, Jesus proved that he was worthy of acceptance as a sacrifice to God. Though not wrathful at Jesus, God accepted his self-offering as atoning vicariously for the sins of many.[61]

"Testing" versus "the Wrath of God"

Even though in my reading of Mark's passion account Jesus is not the *object* of God's wrath, the test that Jesus undergoes when he is "given over to sinners" is experientially *like* the wrath of God: in expressing wrathful judgment (as also in the testing of Jesus), God "hides God's face," granting authority over the persons in question to afflicting agents. To be the object of God's wrath is to be away from the light of God's presence, in the outer darkness, where there is weeping and gnashing of teeth. It is to be in the realm where Satan and his angels attack one without mercy (cf. Matt. 25:41). Jesus finds himself in just such a place as he hangs on the cross. Still, readers of Mark might have supposed that there was a difference between the *meaning* of Jesus' experience, on the one hand, and that of

---

61. The motifs I have discussed in connection with Mark's portrayal of Jesus' passion — especially his willing choice to obey God's will as proof of his worthiness as a sacrifice and as conditioning God's acceptance of that sacrifice — are paralleled in the "Akedah," the teachings about the "binding" of Isaac. Genesis 22:9 indicates that Abraham bound Isaac; but according to later development of the doctrine, Isaac went to the altar willingly and (in some versions of the doctrine) was actually offered as a sacrifice. The sacrifice (or the willingness to be sacrificed) was held to have been accepted by God as atoning for the people's sin. (Several elements in this doctrine are illustrated in *Biblical Antiquities* 40:2, quoted above; see also 18:5; 32:1-4; 4 Macc. 7:14; 13:12; 16:20; 18:11; Jth. 8:26 [which makes reference to the "testing" of Isaac]). There has been considerable scholarly debate about the dating of this doctrine and about possible Christian influence upon it. Dahl makes a good case for influence of the Akedah on Romans 8:32. The scholarly literature on the doctrine as well as primary evidence for its date are thoroughly reviewed in J. Swetnam, *Jesus and Isaac: A Study of the Epistle to the Hebrews in the Light of the Aqedah* (Rome: Biblical Institute Press, 1981); see also the helpful schematization of themes pertaining to the Akedah and of their probable dates of origin in R. E. Brown, 1435-44. Given the disputes about the dating of the origin of various elements of the doctrine and also given the relative infrequency of explicit references in its various attestations to the *testing* of Isaac (see Jth. 8:26; this may, however, refer to other incidents than the "binding"), I have chosen not to defend exemplars of the Akedah doctrine as parallels to support my reading of Mark.

persons who deservedly bear God's wrathful judgment, on the other. The latter tried to save their lives and so destroyed them; they are without hope. "Because the hope of the ungodly is like thistledown carried by the wind, and like a light frost driven away by a storm; it is dispersed like smoke before the wind, and it passes like the remembrance of a guest who stays but a day" (Wis. 5:14). By contrast, Jesus has lost his life, his *psychē,* but by his endurance he will gain it back again. "But the righteous live forever, and their reward is with the Lord; the Most High takes care of them" (Wis. 5:15). Though in the Markan passion account God drew back from Jesus and permitted satanic forces to test him, those forces would not have final control over Jesus' *psyche,* provided that Jesus remained faithful.

Jesus' Arrest and Trials before Authorities (Mark 14:43–15:15)

The arrest of Jesus, when he is "given over into the hands of sinners," marks the onset of his hour of supreme testing. That hour continues in his trials before the Jewish and Roman authorities, through to the moment of his death on the cross. Throughout my treatment of the arrest, the trials before authorities, and the crucifixion itself, I shall focus exclusively on those narrative elements pertinent to Jesus' *peirasmos,* or testing. Specifically, in my discussion of the arrest, I shall highlight the role of Judas, the scripturally governed character of events, and the identity of Jesus' opponents. In my treatment of Jesus before the Sanhedrin, I shall focus on the perversity and blindness of Jesus' adversaries in the trials, Jesus' single-mindedness (especially as it contrasts with Peter's duplicity), and the bearing that Jesus' steadfastness has on the future of the temple cult. In my treatment of Jesus before Pilate and the Roman soldiers, I shall underscore the injustice of Pilate, the irony of the soldiers' mockery, and the perseverance of Jesus. Finally, in my discussion of the crucifixion, I shall interpret the offer to Jesus of perfumed wine, the mockery of bystanders, Jesus' cry of dereliction, and the signs that transpire at Jesus' death (the tearing of the temple curtain and the cry of the centurion).

The Arrest of Jesus (Mark 14:43-50)

Jesus concludes the interlude in Gethsemane by saying, "The hour has come; the Son of Man is *given over* into the hands of sinners. Get up, let us be going. See, *the one who gives me over* is at hand" (14:41-42).[62] Judas's act of delivering Jesus into the hands of sinners marks the onset of the supreme hour of trial; as I have suggested above, the use here of the two forms of *paradidonai* ("give over") will have prompted some ancient readers to interpret this dramatic moment as a transfer of Jesus from the authority of God to that of Satan (see above, pp. 100-102). In such a reading, the blameworthy aspect of Judas's crime was not only (or even chiefly) that he double-crossed Jesus ("betrayed" him, or turned against him), but that Judas acted to give Jesus over into the hands of *ho peirazōn,* "the tester." Though Mark does not expressly mention that Satan inspired Judas (cf. Luke 22:3; John 13:27), Judas's alliance with Satan seems to be presupposed by the woe that Jesus uttered in 14:21 ("It would have been better for that one not to have been born") — in other words, the "one who gives Jesus over" is a child of darkness, destined for perdition.[63] In Chapter 2, I argued that the disciples as portrayed by Mark were partially blinded by sin or by Satan during Jesus' earthly ministry and that Peter was an unwitting mouthpiece of Satan in the encounter at Caesarea Philippi. Judas's handing over of Jesus continues the Markan theme of satanic intervention in the inner circle, but raises the stakes: Judas's apostasy from Jesus exceeds the disciples' earlier failings (and even their subsequent ones: see 14:50; 15:66-72), for Judas has joined the opposition, becoming one who

---

62. Here I use the cumbersome translation "given over" and "the one who gives me over" (rather than the more traditional "betrayed" and "betrayer") because I wish to highlight the continuity between Judas's act of *giving Jesus over* and the following sequence of transfers of Jesus from one authority to another. After interrogating him, the Jewish officials will beat Jesus and *give him over* to Pilate (15:1; see also v. 10); Pilate will then *give Jesus over* to be crucified (15:15). Moreover, the English word "betray" connotes treachery and double-crossing in a way that the Greek term need not. While these connotations seem applicable with respect to Judas's act of "giving Jesus over," they do not seem applicable in the subsequent cases. (See also nn. 30, 32, 33 above.)

63. On punishments to be meted out to "children of darkness" as mentioned in Luke, Acts, and other texts of formative Judaism and Christianity, see S. R. Garrett, *The Demise of the Devil: Magic and the Demonic in Luke's Writings* (Minneapolis, Fortress Press, 1989), 83; see also above, Chap. 1 n. 48.

actively serves Satan's aims.[64] No matter that his role was divinely foreordained, or that God must have authorized the transfer of Jesus; Judas is still held culpable for his treacherous deed (14:21).

Jesus Is Tried by the Sanhedrin (Mark 14:53-72)[65]

The Perversity and Blindness of Jesus' Adversaries

Mark portrays the unnamed high priest, the chief priests, the elders, and the scribes (Mark 14:53) as ruthlessly unprincipled in their treatment of Jesus when he appears before their assembly. At the outset Mark informs the reader that these adversaries "were looking for testimony against Jesus *to put him to death [thanatōsai];* but they found none" (14:55). In other words, they had determined the result of the trial before they had even questioned Jesus.[66] The members of the council are portrayed as doing whatever needs to be done, including the gathering of false witnesses, in order to secure their evil aims. Mark reports that they could not find persons whose testimony agreed, yet they proceeded with the trial, thereby revealing once again their complete disregard for the canons of justice (14:56-59). But by far the most striking indication of their injustice is their mockery and maltreatment of Jesus once the verdict of "deserving death" has been passed. They spit on him, cover his face, and strike him, saying "Prophesy!" This image of the august members of the Sanhedrin descending to the behavior of thugs is nothing short of remarkable.[67] By

64. Mark highlights the active agency of Judas: he "went to the chief priests" with the express intention of giving Jesus over (14:10); he "looked for opportunity" to do the deed (14:11); he had arranged a signal (a kiss) by which he would identify Jesus and had instructed those who went to arrest Jesus on what to do next (14:44).

65. On whether this was a legal trial or an interrogation, see R. E. Brown, 423-26.

66. Cf. D. H. Juel, *Messiah and Temple: The Trial of Jesus in the Gospel of Mark* (Missoula, Mont.: Scholars Press, 1977), 63. R. E. Brown, 433, points out the polemical character of Mark's negative portrayal and comments that "ancient literary accounts of famous trials are most often narrated with a bias."

67. R. E. Brown, 573, writes, "Commentators, horrified that Mark's 'some' seems to refer to the Sanhedrists who have just condemned him, express doubt that distinguished Jewish figures would have acted so callously. That is to confuse historical issues with the intended thrust of a Gospel narrative that has had a hostile view of the chief priests, scribes, and elders from the start."

suborning false testimony and by mocking Jesus, Jesus' adversaries typecast themselves as the blind enemies of the suffering righteous one, who do not share in the higher knowledge of God's plan (see Pss. 22:7-8; 27:12; 35:11-12; and esp. Wis. 2:12-20).

Through the use of narrative irony, Mark underscores the blindness of the council members who try Jesus.[68] At least three of these adversaries' actions in 14:53-65 qualify as ironic. First, the adversaries condemn Jesus based partly on the "false charge" that he had said "I will destroy this sanctuary *[ho naos]*[69] that is made with hands *[cheiropoiētos]*, and in three days I will build another, not made with hands *[acheiropoiētos]*" (v. 58). Mark clearly does regard the charge as "false" — at least, it is false in the way that the accusers and judges construe it. But on a higher level the charge could be viewed as true: in the opinion of Mark's readers, Jesus *had* destroyed the Jerusalem sanctuary and built another — namely, the community of believers gathered in prayer.[70] Second, the high priest condemns Jesus for blasphemy. This condemnation is ironic because in truth Jesus is the one who does *not* blaspheme: despite the severity of his tests, Jesus never curses God.[71] Third, following their guilty verdict, the council members cover Jesus' face and strike him, saying "Prophesy!" The statement is ironic because Jesus *is indeed* a prophet, who has made many valid prophecies. At that very moment, his prophecy that Peter would deny him is being fulfilled (more on this below).[72] Through these uses of irony, Mark

68. D. H. Juel, *A Master of Surprise: Mark Interpreted* (Philadelphia: Fortress Press, 1994), 96-97, also sees Mark's passion account as deeply ironic and stresses that this irony is bound up with the royal imagery of the account.

69. *Naos* (used at Mark 14:58; 15:29; and 15:38) refers to the temple sanctuary proper, which houses the Holy of Holies, whereas *hieron* (used at 11:11, 15, 16, 27; 12:35; 13:1, 3; 14:49) refers to the whole temple complex. See the discussion in Juel, *Messiah and Temple*, 127-28.

70. On the temple charge, see below, pp. 119-24. I shall discuss Mark's treatment of the community of believers as the new temple below in Chap. 4.

71. Moreover, if there was a prohibition among the early Christians against cursing Jesus (as some evidence suggests: see 1 Cor. 12:3; cf. Acts 26:11; James 2:7), then the high priest's charge would seem doubly ironic: in mocking and maltreating Jesus, the council members themselves commit "blasphemy" (see also Mark 15:29).

72. Here the apparent notion is that the blindfolded Jesus should name his assailants; compare Luke 22:64. See the interesting discussion of a similar child's game that may have been known to Mark's readers, in R. E. Brown, 574-76. Brown underscores the irony in Mark's account of the mockery of Jesus: "Although blindfolded, he is the one who sees while his enemies are the ones blinded."

shows that the opponents of Jesus are blind to God's higher truth — a truth to which Mark's readers are privy. Mark's portrayal of Jesus' adversaries as blind lends an ironic cast also to Jesus' prophecy to the high priest: "*You will see* the Son of man seated at the right hand of Power, and coming with the clouds of heaven" (14:62). Here Mark trades on a motif common in apocalyptic and other early Jewish literature, that the suffering righteous will be vindicated before the eyes of their oppressors.[73]

The Sanctuary Charge

Persons are brought forward to bear witness against Jesus. But in the short space of two verses Mark twice informs us that they "bore false testimony" (*pseudomartyrein* [14:56, 57]), and adds that "their testimony did not agree" (v. 56). The substance of their charge was that Jesus had said, "I will destroy this sanctuary that is made with hands, and in three days I will build another, not made with hands" (v. 58). Scholars have found Mark's narration of this "false testimony" to be confusing, first, because the alleged statement by Jesus does resemble (though it is not identical to) a prediction that he had made in Mark 13:2 ("Do you see these great [temple] buildings? Not one stone will be left here upon another; all will be thrown down"); and second, because John's Gospel *does* ascribe to Jesus such a prediction about destroying the temple and building another in three days (2:19).[74] In what way, then, is the temple charge against Jesus "false?"

Raymond Brown has reviewed the evidence and concludes that the historical Jesus probably did make *some* sort of prediction about destroying and rebuilding the temple.[75] Moreover, Brown argues that *Mark* supposed Jesus to have made some such prediction.[76] After all, elsewhere in Mark's

---

73. See, e.g., Wis. 5:1-13; *1 Enoch* 27:3; 63:1-4 (cf. Isa. 49:7); 97:3-6; 108:15; *4 Ezra* 7:36; *2 Bar.* 30:4-5; 51:5.

74. Cf. Acts 6:14; 2 Cor. 5:1; Heb. 9:11.

75. See the discussion in R. E. Brown, 448-60. Brown imaginatively reconstructs the various ways such a statement would have been understood by different groups at different times and places (by followers/opponents of Jesus during his earthly ministry, by followers/opponents after his death but before the destruction of the temple by the Romans, and by followers/opponents after the destruction of the temple by the Romans). He demonstrates how multivalent such a statement could have been.

76. R. E. Brown, 446-47.

Gospel Jesus does display a condemning attitude toward the temple: in cursing the fig tree he symbolically cursed the temple; the death of the tree (like the subsequent tearing of the temple curtain) foreshadowed the demise of the temple (or perhaps of its cult). Further, Jesus had predicted that "not one stone" of the temple would be left on another (13:1-2). Finally, bystanders at the foot of the cross in Mark's account repeat the charge about destruction and rebuilding (15:29-30).[77] Brown argues that in Mark's account the charge is "false" not because it was totally foreign to the Jesus depicted by Mark, but because it was false *in a different way* than the witnesses were claiming. Jesus would "destroy" the temple not by some miraculous sign of the sort promised by apocalyptic false prophets (13:22), but by his death; he would replace it with a community of true believers willing to take up the cross and follow Jesus.[78] The falsity of the charge lies not in what is said, but in the malicious intent of those who utter it and the misconstrual of those who hear it and suppose that Jesus is just another charlatan and doomsayer.[79]

But Mark's readers would have known that the charge leveled against Jesus was true on a higher level. The fig tree/temple-cleansing incident indicates that Jesus *had* rendered the temple sanctuary and its cult obsolete. In cleansing the temple Jesus pronounced his judgment against it; later in the narrative, one infers that the temple will "wither and die" as did the

---

77. R. E. Brown, 446, writes, "How are readers to think that passersby knew about the sanctuary statement? Scarcely from the false witnesses! Would not the readers of Mark assume that the reason that even passersby knew about the sanctuary statement was that in fact Jesus had said something like that?"

78. R. E. Brown, 447, 453.

79. Alternately, Juel, *Messiah and Temple,* 117-25 and 143-57, suggests that the charge may be "false" insofar as, in Mark's view, Jesus has *not* made any assertion with the meaning assumed by the false witnesses (who view the charge as a threat against the temple and an impossible boast). But Juel (like Brown) does think that Mark probably intends for the charge to be understood as prophetic (and hence true) on a higher level: the "temple not made with hands" is actually the Christian community, which is "a temple of a different order" (157). See further Dowd, 54-55 n. 86, adjudicating among the interpretations of the temple charge in Juel, *Messiah and Temple;* E. S. Malbon, "TH OIKIA AYTOY: Mark 2.15 in Context," *New Testament Studies* 31 (1985): 282-92 (arguing that Mark rejects "temple" and affirms "house" — i.e., house churches; see esp. 288); J. R. Donahue, *Are You the Christ? The Trial Narrative in the Gospel of Mark* (Missoula, Mont.: Scholars Press, 1973); Donahue, *The Theology and Setting of Discipleship in the Gospel of Mark* (Milwaukee: Marquette University Press, 1983); and E. Best, *Following Jesus: Discipleship in the Gospel of Mark* (Sheffield: JSNT Press, 1990).

cursed fig tree. Following Jesus' death, the tearing of the temple curtain — "from top to bottom" (15:38) — indicates that the "death" of the temple took place at the moment of Jesus' own death. To be sure, the physical building of the temple remains standing, but the activities within the sanctuary are now declared to be null and void, for as Raymond Brown points out, "rending the veil would mean destroying the special character or holiness that made the place a sanctuary."[80] Brown wishes to restrict the implications of the veil rending: in his view, this symbolic occurrence means only that the temple cult has been destroyed, and does not imply that at his death Jesus entered into the inner shrine of the heavenly sanctuary to offer atonement (as in Hebrews).[81] But the symbol may have been a more complex one for Mark and his first readers than Brown allows. After all, if Mark suggests that the temple cult had ended, then readers would want to know *why*. What had happened in Jesus' death that would make the temple sacrifices unnecessary? Even if Mark had no notions whatsoever about a *heavenly* temple, he and other early readers may have supposed that the reason why the (earthly) temple was rendered obsolete was *because Jesus had made the perfect and once-for-all sacrifice, accepted by God as atonement for the sins for the people.*

80. R. E. Brown, 1101. F. J. Matera, *Passion Narratives and Gospel Theologies* (New York: Paulist Press, 1986), 69, argues that the parable of the vineyard in Mark 12:1-11 conveys a message of polemic against the temple that is closely related to that implied by the fig tree incident. With regard to the rending of the temple veil: there is considerable discussion in the scholarly literature about which veil (i.e., the inner veil or the outer one) is meant. Lane, 574-75, opts for the outer curtain and points out that "the early Church Fathers commonly interpreted the event as a warning sign of the impending destruction of the Temple, confirming the sober prophecy of Ch. 13:2" (citing Tertullian, *Against Marcion* IV.42; Chrysostom, *Homilies on Matthew* LXXXVIII. 2 [MPG LVIII, 826]). Other scholars who interpret the rending of the veil as a portent of the temple's destruction include R. E. Brown, 439, 451, 453; Juel, *Messiah and Temple*, 140-42; Kelber, 82; Matera, 68; Senior, 92. H. L. Chronis, "The Torn Veil: Cultus and Christology in Mark 15:37-39," *Journal of Biblical Literature* 101 (1982): 97-114, contends that the rending of the veil signals the end of the temple not because it is a portent, but because it symbolizes the moment of divine self-disclosure: the centurion looks into the face of Jesus and sees the face of God. Henceforward it is Jesus and not the inner sanctum of the temple that is the true locus of the divine presence. For an argument against any view that the rending of the temple veil portends the temple's destruction, see R. H. Gundry, *Mark: A Commentary on His Apology for the Cross* (Grand Rapids: William B. Eerdmans, 1993), 971-72.

81. R. E. Brown, 1108-9; on how Jesus "destroyed" the temple, cf. Juel, *Messiah and Temple*, 206.

Mark and his early readers would also have understood the second half of the false charge against Jesus (that he would "build another sanctuary, not made with hands" [Mark 14:58]) as true — though not in the physical way that Jesus' opponents would have supposed.[82] Rather, Mark hints that the new "sanctuary" is located *in the midst of the believing community.* It is a temple made of "living stones" — persons who confess Jesus as the son of God and who engage in singleminded prayer.[83] This notion that the church is the new temple of God, a temple "not made with hands," is paralleled elsewhere in the New Testament and other early Christian writings. As Brown points out, in this interpretation "Mark 15:39 [the centurion's confession of Jesus as the "son of God"] would be showing the first new believer after the death of Jesus and thus the commencement of the building of another sanctuary."[84]

Sharyn Dowd highlights an earlier narrative clue that Mark thinks in terms of a "sanctuary" made of persons and not stones: namely, Jesus' remarks after he cleanses the temple and then returns to find the fig tree withered away:

> In the morning as they passed by, they saw the fig tree withered away to its roots. Then Peter remembered and said to him, "Rabbi, look! The fig tree that you cursed has withered." Jesus answered them, "Have faith in God. Truly I tell you, if you say to this mountain, 'Be taken up and thrown into the sea,' and if you do not doubt in your heart, but believe that what you say will come to pass, it will be done for you. So I tell you, whatever you ask for in prayer, believe that you have received it, and it will be yours." (Mark 11:20-24)

The passage poses an exegetical problem, for if the withering of the fig tree prefigures the destruction of the temple, how can it also symbolize the power of confident prayer? Upon first reading, the introduction of the latter meaning seems to muddle Mark's careful use of the withered fig tree as a metaphor for the demise of the temple. Dowd suggests that the author of Mark must have seen "a connection between the rejection of the temple cult portrayed in 11:15-19 and the prayer life of the Christian community,

---

82. See the discussion of Mark's phrases "made with hands" and "not made with hands" in Juel, *Messiah and Temple,* 143-57; also R. E. Brown, 438-44 (Brown is critical of Juel: see 448).

83. Cf. R. E. Brown, 440-41, 453, 1109.

84. R. E. Brown, 1109, cf. 1145, 1152; cf. Kelber, 83; Best, *Temptation and Passion,* 99-100.

for which 11:22-25 provides instruction."[85] Thus Mark could use the single image of the withered fig tree to express two very different points.

Dowd goes on to argue that the instructions for prayer are placed after the withering of the fig tree in Mark so as to answer a question that would surely have arisen following the destruction of the temple: namely, *what is to guarantee the efficacy of prayer?* This question became very pressing among Jews after the temple was destroyed by the Romans in 70 C.E., as Dowd illustrates. In Dowd's view, Mark thought the temple had been rejected by God long before the Romans destroyed it; nonetheless, "because of its traditional role as the guarantor of the efficacy of prayer, the rejection of the temple required a reassertion of the importance of community prayer and the power available to it."[86] Mark uses the fig tree incident both to prophesy the destruction of the temple and to reaffirm the power available to those who utter prayers in the wake of that destruction.

In Hebrews, the "way" that Jesus opens up is the way into the heavenly temple, opened through the "curtain" of Jesus' flesh (Heb. 10:20). In Mark, I suggest, "the way of the Lord" leads directly into the new community, made up of those who engage in singleminded prayer. On this point Mark's perspective roughly parallels that in the Lukan writings, which depict Jesus as the leader of a second Exodus, who brings the people from bondage to freedom and enables them to worship God perfectly "in this place" (Acts 7:7) — that is, in the believing community.[87] The language that Mark ascribes to Jesus in the instructions about prayer quoted above ("Do not doubt in your heart" and "Believe that what you say will come to pass") is used in other Jewish and early Christian discussions of the virtue of *singlemindedness (haplotēs)*. The singleminded person is one who trusts fully in God, and who is wholly committed to the service of God, with no small portion of the soul holding back. By contrast, those who are not singleminded are duplicitous, hypocritical, "two-faced," or "divided in heart." Such persons inevitably put God to the test; moreover, when tested themselves, they are easily led astray.[88] In Mark, Jesus' enemies and even his disciples are portrayed as duplicitous, as I argued in Chapter 2. But

85. Dowd, 43.

86. Dowd, 53.

87. See S. R. Garrett, "Exodus from Bondage: Luke 9:31 and Acts 12:1-24," *Catholic Biblical Quarterly* 52 (1990): 656-80.

88. On *haplotes* (singlemindedness) and its relationship to being tested and testing others, see Garrett, " 'Lest the Light.' "

Jesus' teaching about prayer suggests that *in the new community it shall not be so*. In the new community of Jesus' followers, persons will be able to pray in singleminded fashion, neither putting God to the test nor succumbing to temptations themselves. The new generation — unlike the wilderness generation — will be faithful and singleminded as it follows Jesus on the straight and narrow path. They will not be ensnared by Satan, by trouble or persecution on account of the word, or by the cares of the world, the lure of wealth, and the desire for other things (see Mark 4:15-19). They will pray to God with an uncompromised commitment. They will endure in times of testing, as did Jesus himself.

Jesus as Singleminded/Peter as Duplicitous

Jesus had prophesied that one of his disciples would give him over, that all would desert him, and that Peter would deny him three times. In response they had proclaimed their fidelity to Jesus. Peter had said vehemently, "Even though I must die with you, I will not deny you" (14:26-31). By the time of the trials before the Jewish and Roman authorities, the first two of Jesus' prophecies have already been fulfilled: Judas handed him over and the other disciples fled from him on the occasion of his arrest (vv. 43-45, 50). Now, during Jesus' appearance before the Sanhedrin, the predicted denial of Jesus by Peter begins to play itself out.

Mark stresses the *simultaneous occurrence* of Jesus' appearance before the council and Peter's denials of his lord.[89] First, there is the quick alternation of scenes: immediately after Mark's description of Jesus' being led to the high priest (14:53), the evangelist inserts the notice about Peter's following Jesus (v. 54), and then reverts directly to the story of Jesus' trial (v. 55). Thus one's reading of the trial account is conditioned by an awareness that at that very moment Peter is close by — engaged in another sort of trial. Second, when in v. 66 Mark pans back to the scene with Peter, the absence of any temporal indicator, the use of the present participle *(ontos)*, and the use of the historical present *(erchetai)* all heighten the impression that Mark is describing action simultaneous with what has preceded. One could translate vv. 66-67, "And while Peter is standing below in the courtyard,

---

89. See R. E. Brown, 427-28 (cf. 622), for the argument that we are here dealing with two simultaneous events, rather than two unrelated events that Mark has intercalated (here reading against Donahue, *Are You the Christ?*). See also Lane, 541.

one of the maids of the high priest comes, and seeing Peter warming himself she looks at him and says, 'You also were with the Nazarene, Jesus.'" The point of this emphasis on simultaneity, I think, is to encourage the reader to contrast Jesus' perseverance with Peter's fickleness.[90]

When tested, Jesus models the virtue of singlemindedness. His silence when addressed by the high priest (vv. 60-61) suggests that he will not let himself be distracted by the base plotting of his adversaries.[91] Persevering under the weight of these false accusations, Jesus denies Satan any evidence with which to accuse him before the *divine* tribunal. When the high priest then shifts from the accusations to ask Jesus, "Are you the Messiah, the Son of the Blessed One?" (v. 61), Jesus does not shrink back. He answers boldly, "I am," and prophesies his own vindication at the right hand of God (14:62).[92] The movement from silence to speech is significant: the accusations deserved no response, but the question demands one. The demonic hosts of Satan have known Jesus' true identity since the outset of the story; now, Jesus confesses that identity before Satan's human servants (who remain blind nonetheless). Jesus will not compromise his integrity by retreating from conflict or by denying the truth.

Peter, by contrast, *exemplifies the weakness of will in time of trial that typifies the doubleminded or duplicitous person.* His intent is to stay true to Christ (14:31), but when tested he shows that his primary loyalty is to himself. Three times in Gethsemane he fell asleep. Now, he is questioned three times, and three times he denies Jesus. The word for "deny" is *arneisthai;* for the reader familiar with Matthew and Luke, it calls to mind Jesus' solemn warning:

90. Cf. Juel, *Messiah and Temple,* 67-72; Lane, 543; Senior, 86-88, 102.

91. Cf. R. E. Brown, 463: "The emphatic silence of the Marcan Jesus is a contemptuous rebuke for the low quality of the charade." On whether Jesus' silence when falsely accused before the Sanhedrin reflects the influence of the portrait(s) of the suffering servant of Isaiah 53:7, see R. E. Brown, 464-65; also M. D. Hooker, *Jesus and the Servant: The Influence of the Servant Concept of Deutero-Isaiah in the New Testament* (London: SPCK, 1959), 86-89 (both scholars see minimal influence from Isaiah 53 on this point). Marcus, *Way of the Lord,* 187, sees a similarity between Jesus' silence in Mark 14:61 and the servant's in Isaiah 53:7, but thinks Psalm 38:13-15 to have been the likelier influence on Mark's portrayal of Jesus' silence.

92. On what sense to make of the high priest's question and Jesus' response, both on the historical level and on the narrative level, see R. E. Brown, 467-68, 489. Brown, 489, defends the originality of the reading *egō eimi* (over against the reading *sy eipas hoti egō eimi,* attested in Codex Koridethi, family 13 of minuscules).

"Everyone therefore who acknowledges me before others, I also will acknowledge before my Father in heaven; but whoever *denies* me before others, I also will *deny* before my Father in heaven." (Matt. 10:32-33; par. Luke 12:8-9 [italics added])

The author of *Shepherd of Hermas* seems to echo this saying in instructions about remaining steadfast in persecution, and claims that those who deny *(arneisthai)* Christ are doubleminded:

You, therefore, "who work righteousness," must remain steadfast and *be not double-minded,* that your passing may be with the holy angels. Blessed are you, as many as endure the great persecution which is coming, and as many as shall not *deny* their life. For the Lord has sworn by his Son that those who have *denied* their Christ have been rejected from their life, that is, those who shall now deny him in the days to come. (*Herm. Vis.* 2.2.7-8 [italics added])[93]

Mark does not include the Q-logion about "denying" Christ (Matt. 10:32-33, quoted above) in his Gospel and may not have known of it; he does include a variant saying of Jesus, however:

"Those who are ashamed of me and of my words in this adulterous and sinful generation, of them the Son of Man will also be ashamed when he comes in the glory of his Father with the holy angels." (Mark 8:38)

Mark's readers knew at least his version of Jesus' warning; possibly some of them knew the Q-form as well.[94] Familiarity with the saying(s) would have alerted readers to just how high are the stakes in Peter's encounter with his accusers.

In narrating Peter's denials, Mark stresses the magnitude of Peter's failure, and so increases its poignancy.[95] To begin with, Peter's first denial

93. Trans. K. Lake in LCL, *The Apostolic Fathers,* 2.21.

94. See the discussion of the Markan version of the saying and its relationship to the Q-version in Best, *Following Jesus,* 42-43. Best suggests that *(ap)arneisthai* ("deny") and *epaischynesthai* ("be ashamed") may be translation variants.

95. R. E. Brown, 600, writes that "among the evangelists Mark may have the most careful psychological and theological progression in the phrasing of Peter's responses, moving from claimed lack of understanding and knowledge to denial, on to the cursing rejection of Jesus." Brown details how Mark's narration of Peter's movements in the denial scene serves to dramatize Peter's weakness (602).

includes a double negation (literally, "I do not know nor do I understand what you are talking about," 14:68). This double negation makes the denial seem especially forceful or vehement. Moreover, immediately after the first denial, Mark has Peter leave the courtyard and go out into the gateway or forecourt (*proaulion* [v. 68]), as if he is trying to run away from the dangerous queries. Finally, Mark reports that, when questioned for the third time, Peter "began to curse, and to swear, 'I do not know this man of whom you speak'" (Mark 14:71; compare Luke's mild "Man, I do not know what you are saying" [22:60]). The word that Mark here uses for "curse" *(anathematizein)* is in the active voice but has no stated direct object; it is possible that Mark or his early readers thought of Peter as actually *cursing Jesus*.[96] In any case, the three denials plainly reveal that Peter's commitment to Jesus competes with his commitment to save his own life. He wishes to live by heavenly and earthly measures of goodness at one and the same time; because of his doublemindedness, he fails utterly when put to the test.

Jesus Is Tried by the Romans (Mark 15:1-15)

At the conclusion of the Sanhedrin trial, the chief priests, elders, and scribes "bind" Jesus and "give him over" to Pilate (15:1). Jesus is remanded from one authority to another, but all alike are "sinners." Thus Mark indicates that throughout Jesus' hour of trial he moves and breathes under the control of powers opposed to God.

Mark narrates the appearance of Jesus before Pilate in a manner roughly parallel to the preceding account of his appearance before the Sanhedrin.[97] Here, too, a question about Jesus' identity (in response to which he speaks) is paired with accusations against him (in response to which he remains silent). Here, too, Mark brings another character (Barabbas) briefly to the fore, to serve as a foil for the evangelist's portrayal of Jesus. And, here too, Mark concludes the trial with a description of the mocking of Jesus by his adversaries. Some of the points about the identity and character of Jesus

96. R. E. Brown, 605, cites a number of scholars who hold (as does Brown himself) that *anathematizein* "should be taken transitively with 'Jesus' understood as the object: Peter cursed Jesus and took an oath that he had no personal acquaintance with him."

97. Cf. R. E. Brown, 551.

and his opponents that were stressed by Mark in Jesus' appearance before the council are emphasized also in this account of the trial by the Romans. First, Mark highlights *the perversity and blindness of the Romans.*[98] Mark implies that Pilate was not fully persuaded of Jesus' guilt: Pilate "realized that it was out of jealousy that the chief priests had handed him over" (15:10; cf. v. 14). And yet, Pilate bowed to the pressure of the crowd, releasing a known murderer instead of Jesus (vv. 7-8, 11, 15), and thereby revealing Pilate's own corruptness. There is less irony in the account of Pilate's interrogation of Jesus than in the preceding interrogation of him by the Sanhedrin, and so the theme of blindness is not quite so pronounced as in that earlier episode.[99] But the attached account of the mocking of Jesus by Pilate's soldiers is heavily ironic. This irony brings the motif of blindness — and, thus also, the motif of Jesus as suffering righteous one, tested by adversaries who are blind to God's wisdom — back to the fore-front. Before the whole cohort, the soldiers clothe Jesus in royal purple, crown him with thorns, and salute him as King of the Jews (vv. 16-20). Raymond Brown thinks it likely that Mark intends the scene as a burlesque of the "Ave Caesar" acclamation of the emperor. Be that as it may, I presume that Mark's readers instantly discerned the irony in this scene, for they knew Jesus to be *in truth* the messiah-king of Israel.[100]

As in the account of Jesus before the Sanhedrin, so also in the depiction of the trial before Pilate, Mark stresses *the perseverance of Jesus when tested.* Here, as before, Jesus does not shrink back when questioned about his identity. To be sure, his response to Pilate — "You have said so" — is less forthright than some modern readers would prefer, but the bottom line is that Jesus does not refuse to answer, or deny that he is "king of the Jews." Perhaps Mark intended a touch of irony here, too: Pilate himself has "confessed" Jesus to be king. Next the chief priests come forward and level their charges against Jesus (v. 3); one infers that these are the same false charges as in the Sanhedrin trial. As before, Jesus' silence when accused is

---

98. Contra E. Pagels, *The Origin of Satan* (New York: Random House, 1995), 25-34.

99. Though perhaps the Barabbas incident could be seen as ironic: "Barabbas is the actual guilty person, but it is Jesus who in effect takes his place and dies instead of him" (Best, *Temptation and Passion,* lxvii-lxviii).

100. Regarding the burlesque of the Ave-Caesar-acclamation, see R. E. Brown, 868. On the importance of the royal motif in Mark, see Juel, *Messiah and Temple,* 50-52, 56-57, 81-83, 93-90, and 212; also Juel, *Master of Surprise,* 91-105; on how the motif is expressed especially through irony, see Juel, *Master of Surprise,* 96-97.

not an admission of guilt but a refusal to dignify the accusations with a response. He will not try to change the outcome of the trial by defending himself, for that would run counter to the divine purpose that he endure these tests. To drink the cup that God is extending to him, Jesus must bear whatever injustice is laid upon him. The Barabbas incident highlights the extremity of this injustice: Pilate sentences the righteous Jesus to crucifixion, but permits the one who (by contemporary standards) deserved such death to go free.

The Crucifixion of Jesus (Mark 15:16-39)

The Offer of Wine, and the Mocking of Jesus (Mark 15:23, 29-32)

The soldiers who will carry out the execution bring Jesus to Golgotha, but before they crucify him they try to give him a drink of perfumed wine (15:23), which he refuses. Raymond Brown interprets this gesture as the offer of a painkilling drink; in his estimation, Jesus' refusal to drink the wine attests to Jesus' view that to assuage his pain would be to renege on his commitment to do the Father's will, which entails Jesus' suffering. Brown writes, "For the Marcan Jesus the offer of wine is another manifestation of the *peirasmos* or testing that had begun in Gethsemane."[101]

The dividing of Jesus' garments, the placement of him between two thieves, and the blaspheming and mockery of those who pass by "shaking their heads" (15:24-32) all evoke scriptural portraits of righteous sufferers. The content of the mockery here is ironic (as was the mockery at the end of each of the trials). The first passersby say, "Aha! You who would destroy the temple and build it in three days, save yourself, and come down from the cross!" (vv. 29-30). There is truth inherent in this command, though the mockers do not perceive it, for Jesus *will* "destroy the temple" — indeed, divine judgment against the temple will be signaled not three days hence, but at the very moment of Jesus' death, when the curtain of the temple is torn in two (15:38). There is another ironic aspect to the command: Jesus' ability to save others and his own ultimate rescue by God depend precisely on his *not* trying to "save himself" or "come down from

---

101. R. E. Brown, 942.

the cross." To make such an effort would be for Jesus to put God to the test, and so to fail to endure in his own time of trial. It is, rather, by Jesus' obedient endurance of this hour of testing that he shows himself to be the perfect son of God, who willingly offers himself as a sacrifice to God — and whose *psychē* God will save from the grip of death. Hence the command to "come down from the cross" is — like Peter's rebuke of Jesus at Caesarea Philippi (8:32-33) — for Jesus a satanic temptation to escape suffering. Next the chief priests and scribes say, "He saved others; he cannot save himself. Let the Messiah, the King of Israel, come down from the cross now, so that we may see and believe" (15:31-32). The assertion is ironic because, again, Jesus' sacrifice will be acceptable only if he does not "save himself."[102] The attached third-person imperative to Jesus, that he "come down from the cross now, *so that we may see and believe*" is ironic because of its deep resonance with many other incidents in the Gospel in which the leaders prove themselves to be quite *unable* to "see and believe" the truth about Jesus. In 8:11-13, the Pharisees had asked Jesus "for a sign from heaven, to test him." Jesus gave them no sign on that occasion; neither will he grant one here.

The Cry of Dereliction (Mark 15:34)

Jesus' cry of dereliction — "My God, my God, why have you forsaken me?" — is one of the interpretive cruxes of this Gospel. As Ernest Best remarks, "Whatever the path we take through Mark's story this cry is not the ending we expect. Jesus ought to be courageous and trusting right to the last moment. The cry demands understanding."[103] At least one early reader of Mark's Gospel thought that it deserved not understanding, but correction: Luke ascribes to Jesus a different word from the cross, a word far less disturbing than Mark's "My God, my God, why have you forsaken me." Like Mark's version of Jesus' last saying, so also Luke's "Father, into your hands I commit my spirit" (Luke 23:46) is a citation from one of the psalms of lament (Ps. 31:5). Each of these psalms of lament follows a

---

102. On Luke's portrait of Jesus as "the saved savior," see J. Neyrey, *The Passion According to Luke: A Redaction Study of Luke's Soteriology* (New York: Paulist Press, 1985), 129-55.

103. Best, *Temptation and Passion,* lxii.

similar pattern, in which the speaker laments his suffering at the hands of enemies, proclaims his trust that God will rescue him, and finally, celebrates God's intervention. But whereas Mark has Jesus quote a cry of despair, Luke has him quote a more hopeful expression of the psalmist, an expression of confidence in God's trustworthiness.

One scholarly solution to the problem of Jesus' cry of dereliction follows Luke's lead, insisting that Mark and early readers would have recognized Jesus' cry from the cross as a quotation from Psalm 22 and would have known that the psalm has a positive outcome. They would have inferred that by quoting its beginning, Jesus invoked the entire Psalm; thus, Jesus' cry only *looks* like a cry of abandonment.[104] I consider this to be a solution forged out of desperation. Surely Mark did not intend for his readers simply to substitute the psalmist's happier verses for the cry of dereliction. What could possibly have motivated the evangelist to quote this shocking verse, if in fact he meant to convey Jesus' sense of peaceful gratitude? Moreover, such an assumption fails to take seriously the sequential character of the events described in Psalm 22 and other psalms of lament and the corresponding sequential character of the saving events of Jesus' passion. In other words, in the psalms and in Mark the effecting of salvation does not occur all at once, but by stages that occur in sequence, and the sequence is important. According to the sequence in the psalms (and in Wisdom 2), the righteous sufferer first endures severe tests of affliction; next he calls upon the Lord; finally God hearkens to the sufferer's cry and rescues him. According to the sequence in Mark, throughout his "hour" Jesus endures *peirasmos,* or testing, which climaxes in the supreme test of estrangement from God; next Jesus calls upon the Lord (in the cry from the cross); finally, because of Jesus' endurance and faithfulness, God will rescue him from death.

104. For discussion of this and other attempts by scholars to soften the import of Jesus' cry of dereliction, see R. E. Brown, 1047-51. As Lane, 572, remarks, such explanations "bear the marks of special pleading and are unsatisfactory. The sharp edge of this word must not be blunted." In Lane's reading of Mark, during the "hour" Jesus bore the judgment of God upon human rebellion; this judgment entailed Jesus' full alienation from God. The cry of dereliction expresses Jesus' "unfathomable pain of real abandonment by the Father" (573; cf. D. H. C. Read, "The Cry of Dereliction," *The Expository Times* 68 [1956–57]: 260-62). In my own reading, God's face truly is hidden from Jesus for the duration of the hour of trial, but the reason is because God is testing the disposition of Jesus' soul by stepping aside for a time, and not because Jesus is bearing divine judgment or wrath.

The literary function of Jesus' cry is not to show that Jesus has abandoned or renounced his faith in God. For Mark's earliest readers, *a cursing of God* by Jesus would have been the unmistakable sign that Jesus had forsaken God; Jesus' cry in Mark is not a curse, but a prayer uttered in the words of the psalmist. Rather, the function of this prayer is twofold: first, by its very content, the cry shows Jesus' sense that God is not present to him. Second, inasmuch as the cry of dereliction is a *prayer*, expressed in the words of Scripture, it shows that Jesus continues, despite his aloneness, to reach out to God. *At the moment of the cry, God may have forsaken Jesus, but Jesus has not forsaken God.*[105] Jesus has been "given over" to sinful powers; he can no longer see God or feel God's power in him. God has "stepped aside" to "test the disposition of Jesus' soul" (cf. *T. Jos.* 2:4-7, quoted above). Jesus' anguished cry on this occasion of his ultimate test had ample precedent in the psalms and in the book of Job. Job had cried, "Therefore I will not restrain my mouth; I will speak in the anguish of my spirit; I will complain in the bitterness of my soul" (Job 7:11). But Job had not "denied the words of the Holy One" (Job 6:10), and neither does Jesus.

By standing fast, by refusing to be led astray even in this most severe test of affliction, Jesus shows himself to be truly the Son of God, one who is "tried and true" and worthy to offer himself as a sacrificial burnt offering to God. God accepts Jesus' self-offering as sufficient to atone for sin.[106] This acceptance is symbolized first by the tearing of the curtain of the temple (15:38). The tearing marks the temple as defunct.[107] It is defunct because Jesus has offered the perfect and acceptable sacrifice, once for all. God's acceptance of Jesus' sacrifice is symbolized second by the centurion's cry, "Truly this man was God's Son!" (15:39) This cry signals that the veil drawn over persons' eyes during Jesus' earthly ministry — drawn by Satan and held in place by sin — has been torn also. The centurion is the first of many who will look at Jesus with unobscured vision, who will see him as God sees him. Both of these signs indicate *that God has taken back the*

---

105. Cf. J. Gnilka, *Das Evangelium nach Markus,* 3rd ed. (Zürich: Benziger; Neukirchen-Vluyn: Neukircher Verlag, 1989), vol. 2, 322. There are actually two mentions of cries in Mark (15:34, 37). I agree with R. E. Brown, 1079, that the second reference to a cry may well be a narrative resumption, referring (again) to Jesus' one cry, mentioned already in 15:34.

106. See above, pp. 104-15.

107. Regarding scholarly discussion of the rending of the veil, see n. 80 above.

authority temporarily granted to satanic powers. God now has hearkened to Jesus' faithful cry from the cross. "For he did not despise or abhor the affliction of the afflicted; he did not hide his face from me, but heard when I cried to him" (Ps. 22:24).

Conclusion

In his account of Jesus in Gethsemane, Mark portrays Jesus as deeply troubled — not simply because he knew that God willed for him to suffer and die, but because he knew of the extraordinary "hour" that lay before him. It would be an hour in which Jesus would be sorely tested by Satan and his human allies. Jesus first prayed for the hour to pass and then professed to God that he would obediently drink the cup that God was extending to him. The supreme hour of testing commenced at the conclusion of the time in Gethsemane, when the delegation from the chief priests, scribes, and elders came to arrest Jesus and he was "given over" into the hands of sinners. For some early readers of Mark, this notice about Jesus' being delivered into the hands of sinners would have suggested that God had now remanded Jesus to Satan's authority and withdrawn (or hidden) the divine presence from Jesus. But the transfer to Satan's dominion would not have been seen as final — if Jesus remained faithful, God would take back authority over Jesus' *psychē,* his soul, or life.

In Gethsemane, the disciples slept rather than watch with Jesus and pray; at his arrest Judas betrayed him, and the others fled. Jesus had said that these events were foretold in Scripture, but they were no less shameful for having been predicted. The events continue — and escalate — Mark's pervasive theme of the failure of the disciples. This theme culminates with Peter's three denials of Jesus, portrayed as taking place at the very moment when Jesus was himself standing fast before Jewish authorities.

By his portrayal of Jesus' obedient faithfulness when on trial and by quotations from and allusions to various psalms of lament throughout the passion account, Mark typecasts Jesus as the *righteous sufferer,* who willingly endures tests of affliction and trusts God to rescue him in his moment of utmost need. In the same vein, Mark's stress on the perversity and blindness of the Jewish and Roman authorities identifies them as the *adversaries of the righteous sufferer.* As in the Wisdom of Solomon, so also in Mark, the adversaries of the righteous one were "blinded by their own wickedness," and "did not know the mysteries of God." Mark stresses this blindness through a devastating use of narrative irony: the authorities could not "see" that Jesus would *in truth* destroy the temple and rebuild another edifice in its place; that Jesus would *not* commit blasphemy, but would remain faithful until death; that he was indeed able to prophesy; and that he was the messiah-king of Israel. At the cross, the chief priests and scribes taunted Jesus to come down, "that we may see and believe," but in fact Satan had veiled their sight.

The crucifixion marked the climactic moment of Jesus' hour of testing. He refused the offer of perfumed wine, which would have blunted his pain, for he knew he must drink the cup that the Father was extending to him. He endured the mocking taunts of bystanders. The challenges of these bystanders that Jesus "save himself" and "come down from the cross" were further satanic temptations. "You do not need to suffer so," whispers Satan to the afflicted. The darkness at the time of Jesus' death marks the ascendance of satanic powers and the hiddenness of God. Jesus' cry of dereliction — "My God, my God, why have you forsaken me?" — points to the wide chasm that separated Jesus from God. But this word from the cross presaged victory, for it was still a word of prayer. Until he took his last breath Jesus blessed God and did not curse.

In this reading of Mark, Jesus' crucifixion was the climax of an hour in which he endured the furious and desperate assault of satanic forces. For that hour, God permitted Satan to have full authority over Jesus, while God "withdrew" or "hid God's face." As in Hebrews, 4 Maccabees, Wisdom of Solomon, and Pseudo-Philo, the righteous one's patient endurance of this most extreme hour of testing proved him to be perfectly obedient, and hence fit to offer himself as a sacrifice to God. God accepted Jesus' self-offering at the moment of death as a sacrifice of atonement for human sin, and signaled this acceptance by tearing the temple curtain, which marked the temple cult as obsolete. By his death, Jesus opened a "way" into a new temple or "house of prayer." This new edifice would be a community of believers who — like the centurion who makes confession at the moment of Jesus' death — are able to "see" that Jesus is the very Son of God. These believers would not be doubleminded (as were their predecessors, the disciples), but would engage in singleminded prayer and so resist Satan's efforts to lead them astray from the straight and narrow path.

Mark is not sanguine about what lies ahead for members of this new "house of prayer." The evangelist has depicted Jesus as teaching that severe trials and afflictions line the path in front of believers. But Jesus' warnings about trials and afflictions are balanced by genuine "good news" for disciples on trial, as we shall see in the next chapter.

CHAPTER 4

Disciples on Trial

Like Peter, Mark's readers say to Jesus, "Look, we have left everything and followed you." To such followers, Mark is brutally frank. Those who follow Jesus will face the same sorts of trials that Jesus faced. The command to sacrifice all is not the last step on the straight and narrow "way of the Lord," but only the first. Still, Mark insists, the situation of Jesus' followers is a hopeful one. It is hopeful because by his own endurance Jesus has opened the path through the wilderness and has empowered those who pray to resist all the menacing, seductive forces that would lead them astray. Moreover, though the cost of discipleship is great, so also is the reward. Jesus says to his followers, "Truly I tell you, there is no one who has left house or brothers or sisters or mother or father or children or fields, for my sake and for the sake of the good news, who will not receive a hundredfold now in this age — houses, brothers and sisters, mothers and children, and fields, with persecutions — and in the age to come eternal life" (Mark 10:29-30).[1] Like Job, and like Jesus, the readers of Mark are those who persevere in the way of the Lord, having sacrificed all. But also like Job, and like Jesus, the readers of Mark are those who will receive back all that they had lost, and more.

These "disciples on trial" to whom Mark addresses his message are readers of Mark's own making. That is to say, the role of "tested follower" is one that Mark has constructed and invited his readers to occupy. The

---

1. On this passage, see L. W. Hurtado, "Following Jesus in the Gospel of Mark — and Beyond," in *Patterns of Discipleship in the New Testament*, ed. R. N. Longenecker (Grand Rapids: William B. Eerdmans, 1996), 14.

rhetorical strategies by which Mark has created this role include especially his recounting of Jesus' prophesies about events to come — events that will include the appearance of false messiahs and false christs who will "lead astray, if possible, the elect" and also "suffering, such as has not been from the beginning of the creation that God created until now" (13:19, 22). Whenever Jesus utters such prophecies in the Gospel, it is as if he speaks over the heads of characters in the narrative world and addresses the readers of the Gospel directly. For it is the readers of the Gospel who know Jesus to be the Son of God, whose words are true (1:1, 11; 9:7), and it is they who live in the time period beyond the narrative frame, to which Jesus' prophecies apply.[2] Whatever the real-life context of Mark's flesh-and-blood readers in various times and places, his "constructed" or "ideal" readers are ones who accept Jesus' invitation to take up their cross and follow him, and who do so with full knowledge that they must endure trials of various kinds.

Within the narrative, Jesus most often utters his prophecies to the twelve disciples (or, as in 10:28-31, to Peter as their representative). The disciples do not understand Jesus' prophetic words. Robert Fowler claims that they do not exhibit any "uptake" of Jesus' message, but I would like to argue the point somewhat differently. It is not simply that the twelve disciples fail to "take up" Jesus' message, but that they actively oppose it. In particular, they oppose Jesus' message that he must suffer and that they must likewise live as suffering servants of God.[3] This motif of incomprehen-

---

2. Recent discussions of how Jesus' discourse (especially in Mark 13) points beyond the end of the story include R. M. Fowler, *Let the Reader Understand: Reader-Response Criticism and the Gospel of Mark* (Minneapolis: Fortress Press, 1991), 82-87; D. H. Juel, *A Master of Surprise: Mark Interpreted* (Philadelphia: Fortress Press, 1994), 77-88 (esp. 82-84); N. R. Petersen, "When Is the End Not an End? Literary Reflections on the Ending of Mark's Narrative," *Interpretation* 34 (1980): 163-66; A. Y. Collins, *The Beginning of the Gospel: Probings of Mark in Context* (Minneapolis: Fortress Press, 1992), 73-91. On Mark 13 as a farewell discourse and on its paraenetic function, see W. L. Lane, *The Gospel of Mark* (Grand Rapids: William B. Eerdmans, 1974), 444-45 (with bibliography cited at 445 n. 2; see also the comment at 464 regarding Mark 13:12-13).

3. Fowler borrows this literary critical construct of "uptake" from J. L. Austin, *How To Do Things with Words* (Cambridge: Harvard University, 1975), who describes the "securing of uptake" as the bringing about of understanding of the meaning and force of a locution (Austin, 117-18, cited in Fowler, 18). Fowler consistently explains the disciples' lack of uptake of Jesus' words and deeds by referring to the purported incongruity between the Gospel's story and its discourse: Mark is willing to sacrifice the disciples at the level of the *story* in order to achieve his aims at the level of *discourse* (i.e., vis-à-vis the reader; see, e.g.,

sion/opposition by the twelve disciples makes the question of the disciples' relationship to Mark and to his readers a mystifying one. Did Mark revere the twelve disciples?[4] Did the earliest flesh-and-blood persons who read (or heard) his Gospel revere them? Questions such as these have occupied a number of scholars over a number of years.[5]

Theodore Weeden offered one of the most original and controversial answers to such questions. Weeden argued that the twelve in Mark's Gospel represent heretics known to Mark's community — persons who proclaim a "divine-man" *(theois-aner)* Christology rather than a suffering-servant Christology.[6] The negative portrayal of the disciples was designed, in Weeden's view, to undercut this heretical Christology: Mark "stages the christological debate of his community in a 'historical' drama in which Jesus serves as a surrogate for Mark and the discipes serve as surrogates for Mark's opponents."[7] Influential as Weeden's theory once was, it is now rejected by most scholars (including myself), who find its argument that Mark's earliest

---

pp. 80, 102, 218). My argument here, contra Fowler, is that the failure of the disciples is not simply "a puzzle encountered in the reading of the story" (Fowler, 20), but a problem within the story itself, i.e., at the narrative level. *Within the story,* Jesus intends for the disciples to understand, and rebukes them when they do not. Indeed, I would argue that their persistent failure to understand Jesus is a driving force in the Markan plot (cf. Petersen, 161).

4. Or perhaps one should say the "eleven" disciples, omitting Judas Iscariot. On whether the "twelve" are to be identified with "the disciples" in Mark, or whether "the disciples" ought to be understand as a larger group that includes the twelve, see C. C. Black, *The Disciples According to Mark: Markan Redaction in Current Debate* (Sheffield: JSOT Press, 1989), 273-74 n. 5. Black himself holds that Mark uses the terms interchangeably.

5. For a summary and assessment of the last several decades of scholarly discussion of the Markan portrayal of the disciples, see Black. Black's aim in this study is to evaluate the success of the redaction critical method in Markan studies, using scholarly interpretation of the disciples as a test case. Black categorizes scholarly constructions of the Markan evidence into three types: type I, "the 'conservative' position," which reads the Markan portrayal of the disciples as positive, and assumes its basis in history; type II, "the 'mediate' position," which contends that the Markan picture of the disciples contains both positive and negative elements, and assumes that Mark depended on historical tradition to some extent but also exercised a degree of authorial control over it; and type III, "the 'liberal' position," which reads the Markan portrait of the disciples as either wholly negative or wholly positive, and insists on Mark's complete autonomy vis-à-vis historical tradition. Black's classification system is not perfect but it is helpful.

6. T. J. Weeden, *Mark — Traditions in Conflict* (Philadelphia: Fortress Press, 1971); for a shorter treatment, see T. J. Weeden, "The Heresy That Necessitated Mark's Gospel," *Zeitschrift für die neutestamentliche Wissenschaft* 59 (1968): 145-58.

7. Weeden, *Traditions in Conflict,* 163.

readers viewed the twelve as heretics rather than heroes to be implausible.[8] More recently, scholars influenced by reader-response criticism have argued that Mark's portrayal of the twelve is a more nuanced one, containing both bad elements and good ones. According to this way of reading, the twelve are flawed, and so the reader must use caution in identifying with them. But the twelve are not failures entirely. In Elizabeth Malbon's words, they (together with other followers of Jesus) are "fallible followers" — persons who do their best to follow Jesus, but inevitably fall short. Such a nuanced or variegated portrayal of the twelve would have been encouraging to Mark's readers, who could identify with such less-than-perfect persons and strive to emulate their achievements, while avoiding their failures.[9] I reject this sort

8. To be plausible, theories that Mark denied any hope of redemption for the disciples beyond the end of the narrative would have to construct a historical setting for the audience in which such a hostile stance toward the disciples would have been palatable. M. A. Tolbert, *Sowing the Gospel: Mark's World in Literary-Historical Perspective* (Philadelphia: Fortress Press, 1989) offers no such scenario; Weeden, *Traditions in Conflict;* W. H. Kelber, *Mark's Story of Jesus* (Philadelphia: Fortress Press, 1979), 88-96; and J. B. Tyson, "The Blindness of the Disciples in Mark," *Journal of Biblical Literature* 80 (1961): 261-68, offer scenarios that strike me as theoretically possible, but based on a high degree of speculation and therefore improbable. All of these theories take it for granted that Mark's readers would have been satisfied with the evangelist's supposed portrait of the disciples as ones whose negative fate has been sealed by the time of Jesus' death. But if, as I shall argue subsequently, the early church revered the original disciples of Jesus, then it seems unlikely that readers could even have *heard* the negative account in the way these scholars claim that Mark intended. In Fowler's terminology (on which see n. 3 above), it seems unlikely that such a message would have "secured uptake" among Mark's readers, who would have either: (a) rejected such a portrait as contrary to fact, much as American people once rejected revelations by the media that John F. Kennedy might have committed acts of deceit or infidelity; or (b) resolved the tension between Mark's negative story of the disciples and their esteemed position in communal memory or present reality by assuming that this very contrast was a part of God's design (as in the reading I offer here).

9. E. S. Malbon, "Fallible Followers: Women and Men in the Gospel of Mark," *Semeia* 28 (1983): 29-48, and E. S. Malbon, "Disciples/ Crowds/ Whoever: Markan Characters and Readers," *Novum Testamentum* 28 (1986): 104-30; similarly R. C. Tannehill, "The Disciples in Mark: The Function of a Narrative Role," in *The Interpretation of Mark*, ed. W. Telford (Philadelphia: Fortress Press, 1977), 134-57 (who reads Mark's story of the disciples as ending on a very negative note, but as offering hints about the possibility of their eventual reconciliation to Jesus). See the comments on Tannehill's article in W. T. Shiner, *"Follow Me!" Disciples in Markan Rhetoric* (Atlanta: Scholars Press, 1995), 185 n. 27, offering points to consider when assessing whether readers are likely to "identify" with the Markan disciples in any given pericope. See also the summary and biblical/literary critic's assessment of Tannehill's article by Stephen Moore in *Literary Criticism and the Gospels: The Theoretical Challenge* (New Haven: Yale University Press, 1989), 73-78.

of reading also. To be sure, there are some positive aspects to Mark's portrayal of the twelve: most notably, Mark depicts them as ones who have left everything to follow Jesus.[10] But the positive features of Mark's portrayal of the twelve are overshadowed by the disciples' failure to understand Jesus, Peter's rebuke of Jesus at Caesarea Philippi, Judas's betrayal, the disciples' sleeping in Gethsemane, Peter's denials, and the disciples' flight at Jesus' arrest. Moreover, some of the more striking failures occur at the end of the narrative. In Paul Achtemeier's words, "If there is any progression in the picture Mark paints of the disciples, it appears to be from bad to worse."[11] Thus the reader's *final* impression of the disciples is an unfavorable one.

Mary Ann Tolbert's work *Sowing the Gospel*[12] has the virtue of recognizing (though perhaps also overschematizing) this negative progression in Mark's account; her argument, however, has significant weaknesses. Tolbert argues that in Mark the disciples exhibit both positive features and negative ones, with the positive elements coming early in the narrative, only to be eclipsed by the negative traits in the latter part of Mark's story. Her reading is governed by her overall thesis that the parable of the Sower together with its interpretation (Mark 4:3-20) functions as one of two plot synopses for Mark's Gospel: the twelve disciples illustrate the "rocky ground," those who "when they hear the word, they immediately receive it with joy. But they have no root, and endure only for a while; then, when trouble or persecution arises on account of the word, immediately they fall away." Tolbert suggests that one of Mark's chief aims in painting the disciples as ones who receive Jesus' word, endure for a while, and then fall away was to encourage the audience to ponder which *human character traits* make some ground prove to be fertile and other ground prove to be unfruitful.[13] I disagree with Tolbert's reading of Mark at a number of points, but for my purposes here two points are key: first, the failure of the disciples in Mark does not underscore the *human* traits that hinder

10. For a summary of perceived positive features in Mark's portrayal of the twelve, see Black, 41-43; also Malbon, "Markan Characters."

11. P. J. Achtemeier, *Mark,* 2nd ed. (Philadelphia: Fortress Press, 1986), 105. Cf. J. D. Kingsbury, *Conflict in Mark: Jesus, Authorities, Disciples* (Minneapolis: Fortress Press, 1989), 11; Senior, 32-33, 36.

12. On 195 n. 31, Tolbert briefly critiques Weeden, *Traditions in Conflict;* W. H. Kelber, *The Oral and the Written Gospel: The Hermeneutics of Speaking and Writing in the Synoptic Tradition, Mark, Paul, and Q* (Philadelphia: Fortress Press, 1983); Tannehill; and Malbon, "Fallible Followers."

13. Tolbert, 224.

faith, but *the divinely (or satanically) induced blindness that can be healed only after Jesus' resurrection.* Second, whereas Tolbert argues that "the account book on [the disciples] is closed" by Jesus' abrupt word *apechei* (NRSV: "Enough! [14:41]), I hold that Mark points beyond the end of the period he narrates, to the disciples' reconciliation with Jesus and emergence as church leaders, as "fishers of persons."[14]

In my reading, Mark's depiction of the twelve is negative, but serves a positive purpose: the depiction undergirds Mark's message to "disciples on trial." By portraying the twelve as blind and as inconstant in time of trial, Mark seeks to show that their positive — perhaps even heroic — stature and accomplishments as already known to the readers were entirely postresurrection developments. *Only after Easter would the disciples be given full sight and brought to singleminded faith.* In this reading, it is the *contrast* between the disciples' preresurrection blindness/inconstancy (narrated) and postresurrection sight/singlemindedness (foreshadowed in the narrative and assumed by readers) that is relevant and inspiring. The portrayal of Jesus' revered disciples as abysmal failures before Christ's resurrection magnifies and commends the *grace and power of God* — power that not only moves mountains, but also opens blind eyes, softens hard hearts, and changes fickleness to faithful endurance.[15] "Might not such transforming power be available also to me?" the reader asks. "Might it not transform me, too, from one who is fearful and in danger of deserting the Lord's way to one who faithfully endures in time of trial?"

In the next section of this chapter I shall adduce two sorts of evidence to support the reading suggested here. First, I shall argue that Mark drops strong

---

14. Tolbert, 229. My criticisms of Tolbert's work mark a departure from my earlier, unqualified approval of her thesis (in S. R. Garrett, "Review of *Sowing the Gospel: Mark's World in Literary-Historical Perspective," Princeton Seminary Bulletin* 12 (1991): 100-101). For a fuller critique of Tolbert's book, see Shiner, 17-20; moreover, Shiner's remarks at 223-24, about how recent narrative critical treatments of Mark presume too high a degree of narrative linearity and character development (thereby missing the "episodic" quality of Mark's narration), seem to me applicable to Tolbert's study (on this point see also above, Chap. 2, n. 43).

15. Cf. T. J. Geddert, *Watchwords: Mark 13 in Markan Eschatology* (Sheffield: JSOT Press, 1989), 160. The notion that in Mark's view true understanding is possible only after Easter goes back at least to Wrede (see, e.g., W. Wrede, *The Messianic Secret* [1901; Cambridge: James Clark, 1971]), and has certainly had other defenders (see, e.g., E. Schweizer, "Towards a Christology of Mark?" in *God's Christ and His People: Studies in Honor of Nils Alstrup Dahl*, ed. J. Jervell and W. A. Meeks [Oslo: Universitetsforlaget, 1977], 32-33). See above, pp. 82-87, for additional discussion of the issue.

literary hints that the failed disciples will be restored to Jesus after the resurrection. These hints would surely have been heeded by most early readers, who (as I shall demonstrate) likely revered the disciples and knew of their postresurrection transformation into devoted followers of Jesus. Second, I shall consider traditions about the conversion (or "call") of Saul/Paul, which were used by biblical authors to underscore God's amazing grace and eye-opening power. These traditions about the transformation of Saul might have functioned as a model helping ancient readers of Mark to interpret the analogous transformation of the disciples. In a subsequent section of the chapter, I shall elaborate my contention that Mark constructs his readers as "disciples on trial" — that is, as persons in dire need of God's transforming, strengthening power. Then, in a final section of the chapter, I shall demonstrate how Mark's portrait of Jesus as "tried and true," and hence as a perfect sacrifice before God, serves to reassure readers that the grace and power of God can likewise transform them as they face their own hour of trial.

The Disciples in Mark's Gospel and Beyond

The (Re)turn of the Disciples

At least four passages in Mark hint that the disciples, who fled from Jesus at his arrest, would return to see Jesus and follow him in the period after the resurrection. Their "returning" to Jesus would also be a "turning," or conversion: like the blind man at Bethsaida, they would undergo a second stage of healing, so that they could "see" Jesus clearly and "follow" him unswervingly. The first passage to foreshadow the (re)turn of the disciples is Jesus' promise to Simon and Andrew that he would make them become "fishers of human beings" (1:17). As others have pointed out, this metaphorical promise is not adequately fulfilled within the framework of the narrative.[16] Presumably Mark knows it to have been fulfilled in the era following the close of the narrative. *After the resurrection,* Simon, Andrew,

---

16. See, for example, Shiner, 174-75: "The promise given to Peter and Andrew is devoid of content within the narrative world. It is only with the benefit of hindsight that the listener knows how these disciples became 'fishers of persons.'" Shiner, 175-76, suggests that readers would have interpreted the ambiguous fishing-metaphor in light of their knowledge of the disciples' post-Easter missionary activity.

and the others would engage in the work of catching persons for the kingdom of God. A second relevant passage is Mark 10:39, Jesus' prediction to James and John that they will face a fate like his. As Larry Hurtado remarks, the prediction "anticipates their future faithfulness beyond their immediate cowardice narrated in chapters 14–15."[17] A third passage that anticipates the reconciliation of Jesus and the disciples is Mark 14:27-28: here Jesus quotes Zechariah 13:7 to prophesy the scattering of the twelve, but simultaneously he looks ahead to their regathering:

> And Jesus said to them, "You will all fall away [literally: "be scandalized"]; for it is written, 'I will strike the shepherd, and the sheep will be scattered.' But after I am raised up, I will go before you to Galilee." (Mark 14:27-28)[18]

The quoted passage in Zechariah continues on to prophesy the restoration of a remnant, amounting to one-third of the "sheep" that have been scattered. Significantly, Zechariah informs us that this remnant will be restored *through a process of testing:*

> And I will put this third into the fire, refine them as one refines silver, and test them as gold is tested. They will call on my name, and I will answer them. I will say, "They are my people"; and they will say, "The Lord is Our God." (Zech. 13:9)

Though Mark quotes only Zechariah 13:7, and not vv. 8-9, the evangelist seems to presuppose the full passage: immediately after Jesus' quotation of Zechariah 13:7, Mark narrates the events in Gethsemane, which mark the onset of the period of eschatological testing for the disciples and for Jesus himself (see especially 14:38; also the discussion on pp. 91-94 above). Moreover, the promise of *restoration* in the Zechariah passage seems to underlie Jesus' statement in Mark 14:28, "After I am raised up, I will go before you to Galilee."[19] This statement of Jesus is nothing less than a prophecy of reconciliation between Jesus and his disciples: he will "go

---

17. Hurtado, 23.

18. Senior, 62-63, points out that this passage is connected via the word *skandalizesthai* to 4:16-17, Jesus' interpretation of the fate of the seed falling on rocky ground; so also Tolbert, 154-55.

19. Cf. J. Marcus, *The Way of the Lord: Christological Exegesis of the Old Testament in the Gospel of Mark* (Louisville: Westminster/John Knox Press, 1992), 154-64, for the

before them," which implies that they will "follow" him in the way. A fourth passage that foreshadows the (re)turn of the disciples is Mark's account of the "young man" at the empty tomb (16:5-7). The young man (an angel?) instructs the women to "Go, tell his disciples and Peter that he is going ahead of you to Galilee; there you will see him, just as he told you" (16:7). This passage refers back to the prophecy of reconciliation in 14:28 (quoted above). Thus, the penultimate word of the Gospel (assuming the shorter ending of Mark) repeats the prophecy that the disciples, including Peter, will once again follow Jesus.[20]

---

argument that Mark 14:22-28 includes numerous allusions to Zechariah 9–14. See Marcus, *Way of the Lord,* 159, for discussion of how Zechariah 13:8-9 is echoed in the Markan depiction of the testing of the disciples in Jesus' passion (the point that I am making above). See R. E. Brown, *The Death of the Messiah: From Gethsemane to the Grave* (New York: Doubleday, 1994), 130-33, for an argument similar to the one offered here, that Mark 14:28 and 16:7 are promises of Jesus' return after the resurrection.

20. One way that scholars have avoided drawing the conclusion that 14:28 and 16:7 forecast the reconciliation of the disciples is to argue that they do not refer to resurrection appearances, but to the parousia (see Weeden, *Traditions in Conflict,* 46, for the position and a list of scholars who defend it). But such a reading ignores the anticipation of future service by the disciples (as fishers of persons, as ones who will follow Jesus when he "goes before," and even as martyrs). See R. E. Brown, 132, for other arguments against the parousia reading. On the relationship of 16:7 to 16:8 (". . . and they said nothing to anyone, for they were afraid"), see especially Petersen. Petersen argues that taking v. 8 in a woodenly literal way (i.e., assuming that the women never said anything, and that therefore the meeting prophesied in v. 7 never occurred) forces one retrospectively to view Mark's Jesus and the entire Markan narrative with suspicion, indeed as profoundly unreliable. Petersen argues that reading 16:8 as ironic (rather than reading 16:8 literally and the whole preceding narrative as ironic) produces results that are preferable because they are more consistent with the tenor of Mark's story and the expectations fostered by it: "An ironic reading of 16:8 transforms its apparent discontinuous closure into an artful bridge between plotted times and the unplotted times of Mark's narrative world. Continuity is engendered at the very moment when it appears to have been interrupted. But because the apparent interruption in 16:8 proves to be only an artfully penultimate closure, we must also recognize that the ultimate closure to Mark's story comes in the reader's imaginative positing of the meeting in Galilee — because 16:8 is the bridge between the expectation (re-)generated in 16:7 and the implied satisfaction provided by 'Galilee,' and because Galilee constitutes the imaginative resolution of the story's plot — in seeing Jesus the eleven come to understand what they had not previously understood" (163). Cf. Juel, 107-21. Hurtado, 24, argues that the most logical reading of 16:8 sees it as indicating "that the women said nothing to anyone other than the ones to whom they were sent, thereby explaining why news of Jesus' resurrection did not become public until it was proclaimed through the witness of the Twelve and of others who were chosen by the risen Jesus for this task" (cf. Malbon, "Fallible Followers," 45). On Mark's assumption that his readers knew of Jesus' eventual reconciliation with the disciples, see the works of Petersen and Juel cited above; also Kingsbury,

The weight of external evidence favors a view that the earliest Christians esteemed the disciples, and so would likely have "taken up" Mark's narrative hints about their eventual reconciliation. Even in his polemic in Galatians, Paul conceded that Peter ("Cephas") and James and John were reputed to be "pillars" (of the mother church in Jerusalem [Gal. 2:9; cf. 1 Cor. 1:12]). Moreover, Matthew and Luke (Mark's earliest commentators) both viewed the disciples (excluding Judas) favorably. Each of these evangelists eliminated some of the disciples' more egregious failings from their respective accounts.[21] In Acts, Luke reinforced the more positive assessment of the disciples by portraying them as fearless and authoritative leaders. Such early evidence makes it seem likely that Mark and the first readers/transmitters of the Gospel also revered the postresurrection disciples.[22]

13-14, 113. For the opposite view, that one should not "play the game of trying to guess the rest of the disciples' story beyond Mark 16:8," see Fowler, 79. Fowler contends that to do so "is to fixate on the story level to the neglect of the discourse. The future of the disciples beyond Mark 16:8 is quite irrelevant to the chief aim of the story." But has not Fowler here fixated on the discourse to the neglect of the story? In other words, has he not neglected several rather explicit instances of narrative forecasts (the very sort of literary technique that it is Fowler's aim to investigate)? Fowler does discuss these instances later (248-49), but assumes that because they are not "taken up" by characters within the plotted times of the narrative, they cannot have been intended to function as part of the story: Fowler claims that it is not *the narrative characters* who will follow Jesus to Galilee, but *the reader only* ("'Galilee' is *wherever* one 'follows' and 'sees' Jesus" [249 n. 45; italics original]). I would counter that the characters *did* "take up" the promises of Jesus' appearances in Galilee, but only after the resurrection (i.e., in the unplotted times of Mark's story); their inability to achieve "uptake" of the promises prior to the resurrection is itself an important factor in the events that take place during the plotted times of the story. In literary-critical terms, in Mark's Gospel the anticipations of the disciples' reconciliation to Jesus are a kind of "external prolepsis" (on which see M. A. Powell, *What Is Narrative Criticism?* [Minneapolis: Fortress Press, 1990], 37).

21. Though, significantly, Luke did not edit out the motif of the disciples' incomprehension prior to Easter, but underscored it. See R. J. Dillon, "Easter Revelation and Mission Program in Luke 24:46-48," in *Sin, Salvation, and the Spirit*, ed. D. Durken (Collegeville, Minn.: Liturgical Press, 1979), 244-45.

22. Eusebius ascribes to Papias (the late-first/early-second-century bishop of Hieropolis) a tradition that Mark's Gospel came to be written when persons exhorted Peter's follower Mark to leave them a written statement of Peter's teaching (*Eccl. Hist.* 2.15). If historically accurate, this tradition, too, suggests that the author and first readers/transmitters of the Gospel of Mark viewed Peter and his fellow disciples as authoritative figures. (Imagine the contrary case: if Peter were viewed as a failure or a heretic, promulgators of the Markan Gospel would have masked the Gospel's connection to him, inasmuch as the connection would have undercut the authority of the work.) Even if the linking of Mark's Gospel to Peter is historically inaccurate, Papias's testimony indicates that he and others of his day revered Peter.

When modern critical scholars read Mark, the form of their question is "Why did Mark portray the disciples in such a bad light?" But Mark's earliest readers would have focused, I presume, not on Mark's literary strategies per se, but on *the events depicted in the narrative.* For such persons, the relevant question would have been, rather, "What could it mean that the disciples we know as great leaders once acted so shamefully?" And the answer to this latter question would have been obvious enough: God had opened the eyes of the disciples and had transformed them from ones who misunderstood Jesus, and even hindered him, into Jesus' worthy servants and followers. Well-known traditions about Paul — erstwhile persecutor of the church, turned apostle — might have helped readers to make such an inference.

A Persecutor Turned Apostle

The New Testament contains a number of testimonies about the remarkable transformation of Paul from persecutor of the church to apostle. Many if not all of these testimonies highlight Paul's preconversion misdeeds (or misguided zeal) so as to magnify and extoll God's power and grace in bringing about the change. If known to Mark and early readers, traditions about the contrast between Paul's preconversion and postconversion lives would have offered a model for making sense of the radical change that came over the disciples after the resurrection. Even if not known to Mark and his readers, such traditions offer an analogy to help us discern how the Markan traditions may have functioned for early readers of the Gospel.

Paul himself emphasized his former role as one who persecuted the church. To the Galatians he wrote, "You have heard, no doubt, of my earlier life in Judaism. I was violently persecuting the church of God and was trying to destroy it" (Gal. 1:13; cf. 1 Cor. 15:9; Phil. 3:6). The wording of this passage highlights the extremes to which Paul went as enemy of the church: he persecuted the church "violently," or (more literally) "to an extraordinary degree" *(kath' hyperbolēn);* he "was trying to destroy" or "was making havoc of" *(porthoun)* it (cf. Gal. 1:23). By insisting on his own zeal and violence in persecuting the church, Paul shores up his argument to the Galatians that his present role as apostle was not initiated by any human effort, but by a revelation from God. A mere human would not have been able to arrest and to redirect one so zealous in "pursuing" the church so as to destroy it ("pursue" is another meaning of *diōkein,* usually translated "persecute"). But God, who had set Paul apart before he was born and called Paul through his grace, revealed his Son to him (Gal. 1:15-16). Paul reports further that, when churches received word of his conversion, they were moved *to praise God.* The churches in Judea heard it told that " 'the one who formerly was persecuting us is now proclaiming the faith he once tried to destroy.' And they glorified God because of me" (1:23-24). The point is clear: God's power must be very great indeed to have stopped and "turned" one as dead-set on destruction as Paul! By stressing the severity of his former opposition, Paul makes the point that it was *God* (and not humans) who called Paul into his present service for God. In turn, Paul's emphasis on God's initiative serves to underscore Paul's present authority. He is one appointed by none other than God.

The Acts of the Apostles postdates Mark, but Luke's lingering over the details of Paul's persecuting of Christians, as well as the evangelist's triple narration of the conversion, suggests that this was a well-known story among those to whom Luke wrote — it was a story that the church loved to hear and to tell. At the very least, the detail and repetition indicate that the conversion of Paul from one who ravaged the church to one who labored for it was a critical component in Luke's own understanding of the apostle's identity. Elsewhere I have argued that Luke's stress on the extremity and violence of Saul's attacks on church (Acts 8:3; 9:1, 21; 22:4, 19-20; 26:10-11) and the evangelist's notice that Saul had received "authority" from higher officials "to bind all who called on Jesus' name" (9:14) suggest that Luke viewed Saul as more than a merely human enemy: rather, Saul was acting as an agent of the devil at the time when Christ overtook him. In this reading, the "blindness" sent upon Saul at that time symbolizes his alliance with Satan; later, the restoration of his vision and falling of scales from his eyes mark the end of Satan's jurisdiction over him.[23] In Luke's final account of the conversion, the risen Lord tells Paul that he is sending him to the people and to the Gentiles, "to open their eyes so that

23. S. R. Garrett, " 'Lest the Light in You Be Darkness': Luke 11:33-36 and the Question of Commitment," *Journal of Biblical Literature* 110 (1991): 104. I read the accounts of Saul's conversion in Acts in conjunction with Luke 11:33-36. Consider especially 11:34: "If it [your eye] is evil, your body is full of darkness." Besides the passages discussed here, other New Testament texts that refer or allude to Paul's former persecuting of the church include 1 Timothy 1:13 and Ephesians 3:8 (possibly echoing 1 Corinthians 15:9).

they may turn from darkness to light and from the authority of Satan to God" (Acts 26:18). This commissioning is somewhat ironic, for at the time when the words were supposedly uttered, Paul's own eyes had not yet been opened: he himself had not yet completed his turn "from darkness to light and from the authority of Satan to God." The light had shined on him, but the scales had not yet fallen from his eyes. Jesus was commissioning Saul/Paul to "do unto others" as Jesus was at that very moment doing unto him.

What early Christians seem to have found remarkable about Paul was not that he had once tried to hinder Christ's work, but that Christ had called such a vicious enemy to be his chosen apostle and had turned him from his pursuit/persecution of the church in order that he might follow another "way." The change in Paul dramatized the power of Christ in a most striking and memorable fashion. I suggest that the well-known traditions about Paul's regaining of sight and his turning from persecutor to apostle would have offered readers of Mark's Gospel a paradigm for perceiving and interpreting the analogous change in Jesus' disciples. But even if readers of Mark were unaware of the traditions about Paul's conversion, the popularity of such traditions in the church and their demonstrated function of highlighting the power of Christ/of God make it reasonable to suppose that the Markan disciple-traditions functioned in a similar way for early readers of this Gospel. To be sure, Mark never portrays the disciples as persecuting the church; rather, their failures are ones of inconstancy and incomprehension, of putting Jesus to the test. But, much like Saul in Acts, the disciples as portrayed in Mark *need Christ to heal their blindness.*[24] Readers of Mark's narrative — knowing that in the time of the church the disciples did indeed possess clear, even prescient vision — might well have been moved to glorify the power of God/of Christ because of the change in them.

Remarks in the New Testament about Paul's transformation from persecutor reflect a widespread pattern of speech, identified by Rudolf Bultmann and later termed the "soteriological contrast pattern" by Nils Dahl. In such stylized speech, "the novelty of Christian living is described in

---

24. At least one New Testament author appropriated the Markan material about the disciples in the way I am suggesting: according to Luke's account in Acts, by a time shortly after Jesus' ascension Peter had unmistakably "turned again" to "strengthen the brothers and sisters" (in fulfillment of Luke 22:32, a passage unique to the third Gospel).

contrast to the worldly past according to the scheme: 'formerly . . . now.' "[25] There are numerous examples of the soteriological contrast pattern in the New Testament; one very striking such example occurs at 1 Peter 2:9-10:

> But you are a chosen race, a royal priesthood, a holy nation, God's own people, in order that you may proclaim the mighty acts of him who called you out of darkness into his marvelous light. Once you were not a people, but now you are God's people; once you had not received mercy, but now you have received mercy.

Because the soteriological contrast pattern is so well attested in early Christian writings, we can reasonably infer that the first readers of Mark would have been accustomed to thinking in terms of sharp breaks between "former" lives and lives "here and now." Hence they could readily construe Mark's negative comments about the disciples as descriptions of the former phase of the disciples' existence (what we might call the "before snapshot"), preceding an eventual summons "into God's marvelous light."

In summary, Mark repeatedly foreshadows the "return" (or "turn," i.e., conversion) of the disciples of Jesus. Mark has Jesus prophesy that the disciples would go on to Galilee; there, with newly opened eyes, they would "see" Jesus and serve him by becoming ones who "fished for human persons." If Mark's readers knew the disciples to have been respected church "pillars," then Mark's clues about their eventual restoration would not have been surprising or overly subtle. Instead, for such readers the truly shocking element in Mark's account would have been the evangelist's revelation that the disciples had been such abysmal failures before the passion and resurrection of Christ. Why would Jesus have chosen such unlikely persons to be the first ministers of the church? And what could be the meaning of the change that had subsequently come over them? Readers might have been aided in answering these and similar questions by traditions about Paul, the persecutor-turned-apostle. In any case, the similarity of the plotline in the two sets of traditions (blindness and opposition, followed by obedience and exemplarly leadership) suggests an analogy of function as well. Both the stories about Paul and the Markan

25. R. Bultmann, *Theology of the New Testament,* trans. Kendrick Grobel (New York: Scribner's, 1951), 105-6 (with examples cited); cf. N. A. Dahl, *Jesus in the Memory of the Early Church* (Minneapolis: Augsburg Publishing House, 1976), 33.

account of the twelve served, I have suggested, to magnify the astonishing power and grace of God, which were available even to humble readers of the Gospel as they faced their own tribulations and trials.

The Readers of Mark as Disciples on Trial

Who Were Mark's First Readers?

If we could pose questions to Mark and to the first persons who read or heard his manuscript, we would inquire about their ethnic, cultural, and socioeconomic backgrounds and about their familiarity with the Scriptures and with other traditions about Jesus. We would ask questions concerning the situations that led them to join the Jesus movement, and the reactions of kith and kin. We would ask about contemporary political events and about how Mark and readers thought such events were related to their own doings. We would invite them to describe their expectations for the future. If we had profiles of Mark and of his earliest readers that answered such questions as these, then we would be in a better position to make educated guesses about Mark's overall and subsidiary purpose(s) in writing and about the ways that early readers construed Mark's account. In other words, such information would enable us more knowledgeably to reconstruct the transactions through which the author and earliest flesh-and-blood readers of the Gospel negotiated its meanings.

Regrettably, answers to the sorts of questions posed in the preceding paragraph lie completely beyond our reach. Indeed, we lack sufficient internal and external data to identify even the Gospel's place of origin with any confidence.[26] With respect to the date of composition, most scholars favor a theory that Mark wrote sometime shortly before or shortly after the destruction of the temple in Jerusalem in the first Jewish revolt (i.e., around 70 C.E.). My own opinion is that the Gospel was likely written after the temple's destruction, rather than before.[27] But although we cannot

26. In current scholarly debate there are two major positions on the place of origin of Mark's Gospel: one that locates the author in Rome and one that locates him in geographical proximity to Palestine, possibly in the Roman province of Syria. See J. Marcus, "The Jewish War and the Sitz im Leben of Mark," *Journal of Biblical Literature* 111 (1992): 441-62, for a recent discussion of the evidence.

27. I base this inference on Mark 13:1-2, which I read as *ex eventu* prophecy.

locate Mark's Gospel precisely in space and in time, we can discern patterns of emphasis in hortatory and prophetic passages, and so estimate how Mark viewed the life-context of his readers and the aspects of their situation requiring his pastoral address.[28] I shall argue below that Mark constructed his readers *as ones destined to be put to the test.*

". . . To Lead Astray, If Possible, the Elect"

Mark 13 includes the evangelist's most explicit overtures to the reader of the Gospel, for here Jesus prophesies concerning events that are "about to be accomplished" — that is, events to take place in the period after Jesus' crucifixion, which is itself imminent in the narrative. The prophecies of Jesus in this chapter delineate the faith-context of Mark's ideal readers, located in the post-Easter era.[29] The picture sketched by these sayings of Jesus is of persons enduring the hour of *eschatological trial.* As discussed in Chapter 1, many ancient Jews and Christians believed that eschatological "woes" or "birthpangs" would precede the day of resurrection and final judgment. In Mark 13:8, Jesus foretells wars, earthquakes, and famines and identifies these as "the beginning of the birth pangs" *(archē tōn*

28. Of course, the multiple flesh-and-blood persons who first read and transmitted Mark's Gospel would not have matched perfectly Mark's "ideal" or "constructed" audience. Such persons would have brought various concerns, differing levels of scriptural and theological competence, and many types of cultural knowledge to their reading or hearing of his Gospel. None of them would have heard it precisely as he intended (insofar as he would have been able to identify and articulate all his intentions). Construals of Mark's Gospel by ancient readers would certainly have differed from one another and from Mark's own view; any single reading of the Gospel (ancient or modern) necessarily simplifies, and silences alternative readings. Moreover, though we may focus as sharply as possible on the text, in making our inferences about the location(s) of Mark and his readers we inevitably perceive only what filters through our particular worldview and research lens. Of necessity, even the best-intentioned reader sifts, selects, and orders the data, and his or her own subjectivity enters in at each step. This subjectivity can be limited, but it cannot be completely avoided; it ought to be acknowledged but not lamented. For further discussion of subjectivity versus objectivity in New Testament studies (as well as in the disciplines of sociology and anthropology), see S. R. Garrett, "Sociology of Early Christianity," in *Anchor Bible Dictionary,* vol. 6 (New York: Doubleday, 1992), 91-92; also S. R. Garrett, "Review of *Christian Origins and Cultural Anthropology,* by Bruce J. Malina," *Journal of Biblical Literature* 107 (1988): 532-34.

29. On how chapter 13 points beyond the end of the narrative, see the works cited in n. 2 above.

hōdinōn). That is, the prophesied events signal the painful advent of the new age, which comes about even as the powers of the old age struggle to prevent this "birth." Then, in Mark 13:19, Jesus refers to "suffering" or "affliction" *(thlipsis),* "such as has not been from the beginning of the creation that God created until now" (see also v. 24). This is an allusion to Daniel 12:1, "There shall be a time of affliction [LXX: *thlipsis*], such as has never occurred since nations first came into existence." In Daniel, the "affliction" immediately precedes the resurrection to judgment of the just and the unjust. The implication for Mark's readers — who, again, live in that time when the prophecies are coming to fulfillment — is that they are themselves experiencing the "great tribulation" that precedes the final resurrection and judgment. The author of Revelation describes this period of tribulation as "the hour of trial that is coming on the whole world to test the inhabitants of the earth" (Rev. 3:10). Once the hour of trial is finished, Jesus foretells in Mark, the day of the Son of Man will at last arrive, marked by cosmic signs as prophesied already in Isaiah, Joel, and Haggai (Mark 13:24-27). If the Jewish war against Rome was underway (or already past) at the time when Mark wrote, then Mark may well have been instructing his readers to interpret the traumatic events of that war as the prophesied time of "great tribulation" and informing them that as soon as the tribulation had ended, cosmic signs would be given and the Son of Man would return (13:24-27).

Jesus specifies the forms that eschatological testing will take for his followers. Just as Jesus will be "given over" *(paradidesthai)* to sinners for testing, so his hearers/Mark's readers will be "given over" *(paradidesthai)* to councils, and beaten in synagogues, and called to give testimony before governors and kings (vv. 9, 11; cf. 4:17).[30] Brother will "betray" or "give over" *(paradidonai)* brother to death; fathers will betray children, children will rise against parents and have them put to death (v. 12). As with the repeated references to Jesus' being "betrayed" or "given over" (discussed in Chapter 3 above), so these occurrences in Mark 13 of the verb "give over" *(paradidonai)* signal that *the ensuing events are to be construed as tests.* Jesus' concluding remark in this section, that "the one who endures *[ho de hypomeinas]* to the

---

30. Senior, 38, similarly observes that the use of *paradidesthai* in Mark 13 evokes Jesus' rejection, trial, and death: the future of the community will mirror that of Jesus. On a probable nuance of *paradidonai* for Mark's earliest real readers, see above, pp. 100-104. On the suffering of the followers of Jesus in Mark, see Collins, *Beginning,* 66-72.

end will be saved" (13:13) likewise suggests that the prophesied events are to be interpreted as tests of fidelity, inasmuch as Jewish and non-Jewish texts from this era regularly assume that "endurance" *(hypomonē)* is the appropriate response to testing.[31] Significantly, Luke alters the Markan form of Jesus' saying, having Jesus prophesy instead that "by your endurance you will gain your souls" *(en tē hypomonē hymōn ktēsasthe tas psychas hymōn,* Luke 21:19). Probably Luke introduced the change to erase any suggestion that one must survive until the eschaton in order to gain the prophesied blessing. In Luke's rendering, those who lose their lives (by enduring trials) will gain them back again. Luke may be trading on the convention that God permits Satan to have some sort of limited authority over person's "souls" or "lives" for the duration of the testing, but does not allow him to retain that authority if the tested ones persevere. By enduring, the righteous recapture their "souls" or "lives," which had been temporarily under Satan's control.[32] Though not as transparent as in this parallel Lukan material, Mark's assumptions in 13:13 may be similar.

The eschatological trials of Mark's readers include not only trials of affliction, but also trials of seduction: in the readers' own era, many are coming in Jesus' name, and "leading many astray" *(pollous planēsousin* [13:6]). The word *planan* means literally to pull or draw aside, to seduce away from the straight paths of the Lord. A little later in the discourse, Jesus adds that false christs and false prophets will "show signs and wonders" in their effort to lead the elect astray (13:22). As I have shown elsewhere, various Jewish texts from this era attest to a belief that Satan inspired false prophets and empowered them to do magic, so as to deceive and lead astray into idolatry.[33] In Revelation, for example, the beast from

31. See S. R. Garrett, "The God of This World and the Affliction of Paul: 2 Cor 4:1-12," in *Greeks, Romans, and Christians: Essays in Honor of Abraham J. Malherbe,* ed. David L. Balch et al. (Minneapolis: Fortress Press, 1990), esp. nn. 7, 30; also S. R. Garrett, "Paul's Thorn and Cultural Models of Affliction," in *The Social World of the First Christians: Essays in Honor of Wayne A. Meeks,* ed. L. M. White and O. L. Yarbrough (Minneapolis: Fortress Press, 1995).

32. For discussion of this cultural (interpretive) convention, see above, pp. 102-4. In Luke 22:31-32, Jesus apparently concedes that Satan has been granted authority over the disciples for a limited period of time: later Peter will "turn" and "strengthen the others." I discuss the meaning of these verses in their Lukan context in S. R. Garrett, *The Demise of the Devil: Magic and the Demonic in Luke's Writings* (Minneapolis: Fortress Press, 1989), 137 n. 63.

33. See the discussion in Garrett, *Demise of the Devil,* 13-17.

the earth is called a "false prophet" and is said to use great signs to deceive the inhabitants of the earth, bidding them to worship the beast from the sea (itself an emissary of Satan; see Rev. 13:12-15; cf. 16:13; 19:20; 20:10). In 2 Thessalonians, the coming of the "lawless one" is said to be "apparent in the working of Satan, who uses all power, signs, lying wonders, and every kind of wicked deception for those who are perishing" (2 Thess. 2:9-10). Deuteronomy 13, which underlies such teachings about false prophets, notes that the enticements of such prophets indicate that "the Lord your God is testing you, to know whether you indeed love the Lord your God with all your heart and soul" (Deut. 13:3). So also Mark implies to his readers that they should interpret the appearance on the scene of messianic or prophetic pretenders ("false christs" and "false prophets") as an indication that the readers themselves are being tested.

Mark informs his readers that they will face other sorts of seductions besides false prophets — seductions that typify a (relatively) peaceful situation, in which Christians are going about their daily business without any acute sense of endangerment. In the parable of the sower, Jesus refers to the enticing power of "the cares of the world, and the lure of wealth, and the desire for other things" (4:19), which may choke out the seed before it matures. Moreover, Jesus concludes his teachings about eschatological trial with a warning to "beware, keep alert; for you do not known when the time will come" (13:33). He illustrates with a parable of a man who goes on a journey, having put his servants in charge and commanded his doorkeeper to "watch" or to "keep awake" (*gregorein,* 13:34). At all times the doorkeeper must be vigilant, for he knows not when the master will return. The parable instructs Mark's readers that they too must "*keep awake* — for you do not know when the master of the house will come, in the evening, or at midnight, or at cockcrow, or at dawn, or else he may find you asleep when he comes suddenly. And what I say to you I say to all: *Keep awake*" (vv. 35-37 [emphasis added]; cf. v. 33).[34]

It should not seem odd or even especially striking that Mark envisions his readers as facing eschatological trials that include *both* suffering *and* seduction. In like manner, other New Testament writers warn against both types of trial. The author of Revelation, for example, writes not only to the Smyrnans, some of whom the devil is about to throw into

---

34. The reference to "all" in v. 37 suggests that Jesus' admonition applies not only to his own auditors at that moment, but also to the readers or auditors of the Gospel.

prison so that they may be tested (Rev. 2:10), but also to the Laodiceans, who say "I am rich, I have prospered, and I need nothing" — not knowing that they are "wretched, pitiable, poor, blind, and naked" (3:17). And, on the one hand the author of 1 Peter counsels his readers, "Beloved, do not be surprised at the fiery ordeal that is taking place among you to test you, as though something strange were happening to you. But rejoice insofar as you are sharing Christ's sufferings . . ." (1 Pet. 4:12-13). On the other hand, this same author exhorts his readers "as aliens and exiles to abstain from the desires of the flesh that wage war against the soul" (2:11).[35] Such expectation that trials of faith and perseverance would take a variety of forms is not surprising, given that Satan was presumed by many to have been the (immediate) author of such trials (see above, pp. 32-44). Satan has various tools at his disposal, including not only threats of pain, death, and bereavement, but also enticing but deceptive offers of benefit or pleasure. Thus Satan is like the tyrant Antiochus in 4 Maccabees, who informed his victims, "Just as I am able to punish those who disobey my orders, so I can be a benefactor to those who obey me" (4 Macc. 8:6).[36]

35. In addition to the examples of different types of testing from 1 Peter and Revelation cited here, see 1 Thess. 3:4-5; 1 Cor. 7:5; 10:12; Rom. 16:17-20; James 1:2-4, 12-16; Heb. 12:3-4; 13:4-5, 9. I suspect that anticipations in various New Testament documents of a *variety* of forms of testing reflect social-historical contexts in which suffering and persecution on account of the confession of Christ were sporadic, rather than unremitting. If "trouble or persecution on account of the word" (Mark 4:17) had indeed arisen on occasion, then readers would have known that it could also happen to them. But if such trouble were sporadic rather than continuous, then persons would also have had opportunity for the "cares of the world, and the lure of wealth, and the desire for other things" (Mark 4:19) to threaten their perseverance. Juel, 87-88, argues that Mark was not writing to a readership that faced persecution, but to "a church that has tasted success and found it satisfying." Thus, Juel claims, the message of Mark's Gospel is one not of encouragement during persecution, but of warning to avoid the temptation to overconfidence (see also Juel, 141-42). In my own opinion, such a restriction of Mark's message is not necessary: Mark does offer encouragement to persevere, but recognizes that the "tests" faced by readers may be *either* tests of affliction *or* experiences of seduction by the cares or things of the world. Both sorts of test give occasion to go astray from the straight and narrow path.

36. Compare the insight of Dietrich Bonhoeffer, who writes, "In temptation Satan wins power over the believer as far as he is flesh. He torments him by enticement to lust, by the pains of privation, and by bodily and spiritual suffering of every kind. He robs him of everything he has and, at the same time, entices him to forbidden happiness" (Bonhoeffer, 113).

Echoes of Jesus' story of the absent master (Mark 13:32-37) resound in the ensuing account of Jesus and his disciples in Gethsemane, in which Jesus repeatedly but unsuccessfully instructs three of the disciples to "keep awake" *(gregorein):*

> He came and found them sleeping; and he said to Peter, "Simon, are you asleep? Could you not keep awake *[gregorēsai]* one hour? Keep awake *[gregorein]* and pray that you may not come into the time of trial *[peirasmos];* the spirit indeed is willing, but the flesh is weak." (14:37-38)

Here the disciples' sleeping is not itself a failure *to endure* testing (which has not yet begun for them), but a failure *to prepare for it.* Jesus had earlier tried to impart full vision to the disciples' blind eyes, but was hindered from doing so; here he tries to goad them into wakefulness, but cannot, "for their eyes were very heavy" (v. 40). Their eyes have again been shut, this time to the need — and the rewards — for perseverance in time of trial. Hence the disciples will fail their imminent tests: Judas will betray the master, the disciples will abandon him, and Peter will deny him three times.

The motifs common to the parable of the absent master and the Markan Gethsemane account include the need for vigilance and prayer (so as to avoid entry into testing: 14:38, 39), the suddenness of the return of "the master," and the possibility (realized in Gethsemane) that the master will indeed find his servants "sleeping" when he comes. These themes and several related ones also come to expression in 1 Thessalonians 5:1-10, a passage that rewards careful attention:

> Now concerning the times and the seasons, brothers and sisters, you do not need to have anything written to you. For you yourselves know very well that *the day of the Lord will come like a thief in the night.* When they say, "There is peace and security," then sudden destruction *[olethros]* will come upon them, as labor pains come upon a pregnant woman, and there will be no escape! But you, beloved, are not in darkness, for that day to surprise you like a thief; for you are all children of light and children of the day; we are not of the night or of darkness. So then *let us not fall asleep as others do,* but let us *keep awake [gregorein]* and be sober, for those who sleep sleep at night, and those who are drunk get drunk at night. But since we belong to the day, let us be sober, and *put on the breastplate of faith and love, and for a helmet the hope of salvation.* For *God has destined us not for wrath but for obtaining salvation through*

our Lord Jesus Christ, who died for us, so that whether we are awake or asleep we may live with him.

Here Paul exhorts his readers to "keep awake" and to "be sober" in preparation for the sudden advent of the Day of the Lord. He explains that the way to "be sober" is to "put on the breastplate of faith and love, and for a helmet the hope of salvation." This image of *putting on armor* suggests that Paul wishes the Thessalonians to take up a posture of defense in their period of waiting — defense against "the Tester," who has already tried the Thessalonians once (3:5) and will do so again (cf. Eph. 6:11: "Put on the whole armor of God, so that you may be able to stand against the wiles of the devil"). Those who do *not* remain vigilant against satanic testing, but rather permit themselves to get caught up in the routines of daily life (saying, "there is peace and security") will be subjected to "sudden destruction." Paul is confident that the Thessalonians' destiny does not reside among those who "sleep" and "get drunk," and who will therefore be subject to destruction/divine wrath. Rather, the Thessalonian believers' future is to be reunited with the Lord, who died to obtain salvation for them (cf. 1 Thess. 4:13-18).[37]

I suggest that the Markan parable of the absent master functions much like this Pauline exhortation, to warn Mark's readers *to guard against satanic testing.* The tests to be faced by such readers may take the form of afflictions, of signs and wonders performed by false prophets, or of the cares and distractions of this world. But, whatever the form of the tests, unless readers remain vigilant and pray, they will fail the tests and so be unprepared to greet the master and stand (i.e., be vindicated) before him when he comes. In the Gethsemane account, Mark uses the disciples' failure to "keep awake" as a case in point. The disciples did not remain vigilant and "pray not to enter into testing," but were asleep when the Lord returned. Subsequently, they fail their tests of fidelity.

In summary, Mark constructs his readership as a community of faithful persons on trial. They are tested by great affliction, such as the world has never seen. They are tested by powerful seducers, who do signs and wonders to lead astray, if possible, the elect. They are tested by the soporific routines of daily existence and by fleshly desires. Jesus admonishes his

---

37. Note that Paul uses the word for "sleep" or "falling asleep" *(katheudein)* in slightly different ways in vv. 6-7 on the one hand and in v. 10 on the other: in vv. 6-7 it refers to the failure of moral vigilance; in v. 10 it refers euphemistically to death.

readers — whichever sorts of tests they face — to "keep awake and pray," that they might endure the testing, and so stand before the Son of Man when he comes. In saying that Mark "constructs his readers" as disciples on trial, I am suggesting that the evangelist casts *all readers* (whatever their objective historical situation) into the role of those who "take up their cross and follow Jesus" on the straight and narrow "way of the Lord." Moreover, Mark insists that all persons who follow Jesus on this "way" will be put to the test. Thus Jesus' words to "disciples on trial" as reported by Mark are prophetic and apt also for persons in settings besides Mark's own, even for "comfortable Christians" at the dawn of the twenty-first century. In my reading, Jesus admonishes all of us who call ourselves his disciples us to "wake up," to "watch," to notice that we are indeed being put to the test, possibly in ways that we have not expected or perceived. Jesus calls us to guard against all persons or circumstances that would interfere with preparations to greet the master when he comes. Only when we as Mark's readers heed his invitation *to perceive our own day as a time of trial* can we begin to discern and appreciate the full and appropriate response to testing made by Jesus and extended to all who follow him.

"Tested As We Are" — Mark's Christology and Hope for Disciples on Trial

A New Context for Discipleship

According to Mark, Jesus' followers will indeed be put to the test, but they need not fear. For, when Jesus endured unto death, God accepted that death as the perfect sacrifice. Jesus' offer of this sacrifice and God's acceptance of it now give Jesus' followers *new hope and new power,* so that they might persevere on "the way" throughout their own times of trial. As Ernest Best points out, discipleship for Mark's readers does not simply mean imitation of Christ. "Through his cross and resurrection, which are their redemption, he creates the very possibility of journey for them."[38]

---

38. E. Best, *Following Jesus: Discipleship in the Gospel of Mark* (Sheffield: JSNT Press, 1981), 248. On how the portrayal throughout the New Testament of Jesus as tested shows forth his solidarity with his followers, see J. H. Korn, ΠΕΙΡΑΣΜΟΣ, *Die Versuchung des Gläubigen in der gr. Bibel* (Stuttgart: W. Kohlhammer Verlag, 1937), 76-88.

The two explicit soteriological statements in Mark, namely 10:45 ("For the Son of Man came not to be served but to serve, and to give his life as a ransom for many") and 14:24 ("This is my blood of the covenant, which is poured out for many"), both present Jesus' death as in some sense a vicarious sacrifice. There has been endless scholarly debate regarding the precise mechanism or process by which, in Mark's view, this sacrifice effected salvation. One possible interpretation of the evidence claims that for Mark, Jesus' death was the supreme instance of vicarious substitutionary atonement (parallel to the high priestly sacrifice on the "Day of Atonement"), in which the sin of the people was transferred to Jesus, who then endured God's wrath on account of that sin.[39] A second interpretation (which can overlap with the preceding one but which makes reference to different analogs from the Hebrew Scriptures) is that Jesus' death was a representative atoning death for "the many," in connection with Isaiah 53 and especially with the covenant sacrifice at Exodus 24:8 (alluded to in Mark 14:24).[40] A third possible interpretation reads allusions throughout Mark to Exodus and new-Exodus passages in the Hebrew Scriptures, as well as the Markan account of Jesus' death on Passover, as pointers to Jesus' role as leader of a second Exodus from bondage — bondage not to the Egyptians, but to human sinfulness (or to Satan).[41] A

39. This is the reading, for example, of A. Hultgren in *Christ and His Benefits: Christology and Redemption in the New Testament* (Philadelphia: Fortress Press, 1987), 57-64. He writes, "For Mark the death of Jesus is the means by which one, the crucified Christ, bears the judgment and sentence due to sin on behalf of the many, humanity as a whole, and his resurrection attests that he has been reclaimed by God. And if he has been reclaimed, God has also reclaimed humanity in him" (63).

40. Such an interpretation is offered in M. Hengel, *The Atonement: The Origins of the Doctrine in the New Testament* (Philadelphia: Fortress Press, 1981), 42, 53-54. On the early Christians' "multiplicity of approaches" to the question of Jesus' saving death, a multiplicity that is exhibited by the "astonishing number and variety" of New Testament allusions to Old Testament texts pertaining to sacrifice, see Hengel, 45-47, 52-53.

41. Marcus, *Way of the Lord,* takes very seriously Mark's use of second-Exodus scriptures (especially those of second-Isaiah), though it would be a simplification to describe his complex Christological reading of Mark as merely an "Exodus interpretation." For a less sophisticated (but still insightful) interpretation of Mark that highlights Exodus themes, see U. Mauser, *Christ in the Wilderness: The Wilderness Theme in the Second Gospel and Its Basis in the Biblical Tradition* (Naperville, Ill.: Alec R. Allenson, 1963). Senior, 43-44, 51, notes that the liberation theme is signaled by Jesus' death on Passover; to be sure, Mark doesn't exploit the Passover connection in the rest of his passion account, but still, "in these preparatory scenes, he brings that rich theological symbolism of liberation and hope emphatically before the reader" (51). On the Exodus motif in Luke and Acts, see S. R. Garrett, "Exodus from Bondage: Luke 9:31 and Acts 12:1-24," *Catholic Biblical Quarterly* 52 (1990): 656-80.

fourth possible interpretation, laid out in Chapter 3 above, holds that although Jesus was not the object or bearer of God's wrath, God did look favorably on Jesus' endurance until death, and so regarded that death as a perfect sacrifice that has atoned for the people's sin and has made all other cultic sacrifices obsolete. Although I would not rule out any of the interpretations given above,[42] I have tried to demonstrate that the fourth option coheres particularly well with Mark's narrative as a whole. Such a reading is consistent with the cultic terminology of Mark 10:45 and 14:24. It is also consistent with Mark's portrayal of Jesus as one who endured trials — ranging in severity from the minor to the extreme — beginning with his testing in the wilderness and recurring up through his hour of utmost affliction on the cross. I have argued that in this portrayal Mark employed first-century interpretive conventions pertaining to testing and the endurance of testing (as well as to the effects of such endurance), which would have signaled to readers that Jesus was "tried and true" — one who persevered unto death in time of trial and whom God therefore regarded as a "proven" or "perfect" sacrifice.

Jesus' perfect sacrifice rendered the temple cult in Jerusalem — the old means of atoning for sin — obsolete. Twice in his narrative, Mark signals this imminent change in the status of the temple cult. The first such signal is in the account of Jesus' cleansing of the temple (11:15-19). When Jesus drives out the buyers and sellers in the temple, he says, "Is it not written, 'My house shall be called a house of prayer for all the nations'? But you have made it a den of robbers" (11:17). The incident is bracketed by Jesus' cursing of the fig tree that did not bear fruit (11:12-14) and the disciples' observation that the fig tree had withered (11:20-24). The implication is that the temple — which, like the fig tree, did not bear fruit — will also be destroyed. The second signal that the temple cult will not endure is the tearing of the temple veil at the moment of Jesus' death. Though there

---

42. Nor would I rule out still other readings not given here. The early Christians — including Mark's readers, and very likely Mark himself — took a "multiplicity of approaches" (borrowing Hengel's phrase: see n. 40 above) to Jesus's suffering and death. They viewed these various explanations as complementary rather than as mutually exclusive (by way of illustration, see the comments on Heb. 2:10-18, in Chap. 3, n. 46 above). Some early readers of Mark may indeed have inferred from this Gospel that Jesus bore the wrath of God, or that he gave himself as a covenant sacrifice, or that he was the leader (or: the paschal lamb) in a new Exodus — especially if those readers had some prior familiarity with such explanations. As I noted above (pp. 8-9), there is surely more than one successful path through Mark's narrative, though some paths may be straighter than others.

are certainly other ways that Mark's early readers could have read this symbol, taking it as prefigurative of the temple's destruction is most coherent with the temple-cleansing incident. Mark and his earliest readers would have known that the temple was not to be physically destroyed until decades after Jesus' earthly ministry; the tearing of the veil at the moment of death would have signified that the temple cult was defunct from the moment of the tearing forward.[43]

Because of Jesus' perfect sacrifice, his followers have been saved from the sin that had blinded them. Their newly bestowed vision enables them to walk singlemindedly in the way of God's desiring, and to resist temptations when they come.[44] According to cultural convention among some Jews and Christians of Mark's day, persons who are blind to higher, spiritual truths — who "see" only that which is temporal and perishing — mistakenly suppose that the preservation of the flesh and the satisfaction of desire are the worthiest goals in life. Hence, "when trouble or persecution arises" (4:17), or when "the lure of wealth and the desire for other things come in" (4:19), such persons are easily seduced away from fidelity to God. *But persons whose eyes have been opened are not easily led astray.* They "see" that the weak flesh, with its passions and desires, belongs to the realm of the perishing and is the site of satanic assault and domination.[45] They know that, whatever befalls them, "the souls of the righteous are in the hand of God, and no torment will ever touch them" (Wis. 3:1). Thus, those who have been healed of spiritual blindness are more readily able to persevere in singleminded devotion to God's will.

The "vision" or "knowledge" that the risen Jesus gives to his disciples is not, however, an exemption from testing, nor is it a magic tool that brings successful endurance without effort. With every test to be faced by Mark's readers, there is the genuine possibility of going astray, or else the

43. On the tearing of the temple veil, see further Chap. 3 n. 80. For a concise and useful treatment of the temple-theme in Mark, see F. J. Matera, *Passion Narratives and Gospel Theologies* (New York: Paulist Press, 1986), 65-72.

44. On the Markan theme of new "vision" for the Christian community after Easter, cf. Senior, 151-52. The thematic connection between eyes/vision and singlemindedness was well established in Jewish and early Christian literature, as I elaborate in Garrett, " 'Lest the Light,' " esp. 98-100; E. S. Johnson, "Mark 10:46-52: Blind Bartimaeus," *Catholic Biblical Quarterly* 40 [1978]: 203, 200-201 [on the equation of "salvation" and the granting of spiritual vision]).

45. On the way early readers of Mark might have construed the spirit/flesh dichotomy, see above, p. 94.

test is not really a test. The vision and knowledge that Jesus brings do not erase from those of us who follow him the desire for life or for the good things of the earth; rather, they help us: (1) to put these into proper perspective; (2) to see how the powers that rule this world deceive us into overestimating the value of mundane life and of its pleasures; and (3) correctly to assess that value relative to the worth of salvation and eternal life. Doublemindedness will still arise for those who follow Jesus. Indeed, Mark has shown *Jesus himself* as one who experienced the deepest, most agonizing inner conflict when forced to choose between his own "way" and the "way of the Lord." After Easter, whenever the risen Jesus empowers the "blind" to "see," he does not put up a roadblock at the entrance to the wrong path. Rather, he enables us to see that there is another, better way (as he saw that there was a better way), and helps us to choose the narrow gate and difficult road, by showing us the "life" that lies at its end. When, in Gethsemane, Jesus chose to follow God's will, he moved from "doubleness" to "integrity," and so was able to endure the extreme suffering that would ensue. In the Christian community, those who follow Jesus in choosing God's will are likewise empowered to triumph over duplicity and embody singleminded devotion to God. The choice is not, however, a once-for-all choice, but one that must be made again and again, as believers confront ever-new situations of trial.

The Church — A House of Prayer for All Nations

I have already argued that Mark heralds the community of believers as the "house of prayer for all nations" (11:17), the new temple to be raised up by Jesus (14:58).[46] One can compare 1 Peter 2:4-5, which exhorts readers to "come to [Jesus], a living stone, though rejected by mortals yet chosen and precious in God's sight, and *like living stones, let yourselves be built into a spiritual house,* to be a holy priesthood, to offer spiritual sacrifices acceptable to God through Jesus Christ" (2 Pet. 2:4-5).[47] Mark, who in

46. Above, pp. 121-24. Regarding the argument that Mark sees the new community in terms of the "house" or "house church" (rather than in terms of a "new temple"), see Chap. 3 n. 79.

47. Senior, 26, likewise observes the thematic similarity of Mark's notion of a "living temple" to 1 Peter 2:4ff. (and also to Eph. 2:20).

12:10 likewise refers to the "rejected stone" of Psalm 118, implies that just such a "spiritual house" displaces the temple cult at the moment of Jesus' death, thereby altering forever the setting and the manner in which followers of Jesus will offer up their praises and sacrifices to God. *Singleminded prayer* is the hallmark of the new community, the temple built of living stones. But how might Mark and his readers have understood this notion of "singleminded prayer"? How did one go about praying in such a manner, and what were the consequences of such prayer for daily life? These questions deserve closer scrutiny.

Prayer That Moves Mountains (Mark 11:22-23)

When the fig tree that Jesus had cursed withered, Jesus said to the disciples,

> "Have faith in God. Truly I tell you, if you say to this mountain, 'Be taken up and thrown into the sea,' and if you do not doubt *[diakrinesthai]* in your heart, but believe that what you say will come to pass, it will be done for you. So I tell you, whatever you ask for in prayer, believe that you have received it, and it will be yours." (Mark 11:22-24)

Here Jesus promises that faithful prayer will be answered.[48] But his promise is qualified: *those who pray must not doubt in their hearts.* The word used for "doubt" is *diakrinesthai,* which in contemporaneous discussions about faith or prayer means to waver in one's conviction, to lack confidence that God will do as requested.[49] The word *diakrinesthai* is used in Romans 4:20 in this sense, in Paul's comment regarding the faith of Abraham: "No distrust made him waver *[ou diekrithē tē apistia]* concerning the promise of God, but he grew strong in his faith as he gave glory to God, being fully convinced that God was able to do what he had promised." The author of the epistle of James also uses the term "doubt" in this sense, contending that those who "doubt in their hearts" are "doubleminded" *(dipsychos),* and must not expect to have their prayers answered:

---

48. See the discussion of this passage (drawing on S. E. Dowd, *Prayer, Power, and the Problem of Suffering: Mark 11:22-25 in the Context of Markan Theology* [Atlanta: Scholars Press, 1988]), above, pp. 121-23. On the notion in ancient Judaism of prayer as a means to combat testing, see Korn, 74.

49. In the majority of its occurrences in the New Testament and contemporaneous texts, the word means "to discern" or "to make distinctions, or judgments."

If any of you is lacking in wisdom, ask God, who gives to all generously and ungrudgingly, and it will be given you. But ask in faith, never doubting *[mēden diakrinomenos]*, for the one who doubts is like a wave of the sea, driven and tossed by the wind; for the doubter, being doubleminded *[dipsychos]* and unstable in every way, must not expect to receive anything from the Lord." (James 1:5-8)

For this author, doubt and doublemindedness go hand-in-hand; both betray a heart that is not wholly committed to God.

The notion that "doubt" is sinful may strike modern readers as ridiculous or even offensive, for complex cultural reasons. These reasons include our tendency to understand "faith" as cognitive assent to sets of propositions — propositions that have, for many persons since the Enlightenment, seemed to be problematic. But for ancient Christians and Jews, the problem of duplicity and correlated doubt was more a question of alliance or commitment than it was one of intellect. As Oscar Seitz remarks, "When the doubleminded man approaches God in prayer he wavers or hesitates; his heart is in need of purification because his motives are mixed; his mind is not wholly turned to God because of his desire for other things, especially the wealth and pleasures of the world."[50] Doubt and doublemindedness were thought by Jewish and Christian writers from this era to have several pernicious effects. First, the doubleminded person is easily tempted.[51] Second, doubt fosters a longing to put God to the test — to see whether God (or God's servant) will really perform as promised. Hence, the author of Wisdom of Solomon opens his book with this exhortation: "Love righteousness, you rulers of the earth, think of the Lord in goodness and seek him with singlemindedness *[haplotes]* of heart; because he is found by those who do not put him to the test, and manifests himself to those who do not distrust him."[52] Third, doubt compromises one's ability to endure suffering. The one who

---

50. O. J. F. Seitz, "Antecedents and Signification of the Term ΔΙΨΥΧΟΣ," *Journal of Biblical Literature* 66 (1947): 214. Seitz calls attention especially to James 1:8 and *Hermas Mandate* 9.

51. See above, pp. 22-23, 96-98.

52. Wis. 1:1-2; here I interpret the word for "to distrust" *(apistein)* as equivalent in meaning to the word for "to doubt" *(diakrinesthai)*. I discuss the connection between doublemindedness and putting the Lord to the test above, pp. 22-23, 62), and in Garrett, "'Lest the Light,'" 101-3.

doubts God's promise to save from distess will more easily succumb to the temptation to apostasize, to curse God, or otherwise to disobey God's commands — but it is only the one who endures or stands firm in trials who will receive a heavenly reward (James 1:2-4, 12). Thus, in the *Testament of Job,* when Job's wife exhorts him to "speak some word against the Lord and die," Job says to her that Satan "seeks to make an exhibit of you as one of the senseless women who lead their husbands astray from singlemindedness" (*T. Job* 26:6). Job recognizes that to give in to Satan's temptation by doubting God's eventual mercy would, in Job's own words, alienate him from "the truly great wealth." He would forfeit his heavenly reward.53

Thus, when Jesus exhorts the disciples to "have faith in God," he is exhorting them to have *singleminded faith.* The temple cult will be displaced by the community of persons who pray in *this* fashion — not doubting in their hearts, but believing that what they say will come to pass. But how does one "get" singleminded faith? By what means can one insure that one will not "doubt in one's heart"?

"I Believe — Help My Unbelief!"

In Mark's Gospel, Jesus speaks about singleminded faith on one occasion prior to the withering of the fig tree. When Jesus came down from the mount of transfiguration, he found the disciples with "a great crowd gathered around them, and some scribes arguing with them" (Mark 9:14). It seems that someone from the crowd had brought his demoniac son to be healed; the father had asked Jesus' disciples to cast it out, but they were not strong enough. Jesus then answered, "You faithless [*apistos*] generation, how much longer must I be among you? How much longer must I put up with you? Bring him to me" (4:19).54 At Jesus' command, the man brought the boy, explained his symptoms, and beseeched Jesus to help the two of them. Jesus responded, "If you are able! — *All things are possible* for the one who believes" (9:23 [italics added]). This formu-

---

53. See also *Hermas Mandate* 4.2.6: here an angel exhorts the author, "Believe on the Lord, you who are double-minded, that he can do all things, and turns his wrath away from you, and sends scourges on you who are double-minded" (trans. K. Lake in LCL, *The Apostolic Fathers,* 2.65).

54. On how Jesus' rebukes of "this generation" echo Moses' rebuke of the Israelites in Deuteronomy 32:4-5, 20, see p. 23 (incl. n. 6) above.

lation is similar to the one at 11:22-24, in which Jesus promises that God answers *singleminded prayer.* The similar phrasing indicates that also in this incident with the demoniac child, Jesus is speaking about the urgent need for singlemindedness. After hearing Jesus' proclamation, "immediately the father of the child cried out, 'I believe; help my unbelief!'" (9:24). This petition for Jesus to "help my unbelief" is itself a request for singlemindedness — or, more precisely, for the healing of doublemindedness, of doubt. For Mark's readers, then and now, the incident suggests that *the way to achieve singleminded faith is to ask for it in prayer.* (There is an element of circularity here: one needs to pray singlemindedly, but the very means to attaining singlemindedness is to ask for it in prayer.) The demoniac's father doubted, but received answer to his prayer in spite of his unbelief. His experience gives reason for confidence that God responds also to those who do not feel an inner certitude that their prayer will be answered.[55]

"Take Up Your Cross and Follow Me"

Jesus promises his readers that they will be the "house of prayer for all nations" and that their prayer will be characterized by singlemindedness. Because they devote themselves fully to God, with no fraction of the self wavering in this commitment, they can trust God to support them in times of trial by answering their prayer. Because their eyes are open to the dangers on every side, Satan will not easily lead them astray from perseverance on "the way of the Lord." But Jesus' promises come at a steep price. The price is the entire self, which must be given up for God:

> "If any want to become my followers, let them deny themselves and take up their cross and follow me. For those who want to save their life will lose it, and those who lose their life for my sake, and for the sake of the gospel, will save it. For what will it profit them to gain the whole world and forfeit their life? Indeed, what can they give in return for their life?" (8:34-37)

55. On prayer as the means for healing doublemindedness, see also above, p. 97. The reference to the need for prayer at the conclusion of the healing incident (9:29) confirms that Mark is using the episode to comment to his readers on the efficacy of — and means to — singleminded prayer.

The one who "denies the self" is the one who commits to following God's will, wherever it may lead. Jesus illustrates such self-denying commitment to God's will in Gethsemane, when he prays his twofold prayer:

> And going a little farther, he threw himself on the ground and prayed that, if it were possible, the hour might pass from him. He said, "Abba, Father, for you all things are possible; remove this cup from me; yet, not what I want, but what you want." (14:35-36)

Here Jesus denies his flesh's desire to live, and submits himself to the will of God. In doing so he makes a deliberate choice for "simplicity" or "singleness" of self. Mark does not record a version of the "Lord's prayer" as known from Matthew and from Luke; for Mark, this prayer in Gethsemane *is* the "Lord's prayer." It is a model of how "disciples on trial" ought to pray.[56]

For Mark's readers, there are enormous consequences for praying such a prayer. The earlier passages, about the man whose demoniac child was healed and about prayer that moves mountains, demonstrate that there are *no limits* to what God can do or to what believers can request. The God of Jesus and his followers is not a God inclined only to small miracles! In particular, we who follow Jesus can and should pray to God that we might avoid testing. On the other hand, when we have dedicated ourselves to singleminded service of the Lord, we must anticipate that the Lord may not will to "take away the cup." God may answer such a prayer to avoid testing not by removing the trial, but by giving us the strength to endure it (cf. 1 Cor. 10:13; 2 Cor. 12:9).[57] The price of Jesus' promise is steep, but so also is the reward, for those who lose their lives for Jesus and for the gospel have Jesus' assurance that they *will gain life back again* (Mark 8:35; 10:28-31).

---

56. See Chap. 3 n. 29.

57. In Paul's writings, the Holy Spirit is God's aid to believers who face trials of faith and obedience. In Mark's Gospel Jesus does not say much about the Holy Spirit as aid in time of trial, except in 13:11, where he promises that the one "handed over" to trial before authorities will be given words to say by the Spirit. But it is certainly possible that Mark takes it for granted that the Holy Spirit is present with believers, empowering them to persevere in all sorts of trials.

Conclusion

At the narrative level in Mark's Gospel, Jesus directs his message about impending trials to the twelve and to those who accompany them (that is, to persons in Jesus' own circle). But because Jesus utters these words in a prophetic mode — speaking of things that will come to pass after his own death and resurrection — the words have special relevance to disciples, in the period of Mark's church and even up to the present day. Thus, the "disciples on trial" to whom Jesus speaks in Mark's Gospel include the twelve disciples and all of us forever after who try to follow Jesus on the straight and narrow way of the Lord.

Mark portrays the twelve disciples as blinded by their iniquity, or (some might have inferred) by the devil, for the duration of Jesus' earthly ministry. Because of this blindness, the twelve were led astray in the hour of testing that commenced at Jesus' arrest: Judas betrayed Jesus, the disciples fled, Peter denied Jesus three times. But Mark's earliest real readers, I have argued, probably knew that eleven of the twelve disciples had returned to Jesus after the resurrection and had gone on to become great leaders in the church. Such readers might well have interpreted the postresurrection change in Jesus' disciples as proof of God's amazing grace. The disciples, once lost, had been found; once blind, could now see.

Mark implies that, during the era of the church, the context in which trials take place is fundamentally different than it had been for the twelve during Jesus' earthly ministry. Jesus' atoning death on the cross ransomed Jesus' followers from sin and so healed them of their blindness. No longer can they be easily deceived into thinking that flesh must be preserved and desires satisfied at any cost. Jesus' followers have open eyes; hence they can see Jesus clearly and follow him unswervingly. Moreover they are empowered by God whenever they engage in singleminded prayer (or: prayer for singlemindedness). Such followers constitute a new temple, made of living stones, with "the stone that the builders rejected" at its head. This new temple will be none other than the prophesied "house of prayer for all nations."

Conclusion

(Re)Telling the Old, Old Story

"The way of the Lord" is for Jesus a treacherous path that leads from the river Jordan to the cross. The path is treacherous because foe and friend alike seek to obstruct Jesus on it or to lead him astray from its straight and narrow course. Indeed, the only figures in Mark's Gospel who "make straight Jesus' path" are John the Baptist and the woman who anoints Jesus at Bethany: the Baptist, by preparing the people and by showing through his own example where Jesus' path will end; the anointing woman, by preparing Jesus for his arrival at that goal. All the other major figures in Mark "make a straight path crooked" by hindering Jesus or acting to divert him from the way. Satan initiates Jesus' trials during his sojourn in the wilderness. Human adversaries, blinded to Jesus' true identity, continue the testing in verbal exchanges and demands for signs of God's favor. And even the disciples of Jesus — well-intentioned but likewise unseeing — lay obstacles by resisting his prophecies of suffering and death.

Jesus perseveres throughout all such tests. He perseveres in the wilderness and is ministered to by angels. He endures the testing of his human enemies, never missing a step. He silences Peter when the disciple rebukes him for choosing the way of affliction, rejection, and death. In Gethsemane Jesus falters, but — strengthened through prayer — does not turn aside. Then, at the close of the Gethsemane episode, he is remanded from God's control to the control of sinners, and so enters into the ultimate hour of testing. He is mocked and tried by Jewish and Roman authorities, but still he endures. On the cross he cries out in pain and anguish at the separation

171

from God. But he refuses to sin with his lips; he remains faithful until the bitter end. Thus, by his endurance of all manner of testing, Jesus proves that he is indeed worthy to be called God's "beloved son." For he has chosen the way of God rather than a path of his own desiring. Jesus' choice does not represent the absence of a desire for his own prospering, conceived in human terms — on the contrary, Jesus longs to live! Rather, Jesus' choice represents his *deliberate laying aside* of his own desire in favor of God's desire for him: he prays, "Yet, not what I want, but what you want." God looks upon Jesus' singleminded devotion to God's will, sealed through faithfulness unto death, and accounts Jesus' sacrifice as acceptable and sufficient to ransom the many from their sin. God signals this acceptance by tearing the curtain of the temple, whose usefulness has now come to its end.

Jesus, in my story, is one "tested as we are, yet without sin." My story is itself a retelling or "rewriting" of another story — Mark's story. I do not claim to have laid bare the very mind of Mark or to have nailed down all his intentions in telling his story. On the other hand, I have not been afraid to make educated guesses about "what Mark was up to" at various points. Moreover I do profess to have read Mark in a manner consistent with certain cultural models or "interpretive conventions" that Mark and his readers might have shared.[1] One such cultural model (explored in Chapter 1 above) interprets the suffering of righteous persons as satanic testing. According to this model (which I have elsewhere called the "Job model" of affliction),[2] God permits Satan to put righteous servants of God to the test. God anticipates that the tested ones will persevere in faith and obedience, whereas Satan hopes — and works mightily to ensure — that they will fall away. Other assumptions are often correlated with this model of testing: assumptions regarding, to give examples, the fullness and the duration of Satan's authority over the righteous person, actions that would signal that person's apostasy, and Satan's reaction (typically one of shame) when he must concede his own defeat. A second cultural model that I have posited as relevant to Mark's Gospel (explored in Chapter 2 above)

---

1. Of course, as I have noted elsewhere, these "interpretive conventions" are themselves my own constructions, replicating perceived patterns in ancient texts. See my discussion of "cultural models" in S. R. Garrett, "Paul's Thorn and Cultural Models of Affliction," in *The Social World of the First Christians: Essays in Honor of Wayne A. Meeks,* ed. L. M. White and O. L. Yarbrough (Minneapolis: Fortress Press, 1995), esp. 86 n. 15.

2. See Garrett, "Paul's Thorn," 87-91.

narrates the story of a righteous sufferer who is being put to the test by certain wicked persons. These adversaries test the righteous one because they have first been "blinded" by the devil or by their own iniquity. They focus exclusively on mundane matters, especially the physical suffering and death of the righteous one. Hence, they are unable to perceive the higher meaning of events: that God has destined the sufferer for salvation and eternal life. A third interpretive convention (explored in Chapter 3 above) asserts that if the righteous sufferer obediently endures his or her testing, even unto death, God will regard that death as a perfect sacrifice. In two of the texts analyzed — Hebrews and 4 Maccabees — the vicarious atoning effect of the sufferer's death is made explicit.[3] By interpreting Mark in light of first-century interpretive conventions, I have written a story that may at least bear a family resemblance to the story that Mark's first readers (or even Mark himself) supposed him to have told.

Mark's Story of Jesus and Markan Theology

The path I have followed through Mark's story affords a new perspective on key features of the Markan landscape, including the Gospel's rendering of God, Christ, Christ's death as a saving event, the church, and Christian discipleship. I shall now elaborate each of these points, and then conclude with brief remarks on the opportunity and challenges facing theologians, pastors, and disciples who seek to apply Mark's wisdom to the present.

First, with respect to *Mark's vision of God:* Mark presents us with a God who permits testing to occur. God sends the son, the righteous one, "into the wilderness," where the "wild animals" dwell and where Satan is permitted to assault him so as to lead him astray. At the same time, God permits the sinful to continue on in their sin — in their blindness and hardness of heart — though it means that they will further test the righteous one. God finally even permits the son to be "given over" into the hands of those sinners, with the consequence that God's face is no longer

---

3. These three "interpretive conventions" and correlated assumptions, which I have artificially isolated, actually appear in various permutations and combinations in the ancient texts. For illustration of the point, see my study of thematic overlaps among Wisdom 2, *Testament of Job,* and 2 Corinthians in S. R. Garrett, "The God of This World and the Affliction of Paul: 2 Cor 4:1-12," in *Greeks, Romans, and Christians: Essays in Honor of Abraham J. Malherbe,* ed. David L. Balch et al. (Minneapolis: Fortress Press, 1990), 99-117.

seen, God's presence is no longer felt; this is the ultimate hour of testing. On the other hand, although permissive toward Satan and sinners, God is unyielding toward the son. God calls him to persevere on a straight and difficult path that leads to certain death — without, however, diminishing the son's passionate desire for life. Moreover, Mark teaches, the God who tested the son in such ways will surely also test those who seek to imitate the son's life and to follow in his steps. The life of disciples, like the life of Christ, is to be a life that includes times of testing. Or perhaps we should say with Dietrich Bonhoeffer that the trials of Christ's followers *are* the continuing trials of Christ. The disciples "will indeed suffer temptations, but it will be the temptations of Jesus Christ which befall them."[4]

Second, with respect to *Mark's vision of Christ:* We infer that Jesus' temptations were *real.* Repeatedly during his earthly life, Jesus had to choose whether he would follow God's path or another way; his consistently repeated choice of God's way was not automatic, and it demanded tremendous personal sacrifice. By acknowledging the reality of Jesus' temptations, we deepen our appreciation for him as fully human. Especially in Mark's Gethsemane account, we perceive that Jesus desired life no less than we. "In him was all desire and all fear of the flesh, all damnation of the flesh and alienation from God."[5] Jesus' desire forced a temporary split between God's will and Jesus' will. Jesus was — however briefly — "doubleminded" — that is, he wanted to live according to God's measure of goodness and according to his own, human measure of goodness at one and the same time. Thus he could say, "The spirit is willing but the flesh is weak." For us to assert that Jesus was doubleminded is not to claim that he sinned; rather, it is to declare that he found himself at the fork in the road where sin was a genuine option — at the place of temptation, or testing. In Gethsemane, Jesus decisively renounced the path of his own desiring by choosing instead the way of God. Thus, he attained singlemindedness not by avoiding doublemindedness but by conquering it. His choice for God was then proved, perfected in his judicial trials and in his hour on the cross. His will conformed to God's will until the end — indeed, Jesus cleaved to the purposes of God even when God pulled away from him.

Third, with respect to *Mark's vision of Jesus' death as a saving event:* Mark

---

4. D. Bonhoeffer, *Creation and Fall, and Temptation: Two Biblical Studies* (New York: Macmillan, 1959), 108.

5. Bonhoeffer, 103.

alludes to different biblical images or models that might be used to explain how and why Jesus' death "saves." For example, various interpreters have detected clues that Mark understands Jesus as one who bears God's wrath; or as a sacrifice given to ratify a new covenant; or as the paschal lamb whose sacrifice signals the new Exodus from bondage, the bondage of sin. I myself have highlighted Mark's portrayal of Jesus as tested and have interpreted his death as the culmination of perfect endurance and the basis for God's acceptance of that death as a healing, atoning sacrifice. I hope that in the course of my reading I have succeeded in walking a fine line: arguing for the plausibility (or even self-evidence) of my interpretation within a first-century Christian context, while still avoiding any suggestion that Mark employed but a *single* model for making sense of Jesus' death. Rather, I have contended, Mark and his readers took a "multiplicity of approaches" to solving the mystery of Jesus' death. The reason why it is so hard to pin Mark to a single soteriological model is because the early Christians drew on *various* images or models from scripture and culture in their interpretations of Jesus' death; this variety of approaches was not considered to be a problem. And so the consequences of Jesus' death can be summarized in different, complementary terms: he bore God's wrath for persons; he established a new covenant for them; he ransomed them from bondage; he healed their blindness. Whichever language one chooses to explain Jesus' death and resurrection in Mark, the consequence of that death and resurrection are that followers of Jesus are in a new position vis-à-vis both God and sin/Satan. Thenceforth Christians will not have to rely on their own meager powers as they seek to replicate Jesus' faithfulness in the inevitable trials to come.[6] For believers have been freed from the sin that clings so closely and are empowered through prayer to persevere on the straight and narrow way of the Lord.

Fourth, with respect to *Mark's vision of the church:* With a number of other interpreters, I hold that Mark portrays the church as the "house of prayer for all nations," which — in the wake of the temple cult's demise — is the place where God's faithful people may be found. The distinctive

---

6. The interpretation of Markan soteriology that I have offered here has interesting points of connection with the argument that several or all of Paul's references to *pistis tou christou* refer to the "faith(fulness) of Jesus Christ" as effective for our salvation (rather than referring to *our* faith *in* Christ; this view was anticipated in S. K. Williams, *Jesus' Death as a Saving Event: The Background and Origin of a Concept* [Missoula, Mont.: Scholars Press, 1975], 47-50, and developed by R. B. Hays in *The Faith of Jesus Christ* [Chico, Calif.: Scholars Press, 1983], and by others since).

element offered by my construction is its emphasis on the *singlemindedness* of the prayer carried on in this new "house of prayer." The prayer in which Christians engage is the prayer of persons whose blindness has been healed. (Here I build on the close association in early Jewish and Christian discourse between "singlemindedness" and "singleness of vision.") Those whose eyes have been opened are ones who "see" things as God sees them, who set their minds not on mundane, human things but on higher, divine things. In answer to their singleminded prayer (or their prayer for singlemindedness), they have been granted a clear vision of what is at stake in their trials: they perceive with inner sight the deception Satan uses to try to lead them astray, as well as the "life" and the "salvation" that God grants to those who persevere in obedience and faith. Mark holds that the singleminded vision of Jesus' followers is essential if the church is to stay "on track" as it moves into the anticipated period of eschatological trial.

Fifth, with respect to *Mark's vision of discipleship:* Mark's view of discipleship is conveyed in and through his depiction of the twelve. In Mark's portrayal of Jesus' earthly ministry, I have argued, his disciples are never fully healed of their blindness. Because they remain partially blind, they do not comprehend the necessity of Jesus' suffering, and so do not not help him as he seeks to travel on God's way. Indeed they even put him to the test. In reading the story this way, I place myself with those scholars who perceive Mark's depiction of the disciples as a negative one. Differently than some such scholars, however, I contend that Mark does expect his readers to know — indeed, to take it quite for granted — that subsequent to Jesus' death and resurrection the disciples were redeemed. Readers would have known that after the resurrection the disciples came to singleminded sight and guided others on the way of the Lord. Thus I offer another "solution" to the perennial problem in Markan scholarship of the portrayal of the disciples: in my reading the disciples are not stand-ins for heretics, or fallible followers, or rocky ground that bears no lasting fruit, but *soon-to-be recipients of God's amazing grace.* Blind, they will soon see. In telling their story, I have argued, Mark concentrates on the "before snapshot" — the picture of them while the scales were still on their eyes. But Mark has given strong hints of their eventual healing, hints that would have been taken up by readers who revered the disciples as leaders of Christ's church. By portraying so vividly the failures of the disciples during Jesus' ministry, Mark magnifies and commends the grace and power of God, which was able to transform these outsiders into servant-leaders of the church. Further, by depicting the disciples in such a way, Mark reminds those of us who also claim to be Jesus' followers that we, too, are ones who have been called out of darkness and into God's marvelous light.

But Mark also reminds us that our reception of God's mercy at baptism does not mean that thereafter the uneven places will automatically be made level and the rough places a plain. The evangelist's description of eschatological events in chapter 13 uses a number of terms and images that were closely associated with testing/temptation in Jewish and early Christian discourse. By using such language Mark emphasizes that followers of Jesus must expect to undergo times of testing. Moreover, for us, as for Christ, the tests will be *real:* the spirit will lead us into the wilderness, into solitude, into abandonment. As Bonhoeffer writes, "For a little while the devil has room."[7] Jesus' first disciples failed their tests of fidelity to him because of their habit of setting their minds not on divine things but on human things. "Setting one's mind on human things" doesn't mean that one has no idea what God desires; all too often, one knows God's will but resists giving up one's own vision of the future, if giving it up means that one must suffer or deprive oneself in some way. So Peter vowed that he would die with Jesus rather than betray him; yet, in the critical moment in the courtyard of the high priest, he found that he could not persevere in his intention. As Christians we, too, experience times of severe testing: in such an hour we know the way of God, but another path, a path of our own choosing, impresses itself on our mind, till we think we cannot ignore it. And thus our doublemindedness — our divided soul — threatens to undo us. We lurch first one way and then another, careening now after our intention to follow God's way, and now after our intention to fulfill our own desire. "So the Christian recognizes the cunning of Satan. Suddenly doubt has been sowed in his heart, suddenly everything is uncertain . . . suddenly evil desire is wakened, and suddenly the Cross is upon me and I tremble. This is the hour of temptation, of darkness, of defenceless deliverance into Satan's hands."[8]

---

7. Bonhoeffer, 98.

8. Bonhoeffer, 99. Bonhoeffer does not explicitly bring in the notion of doublemindedness, but his description of the experience of temptation (in the passage quoted above and elsewhere in the cited work) is evocative of biblical descriptions of doublemindedness, especially the description found in Romans 7. Unlike Mark, Bonhoeffer does not highlight *prayer* as a means to conquer in times of testing; rather, he stresses our union with Christ. God has indeed answered our prayer to "lead us not into temptation," for it is no longer *we* who are tempted, but *"Jesus Christ is tempted in us"* (Bonhoeffer, 107 [italics original]).

Prayer — the hallmark of those who inhabit the "house of prayer for all nations" — is the answer that the Jesus of Mark's Gospel offers to this dilemma. Jesus prayed in Gethsemane, when his own distress and anguish threatened to engulf him, and in that way he became victorious over the death-dealing forces. So also, Mark suggests, we who follow Jesus must see that, on account of his endurance, we ourselves may be victorious over the forces that divide us internally and threaten to separate us from the love and the will of God. God regarded Christ's perfect sacrifice as sufficient to ransom us from the blinding power of sin. Therefore our prayers for singlemindedness shall be granted; we shall be enabled to see Jesus clearly and to follow him unswervingly on the straight and narrow way of the Lord.

And what if believers do *not* endure in time of trial? In other words, what if they succumb to the forces that continually confront them with seductive images of power or wealth or pleasure or that assault them with blows of affliction? Surely Mark's Gospel permits us to answer by insisting on the graciousness of God in looking past such human failings. When we put God to the test, God, who could forgive and transform the twelve, will persevere in forgiving and transforming us. God regarded Jesus' willing death as the perfect sacrifice and accounted it as sufficient to atone for human sin — even the sin of those who, having once seen the light, willingly step back into darkness. (Compare the position of Paul, that Christians are no longer enslaved to the power of sin, to do its bidding, though they might willingly — albeit foolishly — put themselves again under sin's mastery [Rom. 6]. Such ones could apparently be "restored" to the community [Gal. 6:1].) Thus by grace God opens person's eyes and by grace God also pardons them should they, nonetheless, go astray.

Mark does not, however, expect that failure to endure in time of trial will *typify* Christian existence. Much more his Gospel anticipates that Christians will meet their inevitable trials with heightened perception (10:51-52; see above, pp. 82-87), with humble prayers for strength and singlemindedness (9:24; see above, pp. 166-67), and with confidence that they can scarcely fail, inasmuch as Christ has already won the victory. Mark's apparent hopefulness that after the resurrection believers will be empowered to endure testing differs from the emphasis of Luther and other Reformation thinkers on Christians' continuing moral weakness. Mark seems to regard endurance in time of trial as the norm for Christian existence (i.e., existence after the resurrection/after conversion) and failure as the occasional but startling exception.[9] For Mark, as for other Gospel writers, testing/temptation recurs even after Easter (or after conversion), because the forces of evil continue to try to undermine God's work, but victory over those forces is guaranteed wherever Christians participate in Christ's accomplished victory over them.[10]

The Old, Old Story — Our Story Too?

At the outset of this study, I suggested that in telling a story of Jesus as "tested through what he suffered," Mark addressed certain questions about perception and imperception that must have pressed upon early converts to Christianity: How could the historical enemies of Jesus have failed to perceive his unique place in God's plan? How could the Christians' *own* enemies be blind to this truth? How could the first disciples of Jesus have been so ignorant and stubborn? How could new Christians themselves once have been so unseeing and obstinate? Finally — and perhaps most pressing of all — how could believers rely upon their own perceptions of right belief and action in moments of personal or communal crisis, when doubt and uncertainty seemed to invade and take hold? In the course of the study I have tried to show how Mark answers these questions through his use of metaphors of blindness and of sight and his portrayals of fickleness and of singleminded devotion to God's will.

In the process of answering these questions, Mark invites readers to find

9. Luther, notably, read the dilemma of weakness of will in Romans 7 as typifying Christian (postconversion) existence. In my reading of Paul, the weakness of will described in Romans 7 characterizes human existence *prior to* conversion, and in fact is the very dilemma from which Christ delivers us (cf. J. C. Beker, *Paul the Apostle: The Triumph of God in Life and Thought* [Philadelphia: Fortress Press, 1980], 216-18, for an interpretation of Romans 7 consistent with my position). Thus my reading of Paul parallels my reading of Mark on this question of whether Christians can be expected to persevere in times of trial. On how Luther's reading of Romans 7 has influenced subsequent interpretations, see K. Stendahl, "The Apostle Paul and the Introspective Conscience of the West," *Harvard Theological Review* 56 (1973): 199-215.

10. For development of this thesis with respect to Luke, see S. R. Garrett, *The Demise of the Devil: Magic and the Demonic in Luke's Writings* (Minneapolis, Fortress Press, 1989); with respect to Ephesians, see C. E. Arnold, *Ephesians: Power and Magic: The Concept of Power in Ephesians in Light of Its Historical Setting* (Cambridge: Cambridge University Press, 1989).

a place for themselves and others in Jesus' story. The evangelist casts members of his audience into the role of "tested followers," ones whose commitment and loyalty to Jesus are tested, but who persevere in times of trial because their eyes have been opened to see the path before them and to follow (or: to aid) Jesus on it. Of course, as I noted in the Introduction, it is possible that readers whose eyes have been opened through the reading of Mark's Gospel will see that they have heretofore been filling another role, such as the role of one who puts Jesus to the test. Moreover, today we may not find it such an easy thing to step into the proferred role of "tested follower." We may find ourselves resisting Mark's narration at various points and for various reasons. For example, one sort of resistance may center on Mark's portrayal (as I have constructed it) of God as a testing God. In the course of teaching Mark's Gospel, I have discovered that many persons do not want to see God implicated, even indirectly, in the "bad things" that so often happen to "good people."[11] Similarly, some contemporary theologians may object to the aloofness of a God who would permit the testing/suffering of Jesus on the cross, preferring instead to see God as one who through Jesus *enters into* the human condition of sin and suffering, healing us from within.[12] A different sort of objection to Mark's story might center on the evangelist's portrayal (again, as I have constructed it) of Jesus as "doubleminded" in Gethsemane, inasmuch as such a rendering of Jesus' words and demeanor may come too close to an assertion that Jesus sinned. The public outcry at Scorsese's film *The Last Temptation of Christ* demonstrated that many Christians are made deeply uncomfortable by any such assertion. Yet another objection may be raised against the optimism I find in Mark that

---

11. I have found that when I rephrase the argument ("What if we said not that God causes trials, but that God would have us *interpret* our times of suffering or our times of forbidden desire as instances of trial?"), objections diminish.

12. Note also that some feminist scholars have objected to the implication of atonement theories that God willed for the Son to suffer, arguing that such a stance by God amounts to divine child abuse and that such notions of atonement have long functioned (and continue to function) to reinforce patriarchal structures in which the weak, especially women, must submit to violent abuse by men. For a quick summary of such views, see L. Van Dyk, "Do Theories of Atonement Foster Abuse?" *Perspectives* 12, no. 2 (1997): 11-13. For a helpful discussion of the place of atonement models in NT interpretations of Jesus' death and in recent theology (including feminist theology), see J. T. Carroll and J. B. Green, *The Death of Jesus in Early Christianity* (Peabody, Mass.: Hendrickson Publishers, 1995), 256-79.

Christians who call on Christ will be empowered to persevere during trials. Such optimism not only is out of sync with a Lutheran and Reformed understanding, but also may seem unjustified in view of the spectacular rate of *failure* to persevere in testing that is exhibited by modern Christians, both in the public eye and out of it.

Just as the early Christians took a "multiplicity of approaches" in their efforts to explain the significance of Jesus' ministry and death, so must we. Therefore potential objections to my interpretation of Mark's Gospel, such as the ones raised above, could play an important and helpful role in any effort at constructive theology that makes use of the interpretation. Such corrections would balance the Markan scheme as I have delineated it. Still, these and other objections would not necessarily invalidate that scheme. For although the Markan scheme (like all such models of salvation) is imperfect, it conveys aspects of the truth in an especially pointed and edifying way. Mark's story of Jesus as "tested as we are, yet without sin" teaches us to interpret our times of suffering or our times of forbidden desire differently — and to respond to such experiences more faithfully — than would otherwise be possible. Our society discourages us from being reflective about such experiences or from striving to meet them with perseverance in the straight and narrow path. Indeed, today we are bombarded with messages that we ought not to suffer (even for a legitimate cause), ought not to deny ourselves, ought in fact to possess whatever eases our pain or offers us pleasure. But Mark does not permit us to choose, unreflectively, the wide and easy path. He informs us that our difficult times are nothing less than a test of our fidelity, or singlemindedness — a test whose outcome *matters to God.* Mark further admonishes us to take care lest we become ones who put others, or Christ, to the test. Finally, Mark reminds us that we are ones who walk in the light. Because Jesus endured in time of trial, the forces that would keep us in darkness need no longer have power over us. God answers our prayers for new vision and enables us to set our minds not on human things but on things divine.

Bibliography

Achtemeier, P. J. *Mark*. 2nd ed. Philadelphia: Fortress Press, 1986.

Amstutz, J. ΑΠΛΟΤΗΣ: *Eine begriffsgeschichtliche Studie zum jüdisch-christlichen Griechisch*. Bonn: Peter Hanstein, 1968.

Anderson, J. C., and S. D. Moore, eds. *Mark & Method: New Approaches in Biblical Studies*. Minneapolis: Fortress Press, 1992.

Arnold, C. E. *Ephesians: Power and Magic: The Concept of Power in Ephesians in Light of Its Historical Setting*. Cambridge: Cambridge University Press, 1989.

Attridge, H. W. *The Epistle to the Hebrews*. Philadelphia: Fortress Press, 1989.

Austin, J. L. *How to Do Things with Words*. Cambridge: Harvard University Press, 1975.

Barbour, R. S. "Gethsemane in the Tradition of the Passion." *New Testament Studies* 16 (1969–70): 231-51.

Barr, J. "The Question of Religious Influence: The Case of Zoroastrianism, Judaism, and Christianity." *Journal of the American Academy of Religion* 53 (1985): 201-35.

Bassler, J. M. "The Parable of the Loaves." *Journal of Religion* 66 (1986): 157-72.

Beavis, M. A. *Mark's Audience: The Literary and Social Setting of Mark 4.11-12*. Sheffield: JSOT Press, 1989.

Beker, J. C. *Paul the Apostle: The Triumph of God in Life and Thought*. Philadelphia: Fortress Press, 1980.

Berger, K. "Die Königlichen Messiastraditionen des Neuen Testaments." *New Testament Studies* 20 (1974): 1-44.

Bertram, G. "παιδεύω κτλ." In *The Theological Dictionary of the New Testament*. Vol. 5. Grand Rapids: William B. Eerdmans, 1967.

Best, E. *Following Jesus: Discipleship in the Gospel of Mark*. Sheffield: JSNT Press, 1981.

Best, E. *The Temptation & the Passion: The Markan Soteriology*. 2nd ed. Cambridge: Cambridge University Press, 1990.

Black, C. C. *The Disciples According to Mark: Markan Redaction in Current Debate*. Sheffield: JSOT Press, 1989.

Bonhoeffer, D. *Creation and Fall, and Temptation: Two Biblical Studies*. New York: Macmillan, 1959.

Boucher, M. *The Mysterious Parable: A Literary Study*. Washington: Catholic Biblical Quarterly, 1977.

Brown, C. A. *No Longer Be Silent: First Century Jewish Portraits of Biblical Women*. Louisville: Westminster/John Knox Press, 1992.

Brown, R. E. *The Death of the Messiah: From Gethsemane to the Grave*. New York: Doubleday, 1994.

Bultmann, R. *Theology of the New Testament*. 2 vols. Trans. Kendrick Grobel. New York: Scribner's, 1951.

Carroll, J. T., and J. B. Green. *The Death of Jesus in Early Christianity*. Peabody, Mass.: Hendrickson Publishers, 1995.

Carson, A. "Putting Her in Her Place: Woman, Dirt, and Desire." In *Before Sexuality: The Construction of Erotic Experience in the Ancient Greek World*, ed. David M. Halperin et al., 135-69. Princeton: Princeton University Press, 1990.

Cathcart, K. J. "Day of Yahweh." In *Anchor Bible Dictionary*. Vol. 2. New York: Doubleday, 1992.

Charlesworth, J. H., ed. *The Old Testament Pseudepigrapha*. 2 vols. Garden City, N.Y.: Doubleday, 1983, 1985.

Chatman, S. *Story and Discourse: Narrative Structure in Fiction and Film*. Ithaca: Cornell University Press, 1978.

Chronis, H. L. "The Torn Veil: Cultus and Christology in Mark 15:37-39." *Journal of Biblical Literature* 101 (1982): 97-114.

Collins, A. Y. *The Combat Myth in the Book of Revelation*. Missoula, Mont.: Scholars Press, 1976.

Collins, A. Y. *The Beginning of the Gospel: Probings of Mark in Context*. Minneapolis: Fortress Press, 1992.

Collins, J. J. "The Mythology of Holy War in Daniel and the Qumran

War Scroll: A Point of Transition in Jewish Apocalyptic." *Vetus Testamentum* 25 (1975): 596-612.

Culpepper, R. A. *Anatomy of the Fourth Gospel: A Study in Literary Design.* Philadelphia: Fortress Press, 1983.

Dahl, N. A. "The Atonement — An Adequate Reward for the Akedah? (Ro 8:32)." In *Neotestamentica et Semitica: Studies in Honor of Matthew Black,* ed. E. E. Ellis and M. Wilcox, 15-29. Edinburgh: T. & T. Clark, 1969.

Dahl, N. A. *Jesus in the Memory of the Early Church.* Minneapolis: Augsburg Publishing House, 1976.

Day, P. L. *An Adversary in Heaven: śāṭān in the Hebrew Bible.* Atlanta: Scholars Press, 1988.

Denis, A. M. *Fragmenta pseudepigraphorum quae supersunt graeca.* Leiden: E. J. Brill, 1970.

Dillon, R. J. "Easter Revelation and Mission Program in Luke 24:46-48." In *Sin, Salvation, and the Spirit,* ed. D. Durken, 240-70. Collegeville, Minnesota: The Liturgical Press, 1979.

Donahue, J. R. *Are You the Christ? The Trial Narrative in the Gospel of Mark.* Missoula, Mont.: Scholars Press, 1973.

Donahue, J. R. "Temple, Trial, and Royal Christology (Mark 14:53-65)." In *The Passion in Mark: Studies on Mark 14–16,* ed. W. H. Kelber, 61-79. Philadelphia: Fortress Press, 1976.

Donahue, J. R. *The Theology and Setting of Discipleship in the Gospel of Mark.* Milwaukee: Marquette University Press, 1983.

Dowd, S. E. *Prayer, Power, and the Problem of Suffering: Mark 11:22-25 in the Context of Markan Theology.* Atlanta: Scholars Press, 1988.

Fish, S. *Is There a Text In This Class? The Authority of Interpretive Communities.* Cambridge: Harvard University Press, 1980.

Forsyth, N. *The Old Enemy: Satan and the Combat Myth.* Princeton: Princeton University Press, 1987.

Fowler, R. M. *Let the Reader Understand: Reader-Response Criticism and the Gospel of Mark.* Minneapolis: Fortress Press, 1991.

Freyne, S. "The Disciples in Mark and the *maskilim* in Daniel: A Comparison." *Journal for the Study of the New Testament* 16 (1982): 7-23.

Garland, D. E. *Mark.* Grand Rapids: Zondervan, 1996.

Garrett, S. R. *The Demise of the Devil: Magic and the Demonic in Luke's Writings.* Minneapolis: Fortress Press, 1989.

Garrett, S. R. "Exodus from Bondage: Luke 9:31 and Acts 12:1-24." *Catholic Biblical Quarterly* 52 (1990): 656-80.

Garrett, S. R. "The God of This World and the Affliction of Paul: 2 Cor 4:1-12." In *Greeks, Romans, and Christians: Essays in Honor of Abraham J. Malherbe,* ed. David L. Balch et al., 99-117. Minneapolis: Fortress Press, 1990.

Garrett, S. R. " 'Lest the Light in You Be Darkness': Luke 11:33-36 and the Question of Commitment." *Journal of Biblical Literature* 110 (1991): 93-105.

Garrett, S. R. "Paul's Thorn and Cultural Models of Affliction." In *The Social World of the First Christians: Essays in Honor of Wayne A. Meeks,* ed. L. M. White and O. L. Yarbrough, ed. Minneapolis: Fortress Press, 1995.

Garrett, S. R. "Sociology of Early Christianity." In *Anchor Bible Dictionary.* Vol. 6. New York: Doubleday, 1992.

Garrett, S. R. "The 'Weaker Sex' in the *Testament of Job.*" *Journal of Biblical Literature* 112 (1993): 55-70.

Garrett, S. R. "Review of *Christian Origins and Cultural Anthropology,* by Bruce J. Malina." *Journal of Biblical Literature* 107 (1988): 532-34.

Garrett, S. R. "Review of *Sowing the Gospel: Mark's World in Literary-Historical Perspective,* by Mary Ann Tolbert." *Princeton Seminary Bulletin* 12 (1991): 100-101.

Geddert, T. J. *Watchwords: Mark 13 in Markan Eschatology.* Sheffield: JSOT Press, 1989.

Gerhardsson, B. *The Testing of God's Son.* Lund: C. W. K. Gleerup, 1966.

Gibson, J. "Jesus' Refusal to Produce a 'Sign' (MK 8.11-13)." *Journal for the Study of the New Testament* 38 (1990): 37-66.

Gibson, J. "Jesus' Wilderness Temptation According to Mark." *Journal for the Study of the New Testament* 53 (1994): 3-34.

Gibson, J. *The Temptations of Jesus in Early Christianity.* Sheffield: Sheffield Academic Press, 1995.

Gnilka, J. *Das Evangelium nach Markus.* 2 vols. 3rd ed. Zürich: Benziger; Neukirchen-Vluyn: Neukirchener Verlag.

Gundry, R. H. *Mark: A Commentary on His Apology for the Cross.* Grand Rapids: William B. Eerdmans, 1993.

Gundry-Volf, J. M. *Paul and Perseverance: Staying In and Falling Away.* Louisville: Westminster/John Knox Press, 1990.

Hamilton, V. P. "Satan." In *Anchor Bible Dictionary.* Vol. 5. New York: Doubleday, 1992.

Handy, L. K. "Serpent (Religious Symbol)." In *Anchor Bible Dictionary.* Vol. 5. New York: Doubleday, 1992.

Hanson, A. T. *The Wrath of the Lamb.* London: SPCK, 1957.

Hanson, P. D. "Rebellion in Heaven, Azazel, and Euhemeristic Heroes in 1 Enoch 6–11." *Journal of Biblical Literature* 96 (1977): 195-233.

Hawkin, D. J. "The Incomprehension of the Disciples in the Markan Redaction." *Journal of Biblical Literature* 91 (1972): 491-500.

Hays, R. B. *The Faith of Jesus Christ.* Chico, Calif.: Scholars Press, 1983.

Hengel, M. *The Atonement: The Origins of the Doctrine in the New Testament.* Trans. John Bowden. Philadelphia: Fortress Press, 1981.

Hengel, M. *Judaism and Hellenism: Studies in their Encounter in Palestine during the Early Hellenistic Period.* 2 vols. Trans. John Bowden. Philadelphia: Fortress Press, 1974.

Holland, D., and N. Quinn, eds. *Cultural Models in Language and Thought.* Cambridge: Cambridge University Press, 1987.

Hollander, H. W., and M. de Jonge. *The Testaments of the Twelve Patriarchs: A Commentary.* Leiden: E. J. Brill, 1985.

Hooker, M. D. *Jesus and the Servant: The Influence of the Servant Concept of Deutero-Isaiah in the New Testament.* London: SPCK, 1959.

Hooker, M. D. *The Message of Mark.* London: Epworth Press, 1983.

Hultgren, A. *Christ and His Benefits: Christology and Redemption in the New Testament.* Philadelphia: Fortress Press, 1987.

Hurtado, L. W. "Following Jesus in the Gospel of Mark — and Beyond." In *Patterns of Discipleship in the New Testament,* ed. R. N. Longenecker, 9-29. Grand Rapids: William B. Eerdmans, 1996.

Jaeger, W. *Paideia: the Ideals of Greek Culture.* Trans. Gilbert Highet. Oxford: Basil Blackwell, 1939.

Jenks, G. C. *The Origins and Early Development of the Antichrist Myth.* Berlin: Walter de Gruyter, 1991.

Johnson, E. S. "Mark viii.22-26: The Blind Man from Bethsaida." *New Testament Studies* 25 (1979): 370-83.

Johnson, E. S. "Mark 10:46-52: Blind Bartimaeus." *Catholic Biblical Quarterly* 40 (1978): 191-204.

Johnson, L. T. *The Letter of James.* New York: Doubleday, 1995.

Joines, K. R. "The Serpent in Gen 3." *Zeitschrift für die alttestamentliche Wissenschaft* 87 (1975): 1-11.

Juel, D. H. *A Master of Surprise: Mark Interpreted.* Minneapolis: Fortress Press, 1994.

Juel, D. H. *Messiah and Temple: The Trial of Jesus in the Gospel of Mark.* Missoula, Mont.: Scholars Press, 1977.

Kelber, W. H. *The Kingdom in Mark: A New Place and a New Time.* Philadelphia: Fortress Press, 1974.

Kelber, W. H. *Mark's Story of Jesus.* Philadelphia: Fortress Press, 1979.

Kelber, W. H. *The Oral and the Written Gospel: The Hermeneutics of Speaking and Writing in the Synoptic Tradition, Mark, Paul, and Q.* Philadelphia: Fortress Press, 1983.

Kelly, H. A. "The Devil in the Desert." *Catholic Biblical Quarterly* 26 (1964): 190-220.

Kingsbury, J. D. *The Christology of Mark's Gospel.* Philadelphia: Fortress Press, 1983.

Kingsbury, J. D. *Conflict in Mark: Jesus, Authorities, Disciples.* Minneapolis: Fortress Press, 1989.

Klauck, H.-J. *Unterweisung in lehrhafter Form: 4. Makkabäerbuch.* Gütersloh: Gütersloher Verlagshaus Gerd Mohn, 1989.

Korn, J. H. ΠΕΙΡΑΣΜΟΣ, *Die Versuchung des Gläubigen in der gr. Bibel.* Stuttgart: W. Kohlhammer Verlag, 1937.

Kuhn, K. G. "New Light on Temptation, Sin, and Flesh in the New Testament." In *The Scrolls and the New Testament,* ed. K. Stendahl, 94-113. New York: Harper & Bros., 1957.

Kuhn, K. G. "Die Sektenschrift und die iranische Religion." *Zeitschrift für Theologie und Kirche* 49 (1952): 296-316.

Lane, W. L. *The Gospel of Mark.* Grand Rapids: William B. Eerdmans, 1974.

Lemaire, A. "Education (Israel)." In *Anchor Bible Dictionary.* Vol. 2. New York: Doubleday, 1992.

Levenson, J. D. *Creation and the Persistence of Evil.* San Francisco: Harper & Row, 1988.

Lewis, T. J. "Belial." In *Anchor Bible Dictionary.* Vol. 1. New York: Doubleday, 1992.

Lührmann, D. *Das Markusevangelium.* Tübingen: Mohr (Siebeck), 1987.

MacIntyre, A. "Epistemological Crises, Dramatic Narrative and the Philosophy of Science." *The Monist* 60 (1977): 453-72.

Malbon, E. S. "Disciples/Crowds/Whoever: Markan Characters and Readers." *Novum Testamentum* 28 (1986): 104-30.

Malbon, E. S. "Fallible Followers: Women and Men in the Gospel of Mark." *Semeia* 28 (1983): 29-48.

Malbon, E. S. "The Jewish Leaders in the Gospel of Mark: A Literary Study of Marcan Characterization." *Journal of Biblical Literature* 108 (1989): 419-41.

Malbon, E. S. "TH OIKIA AYTOY: Mark 2.15 in Context." *New Testament Studies* 31 (1985): 282-92.

Marcus, J. "The Evil Inclination in the Epistle of James." *Catholic Biblical Quarterly* 44 (1982): 606-21.

Marcus, J. "The Jewish War and the Sitz im Leben of Mark." *Journal of Biblical Literature* 111 (1992): 441-62.

Marcus, J. "Mark 4:10-12 and Marcan Epistemology." *Journal of Biblical Literature* 103 (1984): 557-74.

Marcus, J. *The Mystery of the Kingdom of God.* Atlanta: Scholars Press, 1986.

Marcus, J. *The Way of the Lord: Christological Exegesis of the Old Testament in the Gospel of Mark.* Louisville: Westminster/ John Knox Press, 1992.

Marrou, H. I. *A History of Education in Antiquity.* New York: Mentor Books, 1964.

Martin, D. B. *The Corinthian Body.* New Haven: Yale University Press, 1995.

Martyn, J. L. "Epistemology at the Turn of the Ages: 2 Corinthians 5:16." In *Christian History and Interpretation: Studies Presented to John Knox,* ed. W. R. Farmer et. al. Cambridge: University Press, 1967.

Martyn, J. L. *History and Theology in the Fourth Gospel.* Rev. and enlarged ed. Nashville: Abingdon Press, 1979.

Matera, F. J. "The Incomprehension of the Disciples and Peter's Confession (Mark 6,14–8,30)." *Biblica* 70 (1989): 153-72.

Matera, F. J. *Passion Narratives and Gospel Theologies.* New York: Paulist Press, 1986.

Maurer, C. "Knecht Gottes und Sohn Gottes im Passionsbericht des Marcusevangelium." *Zeitschrift für Theologie und Kirche* 50 (1953): 1-38.

Mauser, U. *Christ in the Wilderness: The Wilderness Theme in the Second Gospel and its Basis in the Biblical Tradition.* Naperville, Ill.: Alec R. Allenson, 1963.

Meeks, W. A. *The Prophet-King: Moses Traditions and the Johannine Christology.* Leiden: E. J. Brill, 1967.

Miller, P. D., Jr. *The Divine Warrior in Early Israel*. Cambridge: Harvard University Press, 1973.

Moore, S. D. *Literary Criticism and the Gospels: The Theoretical Challenge*. New Haven: Yale University Press, 1989.

Mullen, E. T., Jr. "Divine Assembly." *Anchor Bible Dictionary*. Vol. 2. New York: Doubleday, 1992.

Neyrey, J. *The Passion According to Luke: A Redaction Study of Luke's Soteriology*. New York: Paulist Press, 1985.

Nussbaum, M. C. *The Therapy of Desire: Theory and Practice in Hellenistic Ethics*. Princeton: Princeton University Press, 1994.

Oates, W. E. *Temptation: A Biblical and Psychological Approach*. Louisville: Westminster/John Knox Press, 1991.

Pagels, E. *The Origin of Satan*. New York: Random House, 1995.

Peretti, F. E. *This Present Darkness*. Westchester, Ill.: Crossway Books, 1986.

Pesch, R. *Das Markusevangelium*. 2 vols. Freiburg: Herder, 1976.

Petersen, N. R. "When is the End Not an End? Literary Reflections on the Ending of Mark's Narrative." *Interpretation* 34 (1980): 151-66.

Pfitzner, V. C. *Paul and the Agon Motif*. Leiden: E. J. Brill, 1967.

Plato. *The Collected Dialogues of Plato*. Ed. E. Hamilton and H. Cairns. Princeton: Princeton University Press, 1961.

Pokorny, P. "The Temptation Stories and Their Intention." *New Testament Studies* 20 (1973–74): 115-27.

Popkes, W. *Christus Traditus: Eine Untersuchung zum Begriff der Dahingabe im Neuen Testament*. Zürich: Zwingli Verlag, 1967.

Powell, M. A. *What Is Narrative Criticism?* Minneapolis: Fortress Press, 1990.

Pritchard, J. B., ed. *The Ancient Near East*. Vol. 1, *An Anthology of Texts and Pictures*. Princeton: Princeton University Press, 1958.

Pritchard, J. B., ed. *Ancient Near Eastern Texts Relating to the Old Testament*. Princeton: Princeton University Press, 1969.

Quesnell, Q. *The Mind of Mark: Interpretation and Method through the Exegesis of Mark 6,52*. Rome: Pontifical Biblical Institute, 1969.

Rahnenführer, D. "Das Testament des Hiob und das Neue Testament." *Zeitschrift für die neutestamentliche Wissenschaft* 62 (1971): 68-93.

Räisänen, H. *Die Parabeltheorie im Markusevangelium*. Helsinki: Finnish Exegetical Society, 1971.

Read, D. H. C. "The Cry of Dereliction." *The Expository Times* 68 (1956–57): 260-62.

Rensberger, D. *Johannine Faith and Liberating Community.* Philadelphia: Westminster Press, 1988.

Rhoads, D., and D. Michie. *Mark As Story: An Introduction to the Narrative of a Gospel.* Philadelphia: Fortress Press, 1982.

Robinson, J. M. *The Problem of History in Mark.* Philadelphia: Fortress Press, 1982.

Ruppert, L. *Jesus als der leidende Gerechte? Der Weg Jesu im Lichte eines alt- und zwischentestamentlichen Motivs.* Stuttgart: KBW Verlag, 1972.

Sanders, E. P. *Paul and Palestinian Judaism.* Philadelphia: Fortress Press, 1977.

Sanders, J. A. *Suffering as Divine Discipline in the Old Testament and Post-Biblical Judaism.* Colgate Rochester Divinity School Bulletin, Special Issue. Vol. 28. Rochester: Colgate Rochester Divinity School, n.d.

Schaller, B., ed. *Das Testament Hiobs.* Gütersloh: Mohn, 1979.

Schulze, W. "Die Heilige und die wilden Tiere." *Zeitschrift für die neutestamentliche Wissenschaft* 46 (1955): 280-83.

Schweizer, E. *The Good News According to Mark.* Trans. Donald H. Madvig. Atlanta: John Knox Press, 1970.

Schweizer, E. "The Son of Man Again." *New Testament Studies* 10 (1962–63): 256-61.

Schweizer, E. "Towards a Christology of Mark?" In *God's Christ and His People: Studies in Honor of Nils Alstrup Dahl,* ed. J. Jervell and W. A. Meeks, 29-42. Oslo: Universitetsforlaget, 1977.

Seesemann, H. "πεῖρα κτλ." In *The Theological Dictionary of the New Testament.* Vol. 6. Grand Rapids: William B. Eerdmans, 1968.

Seitz, O. J. F. "Afterthoughts on the Term 'ΔΙΨΥΧΟΣ.'" *New Testament Studies* 4 (1957–58): 327-34.

Seitz, O. J. F. "Antecedents and Signification of the Term ΔΙΨΥΧΟΣ." *Journal of Biblical Literature* 66 (1947): 211-19.

Senior, D. *The Passion of Jesus in the Gospel of Mark.* Collegeville, Minn.: Liturgical Press, 1984.

Shiner, W. T. *"Follow Me!" Disciples in Markan Rhetoric.* Atlanta: Scholars Press, 1995.

Stendahl, K. "The Apostle Paul and the Introspective Conscience of the West." *Harvard Theological Review* 56 (1973): 199-215.

Stone, M. *A History of the Literature of Adam and Eve.* Atlanta: Scholars Press, 1992.

Stowers, S. K. "4 Maccabees." In *Harper's Bible Commentary,* ed. James L. Mays et al., 922-34. San Francisco: Harper & Row, 1988.

Stowers, S. K. *A Rereading of Romans: Justice, Jews, and Gentiles.* New Haven: Yale University Press, 1994.

Surin, K. *Theology and the Problem of Evil.* Oxford: Basil Blackwell, 1986.

Swetnam, J. *Jesus and Isaac: A Study of the Epistle to the Hebrews in the Light of the Aqedah.* Rome: Biblical Institute Press, 1981.

Talbert, C. H. *Learning Through Suffering: The Educational Value of Suffering in the New Testament and in Its Milieu.* Collegeville, Minn.: Liturgical Press, 1991.

Tannehill, R. C. "The Disciples in Mark: The Function of a Narrative Role." In *The Interpretation of Mark,* ed. W. Telford, 134-57. Philadelphia: Fortress Press, 1977.

Taylor, V. *The Gospel According to St. Mark.* London: Macmillan and Co., 1957.

Tolbert, M. A. *Sowing the Gospel: Mark's World in Literary-Historical Perspective.* Philadelphia: Fortress Press, 1989.

Townsend, J. T. "Education (Greco-Roman)." In *Anchor Bible Dictionary.* Vol. 2. New York: Doubleday, 1992.

Tyson, J. B. "The Blindness of the Disciples in Mark." *Journal of Biblical Literature* 80 (1961): 261-68.

Van Dyk, L. "Do Theories of Atonement Foster Abuse?" *Perspectives* 12, no. 2 (1997): 11-13.

Vermes, G., ed. *The Dead Sea Scrolls in English.* Middlesex: Penguin, 1975.

Weeden, T. J. "The Heresy That Necessitated Mark's Gospel." *Zeitschrift für die neutestamentliche Wissenschaft* 59 (1968): 145-58.

Weeden, T. J. *Mark — Traditions in Conflict.* Philadelphia: Fortress Press, 1971.

Widengren, G. *Quelques rapports entre Juifs et Iraniens a l'epoque des parthes.* Leiden: E. J. Brill, 1957.

Widengren, G. "Iran and Israel in Parthian Times with Special Regard to the Ethiopic Book of Enoch." In *Religious Syncretism in Antiquity: Essays in Conversation with Geo. Widengren,* ed. B. A. Pearson, 85-129. Missoula, Mont.: Scholars Press, 1975.

Wilckens, U. "ὑποκρίνομαι κτλ." In *The Theological Dictionary of the New Testament.* Vol. 8. Grand Rapids: William B. Eerdmans, 1972.

Williams, S. K. *Jesus' Death as Saving Event: The Background and Origin of a Concept.* Missoula, Mont.: Scholars Press, 1975.

Winston, D. "The Iranian Component in the Bible, Apocrypha, and Qumran: A Review of the Evidence." *History of Religions* 5 (1966): 183-216.

Wrede, W. *The Messianic Secret.* 1901. Reprint, Cambridge: James Clark, 1971.

Zaehner, R. C. *The Dawn and Twilight of Zoroastrianism.* New York: G. P. Putnam's Sons, 1961.

Zaehner, R. C. *Zurvan: A Zoroastrian Dilemma.* Oxford: Clarendon Press, 1955.

Index of Authors

Index of Subjects

199

Index of Citations